Listening to Homer

Listening to Homer

TRADITION, NARRATIVE, AND AUDIENCE

Ruth Scodel

THE UNIVERSITY OF MICHIGAN PRESS

Ann Arbor

First paperback edition 2009
Copyright © by the University of Michigan 2002
All rights reserved
Published in the United States of America by
The University of Michigan Press
Manufactured in the United States of America
♾ Printed on acid-free paper

2012   2011   2010   2009   5   4   3   2

A CIP catalog record for this book is available from the British Library.

Library of Congress Cataloging-in-Publication Data

Scodel, Ruth.
      Listening to Homer : tradition, narrative, and audience / Ruth Scodel.
          p.   cm.
      Includes bibliographical references and index.
      ISBN 0-472-11265-1 (cloth : alk. paper)
          1. Homer—Criticism, Textual.   2. Epic poetry, Greek—History and
criticism—Theory, etc.   3. Epic poetry, Greek—Criticism, Textual.   4. Oral
interpretation of poetry.   5. Oral tradition—Greece.   6. Oral—formulaic
analysis.   7. Transmission of texts.   8. Narration (Rhetoric)   9. Audiences—
Greece.   10. Homer—Technique.   11. Rhetoric, Ancient.   I. Title.

PA4037.S4164   2002
883'.01—dc21   2002020292

ISBN 13: 978-0-472-03374-4 (pbk : alk. paper)
ISBN 10: 0-472-03374-3 (pbk : alk. paper)

For Ludwig Koenen

Introduction to the Paperback Edition

This book is in part a long thought-experiment. Scholars of Homer have usually assumed that the *Iliad* and *Odyssey* were originally meant to be fully and completely understandable by everybody. It is not surprising that they think this. While scholars disagree vehemently about exactly how the *Iliad* and *Odyssey* came into existence as the written texts that we now have, they agree that their first audiences typically encountered them as oral performances. We also know that the epics were influential in later Greek culture all over the Greek world, and that they were clearly familiar not just to the educated elite, but to a broad spectrum of the population. For a work to be popular, especially in performance, it must be accessible—most people have to be capable of following it, understanding it, and appreciating it.

So far, I agree. One further step, though, I question. Homeric scholarship has typically assumed that audiences only follow and appreciate performances if they understand almost everything. The *Iliad* and *Odyssey* clearly assume prior knowledge of stories about the Trojan War. They have many characters and refer, often very briefly, to many other people and events of Greek legend. So if we assume that a performance can only be popular if the audience can easily understand every allusion or reference in it, Homer's audiences must have known a vast body of material.

This assumption is, however, demonstrably not true. Many years ago, with my daughter, who was about eight years old, I was watching an episode of *The Simpsons* in which baby Maggie, having led an attempt to recover the pacifiers that the operator of her day-care center has taken away, is confined in a playpen, where she throws a rubber ball against the side (Season 4, Episode 2: "A Streetcar Named Marge"). I commented that this was a parody of a film called *The Great Escape*, and she said, "I know." When I pointed out that she could not possibly have recognized the parody of a film she had not seen, she explained that she had not recognized the film, but had realized that it was a parody of an escape-story. This happens all the time: we may miss jokes or allusions utterly, or understand them generically but not recognize their specific origin, or be a member of the in-group that understands everything. Also, as real members of real audiences, we miss things not only because we have no opportunity to know them, but because we fail to pay attention, or to pay attention the right way. This book summarizes a variety of comparative evidence about how audiences around the world actually behave. In the *Odyssey*, Homer describes audiences who listen spellbound as a singer performs epic. It is not always like that.

So in this book, I try to estimate how much—or how little—a member of Homer's audience would have to know not to get lost. Deliberately, I push the experiment as far as I can: I think that Homer assumed that his audiences would have heard of all his main characters before, but we should not take even this for granted. Homeric scholarship has long been divided between those who believe that some passages or plot-elements in the *Iliad* and *Odyssey* show the creativity of an individual poet and those who argue that everything in the poems is traditional. The debate seems to me to miss something important about oral traditions—that it would be very hard for anyone in an audience to know whether a story was an exact repetition of an earlier version or included new variants. There were many stories, each with many possible versions, and nobody could know them all. In any case, the greatness of the *Iliad* and *Odyssey* does not depend on how much of each poem one person invented. Of course we would like to know exactly when each element in the immense fabric was added, just as we would like to know precisely what events were the germ of the story of the Trojan War. However, scholars tend to make the stakes higher than they need to be.

I work from the hypothesis that these huge epics were composed not for a village, where the same poet performed regularly before the same crowd, but for an audience from different places in the Greek world, people whose experiences of epic might be different. Even those who knew a story already would not know exactly what version of it a poet would tell. Sometimes, I suggest, the poet plays with the audience, confusing them about what he intends. Because I am deeply interested in how people tell stories and make them work, I develop this hypothesis to show how the epics try to include everyone—not only those who know more and those who know fewer stories about the ancient heroes, but also those who are content with local aristocrats and those who hate them.

Acknowledgments

This book began as a paper presented at the conference "The *Iliad* and Its Contexts" at Ohio State University in October 1994, and I thank all the participants in the discussion there. That paper, whose arguments are now scattered through this book, appeared originally in *Arethusa* ("Pseudo-Intimacy and the Prior Knowledge of the Homeric Audience," *Arethusa* 30 [1997]: 201–19), and an earlier version of chapter 3 appeared in the *American Journal of Philology* ("Bardic Performance and Oral Tradition in Homer," *AJP* 119 (1998): 171–94), both published by the Johns Hopkins University Press. The book was largely written during a year of leave supported by a sabbatical from the University of Michigan and a grant from the Michigan Humanities Initiative.

I also thank the students in my *Odyssey* seminar in winter 1999 and, for proofreading the manuscript, Kendra Eshleman. Collin Ganio at the University of Michigan Press has helped valiantly.

Contents

What Are We Talking about
When We Talk about Tradition?

No term appears more often in the study of Homer than *tradition*. But what exactly is tradition, and why does it matter? Most Hellenists have long since accepted that for many generations before the Homeric poems were composed, Greeks had listened to the tales of heroes as bards—ἀοιδοί—sang them.[1] In a tradition of this kind, performers neither memorize fixed texts nor improvise freely. An aspiring performer learns stylized diction, performance style, themes, and the outlines of narratives and recombines them before audiences. Milman Parry and Albert Lord found a living parallel for Homer in South Slavic epic, and many cultures have had such performance traditions. The balance between preparation and memorization, on one side, and spontaneous re-creation, on the other, varies among cultures, genres, and individual performers.[2]

The hypothesis of a tradition of composition-in-performance accounts superbly for a variety of otherwise mysterious phenomena in the epics. The poems are in a mixed dialect nobody ever spoke—a special poetic language—and contain many archaisms. The same poetic language, with modest variation, appears in the *Iliad,* which was probably composed in Asia Minor, and in Hesiod's work, composed in Boeotia. Formulae—for example, Homer's "swift-footed Achilles" and "ships with painted prow"—are ubiquitous. Homer's formulae, however, are not a mere collection of phrases. For an important character, Homer has a formula that fits each of the important divisions of the verse (*extension,* in Parry's terminology) and usually only one formula for each metrical

---

1. The seminal works are Lord 1960 and the papers collected in Parry 1971; the Parry-Lord hypothesis has generated an entire field of oral studies with its own journal, *Oral Tradition.* See the bibliography in Foley 1985. A recent survey is Holoka 1991.

2. See Finnegan 1977.

shape. To be sure, the formulaic system is less crudely economical than Milman Parry thought, since his study of how Homer names heroes did not, for example, include their patronymics.[3] An important character turns out to be not one "essential idea," since, especially in speeches, the character's social roles give him or her identities that the basic formulae do not. Formulae are not just metrical filler, and the rules that govern their use (or their absence) are far more complex than metrical necessity.[4] Even the fixed epithets serve larger poetic, rather than narrowly metrical, functions. Nonetheless, it is a system, though a flexible one, developed under the practical pressure of composition-in-performance.[5] Further, the epics retain traces of Mycenaean material culture, such as the use of bronze weapons (instead of iron ones), and of the Mycenaean landscape, especially in the Catalogue of Ships, even though the social world of the poems is utterly unlike that of the palace bureaucracies of the Linear B tablets.[6] The *Odyssey* represents a working bard who is praised for his ability to sing capably on a specific subject on request and thus probably impromptu. All this has no reasonable explanation except that whether or not the poems themselves were composed in performance, their poetic language and narrative style were developed by poets who re-created and adapted their material at each performance. Thus, whether our texts of Homer are the result of dictation, the memorization of a gradually ossified performance, or the work of a literate poet or poets, they are grounded in an oral tradition.[7]

---

3. See Shive 1987.

4. So, for example, formulae sometimes change to avoid conflict with particular contexts: see Sale 1993, 139–40. Many formulae have rich associations: see Muellner 1996, 12–16, on δαίμονι ἶσος, "equal to a god." Cf. Foley's motto (Foley 1999, 7 and passim): "artis gratia, not metris gratia."

5. Even Visser 1987, which argues that the battle scenes are constructed with single words rather than formulae, shows the impressive economy and extension of verbs meaning "kill."

6. There is intense controversy about whether the poems depict the poet's contemporary social world, a slightly older society, or an incoherent amalgam; but nobody thinks that it represents Mycenean society, and nobody denies that there are archaizing elements. See the summary and bibliography in Raaflaub 1991.

7. Throughout this book, I use the name *Homer* to mean both the *Iliad* poet and *Odyssey* poet, though I am inclined to think that different poets from the same "school" composed each epic.

The Homeric poems are directed toward performance, even if they were composed in writing. Solitary reading did not become a common way of experiencing poetry until the late fifth century B.C.E., long after the Homeric epics were canonical texts; and even then, performance, formal or informal, was usual. Earlier poets may have used writing and hoped that written texts would preserve and transmit their work (as they did), but the written version was a support or a supplement for oral performance.[8] The earliest complete copies of the epics were intended not for readers but either as aids for professional performers or as treasures and sources of authority in performance.

This book identifies narrative strategies by which the *Iliad* and *Odyssey* promote their own authority and render their narratives both intelligible and pleasing to their audiences. The audiences treated here are implicit in the poems, but the discussion rests on the assumption that the poets were experienced, professional epic performers. They based their rhetorical and narrative strategies on their experience of real performance audiences in a traditional genre. By looking at epic performances in other cultures, we can better evaluate how such traditions work in practice, so we can estimate what expectations the poets had of their audiences.

Scholars have debated the term *formula*; often, those who use it define what they mean, knowing it is problematic.[9] The term *tradition*, though, goes relatively unexamined.[10] In Homeric scholarship, it refers diachronically to the history and process of transmission—to singers learning songs and teaching them to other singers. It refers to the rules of the genre and to such conventions as the poetic dialect, the formulae, and the meter. It also frequently means the themes and, indeed, the actual narratives themselves. In this sense, the tradition constitutes a canon. Since this canon could be known to archaic Greek audiences only through performance, the evidence from living oral traditions is essential in trying to understand how audiences hear traditional stories in performance.

Considering tradition as canon, as an inherited repertory, opens questions in many directions. How should our awareness of tradition

---

8. Knox 1985 provides a brief history of books/reading in the period.

9. See Edwards 1986, 1988; Russo 1997.

10. Ben-Amos (1984) discusses seven different meanings in current use. Foley (1995, xii–xiii) cites Ben-Amos 1984 and defines *tradition* as he himself uses it. Peradotto (1997) uses a Bakhtinian model.

affect our understanding of what the epics meant for their earliest
audiences and how they meant it? One school of English Homerists
finds oral theory and the study of the tradition unhelpful for interpre-
tation and pay it little attention, even though they accept the oral
background of the epics.[11] Some reductive prescriptions by oralists,
making tendencies rules, have perhaps contributed to this rejection.
W. Ong lists the characteristics of oral thought and expression, general-
izing both from Homer and from oral compositions from various cul-
tures. K. Stanley then argues that the poems cannot be oral, because they
do not show these characteristics—in particular, because they are criti-
cal and conceptual.[12]

How much does tradition matter? The epic stories were an impor-
tant repository of the distant past for Greeks through the classical
period. So did tradition serve as a guarantor of truth, and if it did, in
what sense did it do so? Are the Muses hypostases of tradition or sepa-
rable from it?[13] How did audiences reconcile different versions of sto-
ries in different performances?[14] It is hard even to understand what we
agree and disagree about until we specify what we are talking about
when we talk about tradition.

Instead of defining tradition, Homerists tend to reify it. One form
of reification operates by ignoring audiences completely and looking
only at the process of composition. The school of Homeric studies
known as Neo-Analysis is a particularly clear example. Scholars have
imagined a Homer who modeled his narrative on earlier texts or, as oral
theory became more orthodox, on earlier oral versions. Yet they have
not thought much about how audiences received these parallel ver-
sions. While this neglect of the audience does not affect the validity of
the arguments, it omits an important dimension essential to under-
standing the aesthetics of Homeric borrowing. The death of Patroclus
imitates the death of Achilles in a way that is thematically important in

---

11. Griffin (1980, xiii–xiv) famously dismisses oral theory.

12. Ong 1982, 36–56; Stanley 1993, 268–79. Although Stanley is sensibly crit-
ical of the circularity of the association of conceptual thinking with literacy, he
seems to assume that the oral poet cannot use language ironically.

13. On one side, such scholars as W. Rösler (1980) and S. Slings (1990) insist
that the epic poet claims that his narrative is true—that, indeed, as Ford (1992)
argues, the Muses provide direct contact with the past. On the other side, Pratt
(1993) suggests that the poems are basically fiction.

14. See Griffith 1990.

the *Iliad*. Patroclus dies wearing Achilles' armor. When Thetis then responds to her son's grief as if she were mourning his death, these details invite even a listener who had not heard a song about Achilles' death to guess at what Achilles' death rituals must have been. There is obvious narrative profit in recognizing the parallel. However, it is hard to say whether the poet hopes for listeners who know more than he tells. For example, at the moment when Apollo knocks off Patroclus's armor, it may be an advantage to know that Apollo will also participate in the death of Achilles. However, the narrator has Hector predict Apollo's role in Achilles' death just before he himself dies (*Il.* 22.358–60). He thus provides potential narrative pleasure, a small shock of recognition, for the hearer who only at this moment sees this particular similarity between Achilles' death and his friend's. In contrast, when Diomedes rescues Nestor, the listener who remembers that Antilochus died saving his father might be disappointed by this unpathetic imitation; yet the recollection that Nestor is traditionally rescued makes the story seem right and appropriate. Once the reception of a particular version of a typical story is at issue, it becomes clear that remembering is not an either-or activity.

The reified tradition is a box containing a finite number of items—including multiforms of tales—although the number imagined is very large. A particularly striking example is Richard Martin's comparison of the tradition to an electronic database.

> The more we learn about actual oral poetries, from Central Asian to Arabic and African to South American Indian, the more obvious it becomes that the traditional audience of an oral performance, the "native speakers," as it were, of the poetry, have, all of them, the mental equivalent of a CD-ROM player full of phrases and scenes. Reading Homer with the aid of a computerized lexical searching program enables one finally to replicate the average experience of the audience Homer had in mind. . . . I would go further and say that the full "meaning," and the full enjoyment of traditional poetry, come only when one has heard it all before a hundred times, in a hundred different versions.[15]

---

15. Martin 1993, 227–28. On the workings of memory, see Rubin 1995.

The electronic database is a misleading comparison because human memory relies on context.[16] Whether in oral societies or the contemporary world, people do not remember in the way of databases searchable with Boolean operators. In a database, everything is equally accessible all the time—whether it appears frequently or rarely, in a memorable passage of story or in a list—whatever the searcher's reasons for conducting the search. When hardware and software are working properly, there is never any question whether a given item of information is part of the database or not. In human memory, the accessibility of an item depends on complex forms of embedding, and there is no pure information.

The rhapsode challenged to provide all the ways he could say "Achilles" in the nominative could surely not have succeeded, because the narrative context and the meter brought the appropriate phrase to mind; he learned to sing but did not memorize the chart of formulae. Different information is available on different occasions. A CD provides fixed storage, while audiences in living oral traditions never stop acquiring new experience and never stop forgetting. Jan Vansina has identified the usual pattern for oral history: three generations accurately remembered, a telescoped extended past, and a mythic time of ancestors. The system is homeostatic: additions drive out the old—though not perfectly so.[17] To be sure, Greek saga, with its roughly three generations of heroes placed between the recent past and the beginnings, does not fit this pattern. Still, we should be wary of treating our few snapshots—the surviving corpus of archaic epic poetry—as if they represented a stable state.

A more serious issue is the romanticization of the relation between bard and audience. Richard Martin is not alone in postulating a supremely competent audience, which has heard many epic performances and paid extremely close attention to them all. In stressing the previously neglected role of the audience, performance theory makes the audience a collaborator in the performance.[18] An excellent performer

---

16. Cf. Lord 1960, 99–100: Makíc "could repeat a song he had heard only once, *provided that he heard it to the gusle* [the stringed instrument used to accompany singing]."

17. See Vansina 1973. For the limits of homoeostatis, see Vansina 1985, 120–23. For similar phenomena in the oral tradition of classical Athens, see Thomas 1989, 95–154.

18. Doherty (1995, 24–25 and n. 37) helpfully warns against some oralist studies' "(projected) nostalgia" for this homogeneous audience. Lord (1960,

must then imply a superb audience, and the Homerist easily slips from reconstructing an ideal experience into assuming that this experience was not only real but universal. Perhaps we imagine the audience thus partly because we are nostalgic for the intimacy and fullness of meaning that the most successful traditional performances possess. Probably more important, students of oral poetry also feel a residual need to defend their subject against any assumption that nonliterate culture is primitive.

A self-questioning anthropology has surely helped folklorists fight against condescending attitudes toward oral culture. However, this recognition of depth and complexity can easily drift into an admiration that patronizes at a more subtle level, by denying oral culture its imperfections. Everyone knows that audiences within our own culture are never perfect. People fail to understand novels and fall asleep in movies, not always because the offering is inferior, but because we as audience are lazy or tired or because the particular cultural product is not exactly what we want at the moment. The product may even have been directed at precisely our own social group, at an audience not much less homogeneous than that at an epic performance in rural Rajasthan. Our neighbors may understand the novel without difficulty and find the film enthralling. Being present at a performance does not mean learning all that it could teach.

J. Flueckiger's account of an unsuccessful performance of the Candaini epic (from Chattisgarh in Central India) is revealing.[19] She sponsored a public performance by a performer named Devlal, who was well known in his own village but not in the locale of this performance. Most of the audience left after less than an hour and a half. Since such performances normally last several hours (although members "may come and go, drink tea and talk, and even fall asleep"), this performance was clearly a failure. Devlal's performance was unusual. He chose an episode other than the elopement of the hero and heroine (by far the most popular), and his audience did not know this part of the story. He also performed unusually. Candaini is performed in two distinct styles:

14–17) describes the "instability" of the South Slavic poet's audience. Although a gathering in a town coffeehouse might include singers who would form a critical audience, the typical audience is easily distracted, and songs are often not finished.

19. Flueckiger 1988.

one sung (*git*), with emphasis on the story; the other (*naca*) danced, and much influenced by Hindi films. Devlal, however, dislikes *naca*, claiming that its performers do not have to know the story and that its audiences cannot follow the story even if they want to. He attempted to include dancing in a *git* performance, but the audience was dissatisfied because they expected a *naca* performance. Such a failure reveals the imperfections of real performances and real audiences. A deviation from the style that the audience expected left them confused and dissatisfied. However, nobody objected to the unfamiliar content.

As scholars, we tend to idealize the Homeric poems' audiences, because we are nervous about attributing complexities and subtleties of allusion and meaning to the poems unless we can believe the original audience recognized and understood them. Since the original audience, whatever the exact circumstances, was a listening (and not a reading) public, we need extraordinarily competent listeners.[20] The *Odyssey* makes this task easier by depicting a world in which listening to epic performers is a supreme pleasure, all performers are highly capable, and the audience is utterly attentive. In general, we assume that the bard cannot survive economically unless he can please his audience and that the audience will demand transparency. W. Wyatt offers a clear statement of the common assumption.

> Had there been any lack of comprehension among his hearers, Homer would have known of it and would either have changed the phrasing of his remarks, or provided more introduction to them, or have later offered an explanation of the confusion. He simply was not in a position to allow perplexity in an audience which would have denied him payment if themselves denied of comprehension and thus satisfaction.[21]

When we examine these assumptions, common sense and the reports of fieldwork should cause us to question and modify them.

Oral traditions can survive without being especially popular with

---

20. For example, Ahl and Roisman 1996 and Pucci 1987 both assume extremely knowledgeable and skilled audiences.

21. Wyatt 1985, n. 10. The underlying assumption is very frequent and often excludes the possibility of later explanation. See, e.g., Heubeck 1954, 20–21; Wilamowitz-Moellendorff 1916, 252.

audiences, if social conditions or institutions perpetuate them. An extreme case is the shadow-puppet theater of Kerala.[22] Most of its performances have no audience except the gods and the troupe itself. Nonetheless, the performers are paid, both by major sponsors and by large numbers of one-rupee contributors who pay to be mentioned during a blessing in the course of the performance. Of course, this tradition is not a good parallel for Homeric epic. Performances without audiences are a common Indian phenomenon; they are possible because those sponsoring them acquire merit, but the merit does not depend on the sponsors' participation or on the presence of an audience. Performances are not always entertainments. The Kerala shadow theater, with its endless commentaries and digressions, perfectly addresses its real and authorial audiences—the performers themselves. Homeric epic, though, was relatively secular, and Greek religion operates on different premises from Hinduism: the Greek gods enjoy the same spectacles as mortals, so human entertainments take place at their festivals. Greek epic presents itself as popular: Penelope calls the contents of the poet Phemius' repertory θελκτήρια, "enchantments" (*Od.* 1.337), and Odysseus praises the delight of listening to a bard at an abundant feast (*Od.* 9.2–11). In the classical period, Plato refers to an audience of "more than twenty thousand" for the rhapsode Ion (535d).

Still, it is well to remember that oral performances reveal a broad continuum of relationships with their audiences, varying from tradition to tradition and even from village to village. Some present the intimacy between performer and audience that Martin describes as the norm. In such traditions, most members of the audience know the stories and the style, and can appreciate even minor variants.[23] Others depend less on this prior knowledge. 'Adwallah, a Bani Hilali singer in Upper Egypt, often discussed the genealogies and background of the epic with the audience before the performance, because the audiences were not thoroughly conversant with the information.[24] Another study of the same tradition, however, found that villagers criticized a performer they had heard on the radio (a superb musician) who had used a rest pattern they did not recognize between lines and who did not follow the story correctly and clearly.[25]

---

22. See Blackburn 1996.
23. See Basso 1985.
24. See Slyomovics 1987, 48.
25. See Connelly 1986, 62–63.

The assumption that a successful oral performance must be fully transparent all the time is simply wrong—many performance traditions, for example, include songs whose performance style renders them incomprehensible. A successful oral performance must be meaningful (a quite different matter), and the audience in most traditions expects to be able to follow the story (but consider the remarks on Candaini in *naca* style). The common further assumption that all members of the audience must have an equal and high level of understanding is simply false. "Popular" does not mean "fully understandable." Pindar and Aeschylus cannot have been completely accessible in a first performance. Modern fictions regularly manage to satisfy diverse audiences. Many children's entertainments, for example, are crammed with sophisticated allusion and parody that engage adults, while the core audience is completely oblivious. Only a tiny minority of those who enjoyed the film *Shakespeare in Love* can possibly have known of the actual person behind the character of John Webster, an unpleasant boy who has a modest but important part in the plot. His character is a "bonus" for the few viewers who know English tragedy well. The practice of literary criticism presupposes that intelligent and careful readers may find in texts worthwhile meanings that other intelligent and careful readers have missed and that it is possible to enjoy a narrative without exhausting it. There is no a priori reason to assume that all members of Homer's audience needed to be sophisticated critics, and the comparative evidence does not support such an assumption—though it certainly suggests that some people may well have been such.

From the Egyptian epic tradition, Slyomovics reports a performance that shows that understanding can fail at the simplest level. An elite member of the audience interrupted the bard 'Adwallah to ask what character was speaking—the audience member had become confused. Other members of the audience teased the questioner, and the poet addressed to him the first insulting aside of the performance (a regular feature of the genre): he was not a competent listener. Not everybody in a real audience is skilled at listening, and not every tradition allows for interruptions (a person of lower status might have been more hesitant). 'Adwallah himself claims that his puns (again, an important feature of the genre) are often difficult.[26]

The minutely competent audience not only would have to have

---

26. See Slyomovics 1987, 73, 78.

vast experience with performances but would have to be extremely at-
tentive to all these performances. Comparatively, the audiences of dif-
ferent oral traditions show a very wide range of attention as well as prior
knowledge. Performance traditions have different levels of concern for
comprehension, and so do different occasions. Audiences differ in their
skill, too. In Bali, for example, the high-caste characters in the shadow
theater speak Old Javanese, which the audience does not understand.[27]
Indeed, some puppeteers do not have mastery of the language them-
selves and try to hide that fact by speaking indistinctly. The servant
characters, in contrast, speak Balinese. By paraphrasing what their so-
cial superiors say, they render the gist of the dialogue comprehensible.
In this case, traditionality is evidently more important than immediate
comprehension. In the Indian Dhola epic, sung sections are not under-
standable, but performers and audiences lay great stress on the impor-
tance of making the plot clear as a whole.[28] A traditional storyteller may
choose to make understanding difficult for reasons particular to an oc-
casion. Folklorist Margaret Mills provides an outstanding example in
her account of a storytelling session she attended in Afghanistan. One
of the two storytellers at the session was a mullah who had had hostile
dealings with the official who organized the session and who helped
sponsor Mills. Both storytellers used the occasion to create solidarity
from which Mills and her Afghan sponsors were excluded.[29] Narayan
has studied a swami who on different occasions told the same exem-
plary story with altered details that gave it a special message for indi-
viduals in the present audience. Some of his regular visitors appreciated
the different nuances of each rendition, but not all did.[30]

The concept of *traditional referentiality*, introduced by John Miles Fo-
ley, can lead to a similar misunderstanding.[31] Foley argues that to treat
performances from an oral tradition or their scripts as individual texts
is inherently misleading, because the underlying aesthetic does not
confine reference to the present performance. While literary produc-
tions are relatively self-contained, relying only on the general cultural
background of their audiences and on their knowledge of genre, oral

---

27. See Hobart 1987, 142–43.
28. See Blackburn et al. 1989, 78–79 (Wadley).
29. See Mills 1989, 13–14, 52–56.
30. See Narayan 1989, 37–42.
31. See Foley 1991.

performances assume a much broader and richer familiarity with the traditions to which they belong. Hence they may be elliptical—events essential to the plot of a narrative may be omitted, taken for granted. Characters have predetermined personalities, and an epithet is enough to make the hero present. Oral performance generates meaning through synecdoche. Indeed, apparently bland language is often rich with precise significance.

This is true and important: Formulae often convey far more than a translation would indicate. Homeric characters are often called "godlike," but the *Iliad* calls a hero "equal to a divinity" (δαίμονι ἶσος) only when the context brings the hero close to fighting with a god.[32] Nothing in the words themselves implies this traditional association. Foley defines such relationships of individual performance to tradition as "pars pro toto." Each performance and each use of a formula are indeed synecdoches. The "whole" tradition, however, is an abstraction.

In emphasizing the poetic function of formulaic language in accordance with traditional referentiality, Homerists use such words as *epiphany, ritual, presence,* and *enactment* to stress the vividness with which the noun-epithet formulae evoke the characters.[33] Such terms are potentially misleading, though, for there are oral traditions that are ritual and in which the hero's spirit literally takes possession of a performer.[34] Homeric epic is not among them. Indeed, the poems depict performance as a secular entertainment, taking place after a meal in a chief's house or at a public gathering that also includes athletics. The formula does not make the hero literally present. Indeed, although it evokes the hero's traditional attributes, it does not necessarily bring all of them to full consciousness in the audience.

It is important, therefore, to distinguish the different aspects of traditional referentiality and the different meanings of tradition within it. The implied audience of Homeric epic has heard epic before. A poet could expect that almost all adults would know one of the things we mean when we speak of "the tradition"—the generic conventions of language and style. They would all know the meter and could understand the peculiar dialect, which was widely diffused and largely, though not completely, standardized. Many formulae would surely be familiar to

---

32. See Nagy 1979, 143–44.
33. For example, Bakker (1997) and Ford (1992) use this kind of language.
34. Tamil bow song is an outstanding example; see Blackburn 1988.

everyone, and many members of the audience would understand their significance beyond the denotative meaning. Listeners would be comfortable with those epithets so fossilized that their denotative meaning was lost. They would also know the narrative conventions—the most important type-scenes, for example—so that everybody who had any interpretive skill would be able to estimate the importance of a feast, a journey, or an arrival by comparing its level to the level of elaboration of other sequences in the performance. People would understand the underlying themes and rules of the narrative, so, for example, they would expect prophecies to be fulfilled. These phenomena were probably generalized wherever epic hexameter existed. The type-scenes and themes and many of the formulae appeared throughout the repertory.

The problem begins when we move to specific narrative content, to stories. Some formulaic epithets, for example, are confined to individual characters. To say that these epithets evoke the whole character is to assume that the audience had heard not just epic but stories about these characters and, indeed, the stories to which the epithets especially pertain. There can be no question that stories about Achilles and Odysseus were featured in performances long before our *Iliad*. For one thing, these characters have formulaic systems that refer to story material the *Iliad* does not tell. Odysseus could not be "much-enduring" and "full of wiles" until the poets were telling the stories in which he displays these qualities, more prominent outside the *Iliad* than in it. Achilles is not especially swift-footed in the *Iliad* (he has difficulty catching Hector, and Aeneas once escaped from him by running [*Il.* 20.188–94]), so this characteristic epithet implies other stories. We are probably safe in assuming that Homer expected his audience to have heard some of these tales before. But scholars tend to assume also that the audience must have heard and remembered vast amounts of specific content. The traditional system is often compared to a language. If the "whole" of the tradition is analogous to a language, we can easily perceive how individual speakers both do and do not have access to the whole. Even though most speakers of a language do not know every word in the lexicon or have mastery of every register, the knowledge of a native speaker is rich with connotation and the ability to generate and perceive meaning. Traditional referentiality does not mean that everyone knows all the same stories, in the same variants.

Homer creates characters using only some of the heroic personality he inherited. The *Iliad* mentions Troilus only once, as Priam lists his best, dead sons at 24.257. The evidence of art suggests that this episode was particularly popular and widely known, at least later.[35] Achilles caught the young man, though Achilles was on foot and Troilus on horseback, and killed him—in a place later specified as a shrine of Apollo. It is very possibly because of this episode in particular that Achilles is called "swift-footed."[36] Furthermore, the intense enmity between Achilles and Apollo may reflect this episode, especially the way Apollo, disguising himself as Agenor, entices Achilles to chase him away from the fleeing Trojans and then teases him (*Il.* 22.7–13). Yet the *Iliad* does not just ignore this story. The episode, in which Achilles shows intense brutality early in the war, presents a real difficulty for the *Iliad*, since the poem consistently implies that Achilles was an unusually generous and noble hero before his anger. He is the only hero who is explicitly said to have taken prisoners, and he buried the fallen Eetion himself (*Il.* 6.417–20). The poet does not want his audience to have Troilus too much in mind, at least not until Achilles is about to become again a man who can pity his enemies, because in his story, Achilles' anger causes his extreme violence.[37] Yet the story may have contributed to the *Iliad*'s greatness. All versions of the story of Troilus pity him as a victim, even though the tradition as a whole does not seem to have shown the interest in the Trojans and sympathy for them that the *Iliad* does. The *Iliad* might not have been possible if the story of Troilus had not already encouraged poets and audiences to pity a Trojan, even though it avoids evoking the tale.

The clearest example of the audience's need to avoid recalling what it knows is the repeated use of Orestes as a positive example in the *Odyssey*. The poem never mentions that he killed his mother along with Aegisthus, although Nestor mentions the funeral feast he conducted for them both (*Od.* 3.309–10), so there can be no doubt that the poet knew the story. The matricide would complicate the paradigm, and the audience must therefore ignore the most sensational part of the story.[38] Similarly, the *Iliad* never mentions that Aeneas accompanied Paris when he stole Helen, although the *Cypria* (Proclus 14–16 Davies) told of the par-

---

35. See Scaife 1995, 189.

36. See schol. A on 24.257; Hölscher 1990, 31.

37. On Achilles' past, see Zanker 1994, 8–9.

38. This argument is taken from Andersen 1998, 145–47; Andersen's views on allusion are close to mine.

ticipation of Aeneas, who is present when the scene appears in Archaic art. The *Iliad* isolates Paris as sole villain.

Thus, unless much of the mythology surrounding the surviving epics is later elaboration or Homer's apparently wide knowledge of the canon had surprising gaps, Homer often suppresses material inappropriate for his own work. Traditional referentiality, when narrative content is at issue, depends on an "activator" in the context. It does not bring even the whole of the audience's experience of the tradition fully "on stage." The *Iliad* poet clearly relies on his audience either not to make all the associations that might be available to them or, perhaps, to join him in ignoring them. For the listener who is reminded of Troilus by Achilles' epithet, the story is a disturbing intertext.

Just as Homer's Achilles, though swift-footed, is not the brutal killer of Troilus, neither epic mentions either how Odysseus pretended to be mad to escape going to Troy or his subsequent murder of Palamedes. Odysseus is "cunning" (πολύμητις), but the *Iliad* needs him to stand, like Nestor, for the common interest and trust in the divine promise that Troy will fall, so it ignores stories in which Odysseus pursues self-interest against the common good. Traditional referentiality and compositional style can cause interpretive problems. At *Iliad* 4.350–55, in response to Agamemnon's rebuke for not entering battle more quickly, Odysseus angrily tells him that he will see "the dear father of Telemachus" among the forefighters. Odysseus is the only hero in the poem to name himself by reference to his son, and the story that Palamedes forced Odysseus to abandon pretense by placing the baby Telemachus in front of his plow is likely to be the generating force behind the expression here: it links Telemachus with a question of whether Odysseus is eager to fight. Telemachus's name (meaning "fighting at a distance") supports such an association. Is this passage an allusion to the story involving Palamedes, a hint the audience should recognize? If so, it works by negation. Odysseus is angry at the suggestion that he could be a slacker, and Agamemnon immediately takes back what he has said. If the passage refers to the story of Odysseus's feigned madness, it implies, therefore, that the story is not true. Yet some hearers may well have heard this tale in the past. Here is a troublesome intertext, the shadow of an aspect of the traditional character that this song does not want to develop. As a shadow, the reluctant Odysseus, like the brutal Achilles, is poetically rich. Such moments modify Bakhtin's assertion that epic is "univocal": Homeric epic is constantly in dialogue with everything the poets inherited.[39] Yet if the audience pursues the intertext so far that the Achilles and Odysseus of the epic become the Achilles and Odysseus of the stories from outside the epic, the *Iliad* no longer works.

There is a more general issue, too. In Rajasthan, the Pabuji epic is performed before an unrolled scroll, the *par*, on which the various episodes are painted.[40] The performer points to the incident that is to be performed on a specific occasion. In such a tradition, it makes sense to speak of the part and the whole in relation to narrative content: the whole is immediately present and graspable. In many other traditions, oral transmission occurs in a complex relationship with a written text. Again, in such traditions, it is not difficult to define what the "whole" is, although caution may be in order, since it is all too easy to identify the tradition with the written version. In other traditions, the situation is more complicated. The Indian Alhā epic is a stable form. Its audiences know it well and often join in singing the final words of couplets. Yet according to its performers, it has fifty-two segments. Only a limited number of these are ever actually performed, and some of the segments performed are far more popular than others. Are the episodes that are never or rarely performed part of the "whole"? If a particular audience has never heard an episode, is it part of their tradition?[41] The Egyptian oral poet 'Adwallah rarely performed the episode describing the birth of his hero, although it was part of the whole epic he had learned from his father. His audiences surely knew the outlines of the story; but they cannot have known this episode as well as they knew those they had often heard.[42] Even in Pabuji, many performers do not know certain episodes.[43]

In other words, some oral traditions—whether these are single-song or multiple-song traditions—have a clear canon, and all the participants, both performers and audiences, are familiar with it. Such tra-

---

39. Bakhtin 1981, 16–17, 61.

40. See Smith 1991; Blackburn et al. 1989, 240–43.

41. See Blackburn et al. 1989, 11.

42. See Slyomovics 1987, 23. Ironically, Connelly (1986) treats three performances of precisely this episode, which seems to have been especially popular among the Cairene audience she studied. In Parry, Lord, and Bynum 1974 (298), Lord quotes the great South Slavic poet Avdo Međedović: in 1950, Avdo had not performed "Smailagic Meho" since 1935, because no audience was interested.

43. See Smith 1991, 17–18.

ditions are both familiar to their audiences and resistant to change. Other traditions have canons with which audiences have only partial familiarity. Still other traditions are less fixed, and the pre-Homeric tradition is likely to have been among these. Writing is one obvious source of fixity within a tradition; a ritual context of performance is another. But many traditions (even many that exist in symbiosis with literacy) are fluid, and in these, the "whole" of the tradition is not easy to identify. In Finland in the nineteenth century, old songs were usually, though not always, transmitted with little change (they had a significant ritual element), but new songs were also composed, based on both recent events and old heroes.[44]

A loose but perhaps helpful analogy to the process of transmission in a fluid tradition is Darwinian natural selection. In any composition-in-performance of an oral poem of the type defined by the Parry-Lord model, variations may occur, either in the story or in the language. If the tale is expanded more than is usual, new details may be added. The singer may make a mistake and accidentally drift from one tale to another[45] or may intentionally graft material from one tale into another, to amplify it. At the level of language, the singer may substitute a phrase for the usual formula, either forgetfully or because considerations of euphony drive the change. Most such variation has no further significance. It appears in one performance but is gone in the next. Indeed, most such variation is probably error and renders the song less successful. Some variation, in contrast, especially at the macrolevel of story and content, represents adaptation to the needs of particular audiences (and is in this respect unlike biological evolution, where all change begins accidentally). Central Asian epic performers satirized aristocrats before audiences of commoners but praised them to their faces.[46] Hesiod's praise of kings inspired by the Muses in the *Theogony* may represent the poet's adaptation of his song for the funeral games of Amphidamas, when many "kings" were surely present and judging the contest.[47]

Traditions as a whole change to fit changing conditions. So the skirmish with Christian Basques that stands behind the *Chanson de Roland*

---

44. See Kiparsky 1976, 95–98.

45. Foley (1990, 359–87) discusses an example.

46. See Nilsson 1933, 189, citing V. V. Radloff. Cf. Lord 1960, 18–19, on a Serbian singer: "When he was with Turks he sang Muslim songs, or his own songs in such a way that the Moslems won the battles."

47. See West 1966, 44.

becomes an immense battle with Saracens, and although the fight still takes place in a rugged mountain pass, the knights fight as if on a plain. Near the poem's end, the trial of Ganelon addresses problems of the poet's own time.[48] African genealogies especially reflect contemporary political conditions, not a "real" past.[49] However, in Greek heroic legend as a whole, there is an immense amount of trivial variation. It is hard to see why different circumstances or audiences demanded different names for Agamemnon's daughters or Oedipus's mother or why—to mention a variant that appears within the *Odyssey*—it would make a significant difference whether Melampus took the cattle of Phylacus or of his son Iphiclus. In contrast, when different poets place Agamemnon and Menelaus in the same household or different ones, in Mycenae or Sparta, the variations are meaningful.

In oral tradition, whatever is lost is lost. Still, a variation may be spontaneously re-created elsewhere and disappear again, like an occasional random mutation. Some variations succeed. They repeat themselves either in a future performance by the same singer or even in performances by others, usually because they improve the response the poet receives from his audience. At this point, they may succeed in being widely diffused or may remain as a personal or local variant. They may remain bound to a particular context or may themselves generate new forms. In general, it seems to be the case that an individual performer stabilizes his performance as he repeats it.[50] If many performers in frequent contact with each other perform the same song, they will tend to conformity, as they "correct" each other. The greatest change takes place at the point of transmission, when a new singer learns a song, especially if that singer then performs independently of others. Traditions thus grow cladistically. In this sense, all multiforms are within the tradition and traditional.

To call every specific version of a story a "tradition," though, again tends to reification. A tradition is an element that enjoys extended transmission over time.[51] Thus, nobody can really know whether an unfamiliar element has ever appeared before. Some elements are clearly

---

48. See Ross 1980, 88–93.
49. See Thomas 1992, 109.
50. See Kiparsky 1976, 95; Jensen 1980, 23–24.
51. Shils (1981, 15–16) suggests that a "tradition" requires two transmissions over three age cohorts.

fixed and very widely known. The epic poets clearly expected the audience to know what W. Kullmann has called a *Faktenkanon,* a set of characters and stories that everyone needed to know to have basic competence in the tradition.[52] Even young children probably knew the names of Achilles and Odysseus. That there was a canon of facts, however, does not define its extent.

At any moment, certain elements may be in flux. A famous case is the Iliadic dual Αἴαντε, meaning "the two Ajaxes."[53] The *Iliad* poet had learned and remembered contexts where the dual referred to Telamonian Ajax and his brother Teucer. However, in the poet's everyday language, the dual could not be used this way, and the poet clearly did not understand the usage. So the poet inserted Oelian Ajax (13.66–67, 202–5) into these scenes. If we had poetry by Homer's students and their students, it would probably have resystematized the usage to refer only to the two men named "Ajax."[54] On the one hand, Teucer would have continued to fight beside his brother: the image of the archer who takes shelter within his brother's great shield is so powerful that the poets would not have forgotten it or the story of Teucer's expulsion by his father after his brother's death. On the other hand, the dual would have generated a consistent theme of the alliance of the two heroes named Ajax, and where it was necessary, new narrative would have been generated to explain that alliance. The Homeric text stands at the transition, and by becoming a (relatively) fixed text, it halted the process.

Two opposing forces work on this process. On the one hand, constant change allows a tradition to adapt to changing circumstances. Stories that no longer speak to contemporary concerns are abandoned; archaic language is modernized. The specific content of an oral tradition can change very quickly.[55] On the other hand, some traditions are very conservative. Generalizations about "oral culture" as flat, homeostatic, and without any real sense of the past can be misleading. Audiences often value traditionality for itself.

Traditionality is not the same as objective tradition. The Scot who

---

52. Kullmann 1960, 12–13.

53. See Wackernagel 1953, 538–46; Page 1959; Janko, *Il. Comm.,* 4:48–49, 68–69.

54. Nagy (1997, 175–84) argues against calling this "confusion" and urges instead a diachronic perspective in which different usages represent different stages of fixity.

55. See Thomas 1989, 131–54, on family traditions.

dons his kilt in the correct clan tartan for a special occasion may well be-
lieve that the costume and its connection with his ancestry are of ex-
treme antiquity. That the kilt itself is relatively modern and that associ-
ation between tartan patterns and particular clans is an invented
tradition of the nineteenth century makes no difference to the cultural
significance of his action.[56] Similarly, genres of oral performance can be
important markers of regional and group identities. Indeed, an impor-
tant study of Indian epic makes this a defining characteristic of the
genre: if the people do not regard a particular narrative and its per-
formance as one of the markers between themselves and others, it is not
an epic.[57] These epics link people to their regions, social surroundings,
and pasts. The belief that the epics have been transmitted from earlier
generations is crucial to their cultural force.

The placement of such an intense value on the genre can make it
more conservative. Egyptian peasants who had moved to Cairo listened
with avidity in the local café to the nightly radio broadcast of the Bani Hi-
lali epic.[58] In the village, they would never have heard the epic through
from beginning to end; being displaced made the epic even more impor-
tant to them than it had been at home. In the uncertain, modern world of
the city, the epic represented tradition. In modern times, states have made
performance traditions of high cultural value conform to centrally prom-
ulgated ideologies (Indonesia has used Javanese shadow theater to pro-
mote birth control).[59] However, if such transformation is to succeed, it
must represent itself as faithful to the inherited core. If the genre changes
too much, it loses the traditionality that provides its power. The kilt and
the connection of particular patterns with clans are modern, but the tar-
tan is a genuinely old Scottish dress, whose value to the new Scottish iden-
tity came from its having been forbidden after the failure of the Jacobite
rebellion in 1745. The presence of archaic, meaningless epithets in the
Homeric system demonstrates the force of traditionality. Metrical con-
venience alone does not explain the preservation of forms that no longer
referred to anything, and the bards could certainly have found another
way than the phrase μερόπων ἀνθρώπων to express "people" in the geni-
tive plural after a word ending in the first long syllable of the fourth foot.

---

56. See Trevor-Roper 1983.
57. See Blackburn et al. 1989, 5–7 (Blackburn and Flueckiger).
58. See Connelly 1986, 65–66.
59. See Sears 1986, 16.

The formulaic system may provide a positive indicator that the *Il-iad* poet inherited particular characters and stories about them.[60] Achilles and Odysseus both have several unique epithets that probably originated outside the particular stories in which they appear: the Odysseus of the *Iliad* does not deserve the title "much-enduring" more than anyone else, so we can be reasonably certain that tales of his difficult return are older than the *Iliad*. Nestor has the epithet Γερήνιος, which by itself confirms his traditional status, since its meaning is obscure; the accompanying ἱππότα, though not unique, is reserved for heroes older than those of the *Iliad*. Agamemnon alone is εὐρὺ κρείων, and he shares the vocative κύδιστε only with Zeus, as well as dominating the usage of ἄναξ ἀνδρῶν, which may be a particularized epithet that the poets extended at moments of need. Hector has ὄβριμος and κορυθαίολος. Locrian Ajax has ταχύς (meaning "activated" and even glossed at *Il.* 14.520–22), but his namesake relies on his patronymic. Still, though Ajax himself has no distinctive epithet, his shield has one, ἑπταβόειον. Patroclus has two epithets, both vocative, ἱππεῦ and ἱπποκέλευθε, used only in *Iliad* 16.

The lack of a distinctive epithet does not prove that a character is recent or invented.[61] Menelaus has no completely distinctive epithets at all, since even his patronymic is shared, but ξανθός (blond) is only once used of another hero, Meleager (*Il.* 2.642). This is probably the extension of an originally unique epithet, and it invites speculation about the traditional character of Menelaus. He is not a first-rank hero in the *Iliad*, but he is brave and responsible, and the narrator shows special affection for him.[62] The poets perhaps adopted this epithet to stress that Menelaus was as good-looking as his rival, Paris. One can also examine the overall formulaic system for a particular character. Diomedes lacks characterizing epithets, but with the help of his patronymics, the bards could maneuver him easily. He is certainly a traditional character, but he was perhaps not as sharply characterized in earlier stories as he is in the *Iliad*.

---

60. This argument goes back to Scott 1921; the argument in this paragraph relies in part on the chart in Parry 1971, 92.

61. Combellack 1950 is a critique of attempts to find Homeric "originality."

62. I do not distinguish "poet" from "narrator" (as Rabel [1997] does), since I do not think that the Muse "takes over" when the poet invokes her and since the audience sees and hears a single source in performance. The poet-narrator, however, is not identical with the implied author, who is sometimes secretive (e.g., about Penelope's motives).

Arguments in favor of the traditional status of a background detail or story are that the narrator alludes to it repeatedly and that its outline is coherent. In the *Iliad*, for example, the sequence of events in the story of Heracles' sack of Troy and its aftermath is known, and the poet can at any time reach for a section of that tale.[63] We expect inconsistency in innovations, just as liars are always wise to avoid details they are likely to forget in later retellings. Retelling and practice tend to stabilize a narrative. Inconsistency, though, cannot prove innovation, since minor inconsistency can also be the result of the poet's failure to select a single version of a story he has heard told different ways. Inconsistency that seems to depend on the needs of the immediate context is more likely to represent the poet's adaptations, while inconsistencies that make no difference probably indicate inherited variants.

Scholars looking to distinguish the traditional from the innovative frequently look at the position of a narrative element within the whole of Greek heroic legend. If it seems essential to the story as a whole—as Helen is essential to the story of the Trojan War—it is likely to be traditional. Characters who appear in the Epic Cycle and elsewhere are less likely to be Homeric inventions, especially when their roles do not seem plausible as glosses on their Homeric ones. Furthermore, a "fact" mentioned where it has little to contribute to the context is likely to be traditional. Neither Protesilaus nor Philoctetes plays any role in the *Iliad*. Yet the Catalogue of Ships mentions their absence. They are surely traditional figures, for a narrator would hardly invent characters just to explain why they are absent. In contrast, scholars often suspect innovation where they see a "fact" that is not important to the narrative progression, that is mentioned only once, that appears only in Homeric epic or in authors they believe are likely to be relying on Homer, and that is highly relevant to its context. W. Kullmann, for example, argues that when Achilles offers as a prize at *Iliad* 23.826–35 a huge lump of iron that Eetion of Thebes used to throw, the lump of iron, but not the killing of Eetion, is invented for the occasion. Similarly, he treats death within the *Iliad* as an indicator that the character is a Homeric invention—the poet could not kill those who needed to perform deeds later in the saga.[64] While it is certainly likely that the poet felt constrained not to kill char-

---

63. See Lang 1983; Edmunds 1997.

64. Kullmann 1960; 14, 291 (on Eetion); 58–63 (on survival/death as a criterion).

acters whom he knew as participants in later events, those who die are not necessarily inventions, and not all who survive must be inherited.

Perhaps the most common and generally accepted criterion is the assumption of transparency: passing allusions that do not make complete sense without extraneous knowledge are taken to be by definition traditional.[65] If we doubt the transparency of Homeric narrative, the other criteria at their best can provide guidelines only about whether an element is objectively traditional, whether the poet learned it from an earlier performance. What matters for an audience at the moment of performance, though, is not whether a particular story, phrase, or performance mannerism actually goes back to remote antiquity or is a recent development. An oral culture cannot verify that anyway, unless there is a radical break in style. The audience recognizes continuities with their lived experience of earlier performances. For individual members of a given audience, "the tradition" is what they have experienced: the stories they have heard, performed as they remember earlier performances, perhaps enriched with commentary about the tradition from their elders. It includes both performance tradition and oral tradition: both what they have heard in specially defined situations in which someone took responsibility for a performance and what they have heard informally, outside such a frame—often in narrative summary.[66]

G. Nagy allows traditional referentiality (though he does not use that terminology) the widest possible scope without positing an implausibly capable audience.

> From the standpoint of oral poetics, each occurrence of a theme (on the level of content) or of a formula (on the level of form) in a given composition-in-performance refers not only to its immediate context but also to all other analogous contexts remembered by the performer or by any member of the audience.[67]

If the analysis is trying to establish the possible range of traditional referentiality, this is an appropriate assumption. However, by assuming

---

65. Kullmann (1960, 13–17) gives a particularly clear statement of this principle; he allows as the only exception the possibility that the poet could accidentally refer to an innovation as if it were known. Danek (1998) uses the principle consistently.

66. On this distinction, see Flueckiger and Sears 1991, 6.

67. Nagy 1998, 81.

the relevance of any analogous context anyone remembered—and in scholarly practice, this must become any analogous context that was possibly available to be remembered, since we have no access to these memories—it studies the performance only from the perspective of the most experienced listener. Thus, the experiences of both the authorial audience and the real ordinary listener disappear.

Audience members knew well aspects of the tradition manifested in the core repertory of their local performers. For other aspects, their knowledge may have been no more than an outline of the tale. Other branches of the "same" tradition are irrelevant if the audience does not know about them. The *Iliad* poet may have known and performed a full-scale song about Heracles' adventures on Cos. However, he may have known this tale only in abbreviated form, if other songs mentioned these adventures in passing. Or perhaps he heard a summary in oral tradition outside the performance context. Similarly, the *Iliad* poet's audience probably recognized the outline of this story as traditional, but that does not tell us what place it had in their tradition.

This is not to deny the importance of traditional referentiality at the level of narrative content. Often, the poet neither followed a narrative multiform (applicable to any hero) nor imitated a single-model episode. The most famous events associated with a hero—often the nature of the hero's death—create a core heroic personality. The "personality" is, in effect, the hero's fate, and the bards could reduplicate it in different situations. Thus, the funeral games for Patroclus seem to echo the heroes' return stories:[68] Telamonian Ajax, doomed to kill himself after Achilles' armor is awarded to Odysseus, is wounded fighting against Diomedes; Locrian Ajax, who will die miserably at sea, falls into a pile of manure. The games, though, are more generally emblematic of the way the heroes are. Diomedes wins the chariot race; he is a winner throughout the poem. Teucer loses the archery contest, both because he does not make a major kill in the poem and because he will be exiled by his father when he returns from Troy; Teucer is unlucky. The audience may or may not know all the particular stories that have defined a hero's fate, but when new stories match old in this way, traditionality endures.

One of the most intense and contentious debates in Homeric studies concerns the extent of narrative innovation in the many paradigmatic tales the characters tell each other. On one side, M. Willcock has

---

68. See Whitman 1958, 263–64.

argued, in a very influential article, that many character narratives have been so modified to fit their immediate contexts that they may properly be said to be Homeric inventions.[69] Not just minor details are invented. Willcock argues that the poet has invented precisely the details that make the story paradigmatic. In his most convincing example, Achilles persuades Priam to eat.

> For even beautiful-haired Niobe remembered food, when her twelve children had died in her halls—six daughters and six sons in their youthful vigor. Apollo killed the boys, by shooting with his silver bow in his anger at Niobe, and Artemis, shedder of arrows, killed the girls, because she [Niobe] had compared herself to Leto of the lovely cheeks. She said that Leto had borne two, while she herself had given birth to many. So those two killed them all. For nine days, they lay in their gore, and there was nobody to bury them—the son of Cronus had made the people stones. On the tenth day, the gods of heaven buried them. And she remembered food, when she was tired of weeping. Now, among the rocks in the lonely mountains in Sipylus, where they say are the beds of the nymphs who play around Achelois, there, though she is stone, she broods over the griefs she received from the gods. (24.602–17)

Nobody telling the story of Niobe outside this particular context would have interrupted her mourning with a meal.[70]

The narrator does not draw audience attention to any innovation in such paradigmatic narratives. Nothing encourages the listener to try to distinguish details heard before from unfamiliar ones. The auditor is not supposed to admire the poet's cleverness or consider Achilles as an inventor, noticing the fictional qualities of his rhetoric.[71] The competent listener instead concentrates on the similarities and differences between Niobe and Priam, considering how well the paradigm works.

When Antinous tells the story of the centaur Eurytion (*Od.* 21.295–304), he reveals his stupidity by misapplying a traditional story, not by fictionalizing it. Characters may argue about the application of a para-

---

69. Willcock 1964; cf. Kakridis 1949, 99–103. Willcock (1977) also argues for invention; see also Jones 1992, 1995; Andersen 1977.

70. Hansen (1982, 102) sees the meal as rationalizing inference.

71. Edmunds (1997) argues for this distinction.

digm. Sthenelus, for example, does not agree when Agamemnon tells a story about Tydeus to show Diomedes is inferior to his father; Sthenelus says that Agamemnon is lying although he could tell the truth (μὴ ψεύ-δε᾽ ἐπιστάμενος σάφα εἰπεῖν, *Il.* 4.404). He does not deny the truth of the story Agamemnon has just told but places it within the wider narrative context of the failure of the Seven against Thebes and the success of their sons (4.405–10). Again, it is the application of the story that is open to dispute.

Odysseus and Nestor both evoke the day Achilles left his home to sail to Troy. According to Odysseus, however, Peleus warned Achilles against strife and anger (*Il.* 9.252–58); according to Nestor, Menoetius told Patroclus to give Achilles good advice, while Peleus told Achilles only "always to be best" (*Il.* 11.783–89). Neither Odysseus nor Nestor can be an unreliable narrator, especially since Patroclus was present at the original occasion and for both retellings. The departure sequence, including the father's final advice, is clearly a traditional type-scene, while the exact contents of the advice depend on what the son later needs to have heard. Neither Patroclus nor the external audience should care about inconsistency or the literal truth (i.e., fidelity to earlier versions/objective traditionality). The hearer must rather evaluate the advice given, its appropriateness within both the genre of such advice and the present context, and the internal audience's response to it.

On the other side, G. Nagy argues that these tales, so rhetorically fitted to their contexts, are not invented but selected from the rich variety available in the traditional story hoard.[72] This argument quickly runs into the danger of an infinite regress: all stories have either actually happened in the world or been invented at some time or other. The canon of Greek heroic stories clearly shows many of the processes by which storytellers created it over time. Neo-Analysts have argued that various incidents in the Homeric poems were modeled on events elsewhere in the cyclic epics or the tradition generally: Diomedes' rescue of Nestor on Antilochus's, Hector's death on Memnon's, Achilles' anger on Meleager's, Patroclus's funeral on Achilles'.[73] Within oral theory, we can understand these parallels without positing fixed texts, and we can

---

72. Nagy 1992; 1996b, 132–38. But Nagy (1996b, 19) also comments that "the here-and-now of each new performance is an opportunity for innovation, whether or not any such innovation is explicitly acknowledged in the tradition."

73. For a survey of Neo-Analysis, see Clarke 1986.

even appreciate their importance without necessarily attributing priority to one story or another. Such parallels, like the doublets within the poem—Thetis rescues both Hephaestus and Dionysus; both Zeus and Hera throw Hephaestus from Olympus—show how analogy and recombination generate new stories.

The epics did not survive uncontaminated from a remote past. The leaders of the Trojan War as we know it are Peloponnesian, but many of the most important heroes come from central and northern Greece.[74] M. L. West has convincingly argued for a "band of saga" in the late Mycenaean period going from Pylos through Aetolia and Thessaly.[75] Poets and storytellers clearly combined distinct strands of story to make the Trojan War. The process of syncretism and reorganization has developed a Nestor who is firmly rooted in Messenia but who belongs to a northern family and claims to have fought alongside the Lapiths. Exploits once local were transferred to the composite tales. Hector has many Boeotian victims, and there was a tomb of Hector in Thebes. Some scholars have even thought that Hector must have entered the Trojan saga from Boeotia.[76] This is very unlikely, but we may wonder how the Trojan hero acquired these associations. Diomedes may have made his way from the Theban story into the Trojan, where he develops as a lesser Achilles (in most of our *Iliad*) or a lesser Odysseus (in *Iliad* 10 and elsewhere).

The Trojan story, as it grew, surely required constant growth of this kind. The more Greek heroes needed opportunities for heroic action, the more Trojan heroes had to be developed as their opponents. Often, the question is how recently these transformations occurred. According to the Hesiodic *Ehoeae* (frag. 140 M.-W.), Sarpedon is the son of Zeus and Europa, so he would be too old for the *Iliad*. His role is not necessarily the invention of the *Iliad* poet, but a bard brought him into the Trojan story, perhaps, as R. Janko suggests, to provide Patroclus with a sufficiently impressive opponent.[77]

Along with their archaizing, the epics show the influence of cultural developments at least to the end of the eighth century. They contain sto-

---

74. See Lang 1995, 159–61.
75. West 1988, 160–61. I do not, however, see why Odysseus and Oelian Ajax should be primary while Menelaus is not.
76. See Bethe 1927, 76–83.
77. Janko, *Il. Comm.*, 4:370–71 (on 16.419–683).

ries that came into the Greek world from the Near East, almost certainly after the severe recession in economic life and cultural contacts that followed the Mycenaean collapse. Phoenicians appear in the *Odyssey*. They are "orientalized," shown only as tricky raiders and sources of luxury goods, but they are no inheritance from the Bronze Age. The allusions in the *Iliad* and *Odyssey* to Sicels and to Egypt suggest poets who were eager to incorporate the allusions to faraway places that the expansion of the eighth-century "renaissance" provided. The *Iliad* appears to allude to the language of sepulchral epitaph.[78] If we choose to date the *Iliad* near the end of the eighth century and the *Odyssey* not long after, we must assume that the epics absorbed new material very rapidly. The *Iliad*'s surprising sympathy for the Trojan enemy requires that the poet avoid the formulae he has inherited and narrate in territory for which his formulaic system is weak and therefore likely to be recent.[79]

Although Willcock and others are correct in finding Homeric innovation, they emphasize it too much. When we stress Homeric innovation, we risk applying an inappropriate romantic aesthetic to the epics, identifying their excellence with the poet's originality. When Nagy insists that Homer's storytelling is based in tradition and seeks to downplay the role of innovation, he is opposing that romanticization, with good reason. The ability to create appropriate variants for particular uses is one feature of Homer's art and a proof of poetic skill, but it is itself doubtless a traditional procedure. Emphasizing the innovation distorts the standards of the poems themselves. Furthermore, it is worth remembering that Homer's Niobe, after she eats, incongruously turns to stone. That is her traditional end, and the poet retains it, despite his dislike of magical transformations.[80]

Nagy, however, seeks not only to de-emphasize innovation but to deny individuals any significant role in composition; he and his followers attribute as much as possible to the tradition rather than to individual creators within it.[81] The tendency is most striking with Hesiod, because he makes what appear to be autobiographical statements.

---

78. See Scodel 1992a.

79. See Sale 1987.

80. Aristophanes of Byzantium and Aristarchus athetized the lines, as have several Analysts. Some have pointed out that Niobe's mourning parallels Priam's future mourning for Hector, but petrifaction makes her mourning eternal. See Richardson, *Il. Comm.*, 6:340, with bibliography.

81. Nagy (1996a, 20–22) answers criticism on this point from Carey (1992).

Many scholars have questioned whether Hesiod really met the Muses while tending sheep and whether the *Works and Days* is a transparent representation of a real dispute with a real brother. Some critics treat all apparently autobiographical remarks in Hesiod as traditional generic markers: they argue that "Hesiod" is no longer a bounded individual, that his father did not necessarily come from Cyme (being an immigrant is a poet's persona), and that his trip to Euboea is likewise about poetry.[82] According to the view behind these arguments, later poets— Theognis and even Pindar—also become less individual voices than names for branches of a tradition. One cannot disprove many of these suggestions, but Hesiod's claims that his father came from Aeolic Cyme, that he lived in Ascra, and that he won a tripod at the funeral games of Amphidamas are far likelier to have been truths shared as relevant to the context than eccentric traditional fictions.[83] Whereas if constantly looking for Homer's own inventions looks suspiciously like a reflex of a view of poetry that values individual genius and originality above all other qualities, denying individuals any significant role in composition excessively privileges tradition over individuals.

We cannot know and do not really need to know at exactly what stage in the process of creation a given element first appeared. Much of what some scholars call "invented" might better be called "contextually bound." Homer may very well have invented a given detail in a subordinate narrative that serves the rhetorical purpose of its immediate context, but so may his teacher, his teacher's teacher, or another bard from whom he adapted this section. Someone invented it. However, what matters more is that its transmission is bound to its context, without which it has no function and makes little sense. Nobody heard Homer's version of the Niobe story except in a consolation scene and probably in a scene in which Achilles consoled Priam—in a very close relative of our *Iliad*. Contextually bound material is less likely to be familiar to everyone than is material that might appear in many stories and versions. The other side of "invention" is the dissolution of contextual bonds: the bards remove heroes from their original contexts or give one hero an exploit modeled on those of another, as the bards brought Sarpedon to

---

82. See Nagy 1990a, 48–49; Lamberton 1988, 11–37; Martin 1992; Rosen 1990. The schema of Nagy (1990b, 80) is probably valid, but I see no reason why Hesiod should not belong to stage 1.

83. On the motives for such self-presentation, see Griffith 1990.

Troy and as Diomedes and Patroclus both probably echo Achilles when Apollo must threaten them to stop their assaults.

The *Iliad* relies heavily on such invention—that is, recombination—in battle narrative. The bards needed large numbers of minor characters for killing by the major ones, either in the lists of victims or in the brief duels. Some of these killings were probably traditional feats, perhaps treated at full length in other songs, but they can hardly all have been remembered.[84] Many of these characters were drawn from the catalogues the bard had memorized. The poet recycles many names of victims. For example, Hector kills Orestes and Oenomaus in successive line ends at *Iliad* 5.705–6, but at 12.139–40, again at line end, two warriors with these names fight beside Asius. Leonteus kills Orestes at 12.193–94, while Idomeneus kills Oenomaus at 13.506–8. The association of the names is separate from the context in which the names are used.[85]

The details of the victims' biographies may be thematically organized to fit a particular context. In his *aristeia,* Agamemnon kills first Bienor and Oilius, who have epithets but no patronymics or biographies, and then two sons of Priam, Isus and Antiphus, whom he recognizes because they had once been captured and ransomed by Achilles (*Il.* 11.101–20).[86] Then the sons of Antimachus beg Agamemnon to spare them for ransom. By mentioning their father's name and wealth, they doom themselves, since their father took a bribe from Paris and urged that Menelaus and Odysseus be murdered when they came as ambassadors to Troy (11.122–42). Finally, he kills two sons of Antenor, the Trojan elder who urges Helen's return: but the son whose death is expanded grew up with his grandfather in Thrace, and the particular histories of slayer and slain have no effect on the event (11.221–63). The sequence as a whole emphasizes Agamemnon's relentless hatred of the Trojans (evident also at 6.53–60). Even though he cites his reason for not sparing the (innocent) sons of a Trojan who particularly deserves his ha-

---

84. At *Il.* 5.43–47, Idomeneus kills Phaestus; but it is likelier that the poet associated the Cretan hero with a Cretan place than that this is a genuine reflection of Cretan saga. It is even less likely that Hector was originally Boeotian. See Bowra 1930, 76–81.

85. See Beye 1964.

86. Wilamowitz-Moellendorff (1916, 185; cf. Leaf 1900–1902, ad loc.) would treat *Il.* 11.101–12 as interpolated because Agamemnon's recognition is irrelevant—it has no narrative consequences. Within this series of killing, this inconsequentiality may be precisely the point.

tred, he actually kills all equally.[87] Agamemnon's passionate hatred for
all Trojans stands in contrast to Achilles' earlier generosity and so pro-
vides a thematic twist: when he finally returns to battle, Achilles is as re-
lentless as Agamemnon. Agamemnon may or may not have been a par-
ticularly ferocious warrior in earlier epic, but the poet develops this
aspect of his traditional personality relative to Achilles' and arranges his
Trojan victims accordingly. Like the details of paradigms, these Trojans
and their fates are contextually determined expansions of the traditional
characters of their fathers. The minor warriors thus reveal particularly
clearly how the poet "invents" his narrative by using both generalized
traditional resources, such as associations among names, and themes
unique to his own story.

Invention, in this sense, exists in Homer. This whole debate,
though, suffers from a reification of tradition. If nobody has access to all
previous performances, nobody can know for certain what is tradi-
tional. An audience can judge only whether a story is familiar or unfa-
miliar. If a story is unfamiliar in its exact details but uses familiar mate-
rial, as the Niobe story does, it will sound traditional. Adaptation of
stories to particular contexts is itself a traditional practice, conducted
within traditional parameters. The opposition between tradition and in-
vention thus partially collapses, though only partially—there will al-
ways be a limit for innovation beyond which audiences will refuse to
recognize traditionality.

When the singer of tales performs, singer and audience consciously
participate in a traditional form. They are fully aware that by listening
and performing, they are doing as people have done before them, re-
reenacting the mode of performance, the formulaic technique, some of
the formulae themselves, and (at least in large part) the content of the
tales. This consciousness of participation in a chain of transmission is
crucial to the authority of the song—although, as we shall see, the
Homeric Muses provide an alternative authority. Yet historians know
very well that among the most cherished traditions of a people may be
recent inventions. "Tradition" is in constant flux and will be redefined
as its context changes.[88] For those inside the tradition, what matters is
that they are able to feel that the performance is traditional, that it re-

---

87. See Strasburger 1954, 69–72, developing Schadewaldt 1966, 47–50 .

88. In the terminology of *The Invention of Tradition*, "tradition" corresponds
to what Hobsbawn calls "custom" (Hobsbawn and Ranger 1983, 2–3).

peats crucial elements of performances of the past. Traditionality does not depend entirely on objective tradition. It is a cultural construct, the social memory of the past. Still, it cannot be sustained without the truly familiar, the actually remembered. This aspect is not trivial or merely decorative. It is relatively easy to catalogue a list of archaic words, practices, and objects (e.g., a boar's-tusk helmet) and dismiss them as devices for creating "epic distance."[89] For the historian who needs the epics as evidence about the context of their origin, this is an appropriate procedure. From this perspective, devices that create "distance" are an unimportant residue. However, if we are asking not what the world outside the performance arena was like but how the audience understood the epic world, we need to consider the balance between the epic's distance and its accessibility. Any successful performance of narrative, oral or written, must speak meaningfully to vital and contemporary concerns of its audience, but the possible negotiations are many and varied.

Audiences can be capable of ignoring change from performance to performance if the circumstances demand it. In Upper Egypt, the epic performance itself has powerful cultural authority, but the poet himself is an outcast of very low status. In most other social situations, however, the prestige of speech depends directly on the prestige of the speaker. Hence, the audience has a stake in treating the poet as a mere mouthpiece for the tradition. It ignores the poet's active role in recomposition and treats each performance (apart from the direct addresses to the audience) as a verbatim repetition of a memorized text. Small differences among performances, obvious to the specialist outsider, are invisible to the local audience.[90] Where audiences notice differences, they may reject the performance.

In a culture with a fertile, fluid tradition of epic performance, a performer may learn about variants from other localities and introduce them into his own repertory. These function as innovations from the perspective of an audience not familiar with them already. This can be an important issue for the working bard. A performer does not need to be scrupulous about providing background information as long as the audience knows the story already and knows it in a form close to the one in which it is currently being told. If the story is significantly different from versions familiar to the audience, the performer needs to be as

---

89. See Morris 1986.
90. See Slyomovics 1987, 19.

meticulous as if it were completely new—perhaps more so, because he also needs to be prepared for conscious resistance to the unfamiliar.

At the same time, the audience may come to accept the introduction of new variants as itself a traditional procedure. Diachronically, as singers constantly both transmit what they have learned and innovate, some elements are older than others. Synchronically, when members of the audience recognize any element as already familiar, whether it is a verb form, a feast scene, or a hero's death, we may call it "strongly traditional": these are the elements that establish the traditionality of the performance. The audience may believe, rightly or wrongly, that a particular element is very old and may value it for that reason. At the other end lies the "strongly innovative": material that almost everyone recognizes as new, even if it bears a clear resemblance to the familiar. Pindar, for example, comments on his own innovations in performance style (*Ol.* 3.4–6) and polemically marks his new story about Pelops as new (*Ol.* 1.36), while comparing this new story to the familiar tale about Ganymede and also summarizing the story he rejects. Pindar distorts the objectively traditional story for his own purposes as he summarizes it. Like traditionality, innovation is a rhetorical position. In between lie all the shadings of the "traditional," from stories familiar in all except peripheral details or familiar epic words in unfamiliar inflectional forms to stories unfamiliar in themselves but formed of familiar elements and consistent with the already known. Homeric poetry is strongly traditionalist, never acknowledging that any aspect of its story is not old.

The Javanese *wayang kulit*, or shadow-puppet theater, is a useful point of comparison for issues of tradition and audience, although its performance style is very unlike that of Greek epic.[91] The tradition is of very long standing and has been fostered by the royal courts, but it is also strongly rooted in the villages. It is widely regarded as *the* Javanese performance and is important in Javanese identity. The stories are epic, mainly derived from the *Mahabharata*.

A wayang performance is typically sponsored by a family in connection with a life-cycle event or in fulfillment of a vow; some performances also take place for potential crises. A screen replaces one wall of the family house. Invited guests sit inside the house and see the per-

---

91. De Vet (1996) cites Balinese shadow theater along with other Balinese genres; Thornton (1984, 9–10) cites the stamina of the Javanese and Malay performers as parallel for Homer.

formance from the shadow side. Outside, behind the puppeteer, or *dha-lang*, and the gamelan orchestra, as many as two hundred people may watch from the puppet side. The audience is primarily, but not exclusively, male. A night wayang begins around nine and continues until morning. The invited guests must leave around midnight, since anyone staying longer would appear to be demanding more food. Some guests remain and continue to watch from the puppet side. While most performances occupy one night, some multinight performances present a larger sequence.

Dhalangs are composers-in-performance on the Parry-Lord model. Only in a recent, innovative variety of performance developed at the government academy on Western models is there a written script. The dhalang improvises constantly, adapting his show to the occasion and to the response of the audience. A patron, for example, may ask for a performance with many jokes rather than a solemn one. Dhalangs regularly invent stories, using the traditional characters and story types in slightly new arrangements. Their terminology distinguishes "trunk" stories from "branch" stories, and although their definitions of these terms differ, they recognize a canonical structure that is not changeable as well as considerable room for invention. Moreover, the stories from the earlier parts of the epic tradition have fallen out of the repertory. Audiences are not familiar with the characters who do not belong to the generation of the Pandawas and Korawas, so dhalangs may transfer to them tales originally associated with earlier figures.[92] In other words, the dhalang knows the tradition better than most of the audience and uses this superior knowledge. One dhalang describes his practice as follows:

> It's usually easy for me. I'll describe my own experience. Mas Tikno, we'd like the story Sang Sang Kencana Anting Retno. Now in this case, I've never heard of that story. Actually I feel rather surprised. Ha, what is this Sang Sang Kencana Anting Retno story? Well, Sang Sang Anting Retno, what could that story be? Then suddenly I get some ideas. Since these people like fancy puppet movements and clown scenes, I'll use a story that highlights those things. Therefore the result is like this. I took a Mask Play story but I changed the name of the boon. It's just a starting point. In the first scene, if I'm not mistaken, there's the visitor to the kingdom, but

---

92. See Sears 1986, 126.

maybe I'll change it to another. That's how it's done in the per-
formances. Most puppeteers who create stories take things from
their own imaginations.[93]

The speaker defines "imagination" as practitioners of traditional narra-
tive do; it is the ability to adapt material from one story to another.

Not only are the plots and characters in a wayang performance
highly stylized, but so is the sequence of episodes. Every play begins and
ends with a scene in an assembly hall. The first scene presents a king-
dom at peace, and only after an extended picture of its peace and pros-
perity does a messenger enter to announce the problem that will drive
the story. There is always a scene in which the hero must travel through
a forest and fight with ogres, and after midnight, there is always a bat-
tle. The heroes' servants always have clown scenes. Indeed, invented
stories follow the usual scheme more rigidly than do old ones.[94] This is
a necessity for audience comprehension, especially because the wayang
has an audience whose attention level is extremely variable. During the
opening set in the assembly hall, the audience is noisy. People are still
arriving, and those present are chatting and being served food. Only
when the real dramatic action starts do they really begin to watch. As the
night wears on, many members of the audience outside become tired
and go home; many fall asleep. By morning, usually only a few young
men are still watching. Much of the audience may doze or gamble dur-
ing less favorite sections. They will rouse themselves for a battle—bat-
tles are especially popular—or a funny clown scene. Only connoisseurs
regularly watch a performance from beginning to end. The plots need to
be stylized and episodic to accommodate this kind of audience.

Despite the apparent lack of emphasis on narrative progress in per-
formance and despite the episodic qualities of the narrative, audiences
judge dhalangs not only for their voices and their skills in manipulating
puppets but for their ability to make a coherent story out of the main
plot and subplots and to bring the whole to a satisfying conclusion. The
relationship between performer and audience is not less complex in an
oral culture than in a literate one. Javanese say a dhalang should be im-
pervious to outside influence, should never turn his head during per-
formance, and should not make jokes about anyone present. Yet prac-

---

93. Quoted in Sears 1986, 120.
94. See Keeler 1987, 194–95.

ticing dhalangs also stress the importance of gauging audience response. The most famous dhalang of the 1950s, Ki Poedjosoemarto, was widely praised for his pure and classical style, but spectators did not remain long after midnight at his performances.[95] Ki Poedjosoemarto was still remembered and respected in the next generation; sponsors hired him even though audiences did not enjoy his shows as much as those of less refined dhalangs. Even in oral culture, popularity in actual performance is not the only guarantor of success. Even in a tradition that stresses entertainment, performances serve the goals—spiritual and social—of their patrons, and audience taste is not the only factor that causes success or failure.

Many individuals in the typical audience of a wayang performance do not have an encyclopedic knowledge of the tradition. Everyone knows the major heroes and the main outlines of the *Mahabharata* tale, and everyone knows how wayang is structured. All Javanese (at least all male Javanese) learn how to watch wayang. Beyond this basic knowledge, however, there is a wide range of familiarity. Not everybody likes wayang very much, and not everyone has equal opportunity to see it. Because the social rules do not demand close attention throughout a performance, the audience does not learn as much from each performance as one might expect.

The situation of the dhalang quoted above was atypical—the patron wanted a story the performer did not know. However, the dhalang was able to generate a "new" story that satisfied the patron. The dhalang could innovate traditionally. Real-life performances in the world of Homer probably resembled wayang in several crucial respects. Not everyone had the same knowledge, but the performer expected familiarity with the genre itself and the core stories. Individuals had varying knowledge of the tradition. Most people would have had the opportunity to hear only a restricted number of performers on a regular basis, and the repertory of an individual performer was likely to be limited. Patrons in a given region would have their own preferences, which would further limit the familiarity of the audiences in that region with stories those preferences excluded.

The Homeric epics imply an immense repertory, if we assume that every story to which they allude was a possible subject of epic song— an assumption supported by the fact that many stories mentioned in

---

95. See Keeler 1987, 184–85.

Homer were indeed treated in other epics. First, the Trojan story itself could provide many episodes suitable for separate performance, as indicated by the first song of Demodocus (*Od.* 8.73–82), whether or not it represents a "real" tradition. W. Kullmann divides Proclus's summary of the Epic Cycle into 130 paragraphs.[96] Many of these could furnish a performance by themselves, although others would be likelier to be combined. Of course, Trojan stories were not the only ones available. The *Odyssey* alludes to the Argo as "known to all" (12.70); the various adventures of Jason's crew could fill many separate evenings of narrative, as Apollonius' four books demonstrate. Heracles also provided a wide selection by himself. The Homeric epics mention the Trojan War, the adventure on Cos, the murder of Iphitus, and his descent into Hades. Then there is the Theban saga, well-known to the *Iliad,* including the stories of Oedipus, the Seven against Thebes, and the Epigoni. The tales of Nestor imply a Pylian tradition, and he associates himself with the Lapiths in their battle with the centaurs (*Il.* 1.260–73). The epics do not tell of Peleus's heroic deeds, apart from his marriage to Thetis, but the poets probably knew them, since Peleus is cited as one before whom all the leaders should be ashamed of their cowardice (*Il.* 7.125). The *Odyssey* briefly tells the stories of Melampus (there was a *Melampodia* attributed to Hesiod) and his descendent Theoclymenus (11.287–97, 15.223–56, 271–78). The Cretan adventures of Theseus are known in the *Odyssey* (11.321–25). Also available for epic performance were the stories of heroes who do not belong to any of these cycles, such as Meleager, Bellerophon, Orion, Lycurgus, Otus and Ephialtes, Amphion and Zethus, the Dioscuri, and Areithous. The epics by themselves imply hundreds of possible songs, and not all performers performed strictly epic material. The corpus of Hesiodic poetry offers theogonic and wisdom poetry, as well as epic material in genealogical, catalogue form.

Avdo Međedović, the finest representative of his tradition that Parry and Lord met and an extraordinary master singer, had a repertory of fifty-eight songs.[97] Most singers from Novi Pazar had much smaller repertories. Ramo thought that he had once known thirty songs but that he only remembered ten when Parry and Lord worked with him; in fact, he knew six.[98] One Croatian singer knew ninety songs (for a total of

---

96. Kullmann 1960, 52–57.
97. See Parry, Lord, and Bynum 1974, 6–7.
98. See Parry and Lord 1954, 53–55.

about double the length of the Homeric poems combined), and several knew fifty.[99] A singer in the tradition of the Turkish minstrel tale learned thirteen songs during his apprenticeship and twenty or twenty-five more later, in the army.[100] In a one-song tradition, the singer may know an epic that would require over a hundred hours to perform—four times the *Iliad*. The Kirghiz Manas cycle, collected by Radlov in the nineteenth century as an "induced" epic, is about 250,000 verses. Two different singers performed it at this length, probably the longest such performances known.[101] The possible repertory of a single performer is thus considerably larger than the Homeric epics. However, the corpus of possible songs the epics imply is very large for any individual and much too large to have been the norm for performers.

Epic performance is very unlikely to have been the only form in which Greeks told their stories, though Homerists often slip into calling it the only medium of fame. Just as epic has evidently appropriated the material of folktales and travelers' tales, so the broader oral tradition will have appropriated stories from epic. Still, it seems to me extraordinarily unlikely that even an exceptionally well-trained bard had heard full-length versions of all these stories. Nestor's stories imply a rich Pylian tradition, but it is probable that many bards knew Nestor only as a character in Trojan stories and so knew his youthful deeds only from summaries. It is even less likely that every member or even the average member of Homer's implied audience would have known all the stories in detail. In any case, the audience's experience cannot have included all stories previously told.

The issue may be one not of poetic invention but of borrowing from traditions with which not everyone in the audience is familiar. The Homeric epics, for example, show the relatively recent influence of Near Eastern literature.[102] New mythology has been not only Hellenized but incorporated into the traditional epic framework. The cosmogonic function of Tethys, for example, may not have been familiar to everyone in Homer's audience. It was not an invention but a borrowing from the

---

99. See Bowra 1930, 49.

100. See Moyle 1990, 97–98, 106–8. In this tradition, it appears to be learning the sung portions of the tales that is difficult; the narratives are so similar that learning them receives little attention.

101. See Chadwick and Zhirmunsky 1969, 279–80, 304–6.

102. See Burkert 1992, 88–120 (on Tethys, 91–93); and West 1997.

Near East. Nonetheless, for anyone who had never heard this particular version of this particular story, it would have been "original." Would Homer's audience have been able to distinguish Homer's own invention from borrowings from other branches of Greek tradition or from non-Greek traditions?

The preceding comparison with wayang points in another direction, too. Not everybody pays constant attention in a long performance. Like dhalangs, bards probably often had audiences whose attention varied. Wayang solves this difficulty through fixed structure. Homer responds to it also. Like other archaic narrative, epic usually gives expository information only at the moment it is required. Odysseus's scar is a perfect example. The narrator does not mention the scar until the moment before Eurycleia recognizes the hero, when Odysseus himself remembers his scar and the danger it presents (*Od.* 19.390–91). The narrator must guard not only against the possibility that the audience may forget what he has already said but against the possibility that some may miss it in the first place. Archaic narrative technique is an adaptation to this problem.

The Homeric epics are crammed with recapitulations and predictions. These are rarely precisely accurate, and they do not replace the full experience of hearing the poem. Still, they provide an ongoing flow of information about where the story now stands and where it is going. Even misdirections mislead only in part. The *Iliad* falsely implies that Hector will burn the Achaean ships. Although he does not, he almost does; Homer points in the correct general direction the narrative will take without revealing all outcomes or details.

Perhaps the most difficult recapitulation to explain is the one Achilles gives his mother at *Iliad* 1.365–92.[103] This comes very early in the narrative. It is not necessary within the mimetic world, since Thetis has prophetic and presumably clairvoyant powers; Achilles himself remarks that she knows already what has happened (1.365; the "reminding" aesthetic allows him to tell her anyway). The recapitulation does not convey Achilles' emotional state to the audience (as does the end of the speech at 1.408–12). Achilles pushes the limits of a mortal speaker in describing Apollo's response to Chryses' prayer, but does not quite exceed them, since it would not be difficult to infer how the events must

---

103. Wilamowitz-Moellendorff (1916, 252–53) compares the passage to a Menandrian prologue.

have taken place. The speech gives twelve lines to Chryses' visit to the Greek camp and prayer—lines that echo closely the poet's own—and only eleven to the plague and quarrel itself.[104] Kirk wonders if the speech was not originally an alternative to the beginning of the poem as it now stands, but it is hard to imagine an *Iliad* that begins much later in the tale than does our extant one.[105]

If, though, we consider a listening audience who did not know this story already, the beginning of the *Iliad* is extremely demanding. The hearer must follow the story while reconstructing its antecedents, a task requiring considerable narrative competence, especially because Chryses' failure is partly the result of his ignorance of how the Achaeans have divided their booty, an ignorance the audience may share. Also, Greek audiences may well, like Javanese audiences, have been inattentive during the opening hymn, only settling down to listen carefully when the real action begins. The action in the *Iliad* begins very quickly. In performance, some listeners would not concentrate soon enough. This early recapitulation, which includes a careful mention of the division of spoils, helped anyone who was actually confused. This clarification, setting events in chronological order, would make everyone confident of understanding the sequence of events correctly. Once the antecedents were clear, the poet could recapitulate the action itself more briefly and with a more obviously limited character perspective. If any of this material was new to the audience or differed from a familiar story, the repetition not only made it clearer but gave it greater authority—when Achilles tells it, it has already been heard. Like a dhalang, the bard had to manage sometimes contradictory demands, having to maintain standards while pleasing a crowd and to appear aloof while reacting to the audience. With Achilles' recapitulation, he helps the audience follow without appearing to condescend to them. However, the Homeric bard did not have the dhalang's freedom of imagination. Wayang's fixed structure, music, and familiar puppets representing a limited set of characters help sustain traditionality even when the plot is new. Homer had

---

104. Rabel (1997, 48–51) argues that while the narrator implicitly compares Achilles to Apollo, Achilles himself uses Chryses as a paradigm. But both Achilles and Chryses follow a traditional pattern, and I am not convinced that the Apollo/Chryses distinction is significant or that a listening audience would notice it.

105. Kirk, *Il. Comm.*, 1: 91–93 (on 1.366–92).

a harder task in simultaneously adapting to present needs and maintaining traditionality.

M. Nagler has said, "All is traditional on the generative level, all is original on the level of performance."[106] This is true, but we cannot simply evade or trump the controversies about tradition and innovation by turning this formulation into a mantra. In one sense, we can perhaps say that even passages a bard has clearly memorized (i.e., which he performs with exactly the same words many times) are recomposed at the moment of performance (as in Borges's "Pierre Menard, Author of *Don Quixote*"), but there are real differences, for both performers and audiences, between exact repetitions and variations. Albert Lord tended to exaggerate the level of observable recomposition in different performances and to discount instances of memorization, because memorization was not what he wanted to find. Some singers learned a song, perhaps from a book, and sang it exactly as they learned it; others did not. The differences are real. Attempts to treat all oral performances and all elements of performances as equally traditional and original accept a mystification.

The Homeric audience believed that the stories were basically true. By pretending that each version is the same as others told before, the audience could ignore truth-threatening changes. Poet and audience thus had a shared interest in regarding the content of each performance as fully traditional. Nonetheless, the narrator had no easy task. Just as modern readers of fiction are willing to believe but will nonetheless reject a narrative that offends their sense of what is believable, so the audience of Homeric epic did not scrupulously worry about what it had heard before, but the hearers expected what they heard to accord in essentials with earlier renditions.

While the poets adapted their stories to present circumstances, they never mark innovation as such. Invention within traditionalizing poetry must be invisible. A usable past may need to be reinvented all the time, but if the society knows that its myths are mythic, they will not be very useful. Constant innovation may be necessary, but if the poetry itself does not value invention, modern scholars must be cautious in judging its function. If the rhetoric of Homeric epic discourages attention to originality, perhaps scholars, too, should direct less attention to finding or denying it.

---

106. Nagler 1974, 26.

Textualization and the Newest Song

Oral poets usually perform for audiences whose tastes and responses they can hope to predict. Often, the audiences are local, and a poet may perform many times for the same individuals and come to know their tastes precisely. In some traditions, much of the liveliness of particular performances comes from spontaneous interaction between the poet and members of the audience.[1] Even when the poet does not personally know the audience, each audience is like others he has known. The poet can use his knowledge of the audience's social standing, wealth, family connections, political affiliations, and gender, as well as of the particular occasion for the performance, to render his performance appropriate and acceptable. Often, there is a single patron, whose satisfaction is paramount.

Performers therefore have special problems when they face unfamiliar audiences. The dhalang faced with a request he could not fulfill at least knew what kinds of plays his audience liked. In his own district, a performer can introduce innovations gradually, relying on the confidence his audience has in him and developing their taste along with his own. Of course, sometimes poets fail, not because they are incompetent in their traditions, but because they do not achieve rapport with a particular audience. Devlal's performance of the Candaini epic discussed in the preceding chapter failed because he and his (unfamiliar) audience did not share expectations.

The Homeric poems are often called "Panhellenic" in orientation. They address no particular audience and were thus available for all Greeks. Composed as texts, they were created to be performed and reperformed for audiences widespread in space and time. Homeric epic thus confronted not only the challenges inherent in a developing genre but the even greater challenge of a large and unknown audience.

---

1. The audience of Alhā sings along at verse end (see Blackburn et al. 1989); 'Adwallah teased individual audience members as part of the performance (see Slyomovics 1987).

It is not possible to discuss the audience for which the poets composed without trying to decide what the circumstances of composition were. The older form of this issue was the Homeric Question, the debate over whether each epic was the product of a single author or of a process in which poets incorporated and adapted earlier texts. Oral theory transformed the Homeric Question. The question became whether the poems are genuine oral compositions and, if so, how they became written texts. If the poems' view of their audiences is in question, however, the real issue is not the technology by which the poems were composed but how and why they came to be stable texts, particularly at the level of story. Pabuji is textualized without being written; the episodes and their order are fixed, and even the couplets are standard; variation appears mainly in inclusion or omission.[2] The Serbo-Croatian Muslim tradition was less rigid, with frequent variation in the actual narrative.[3] Still, singers could list the songs that they knew, and many performed the same song on different occasions with some variation at the verbal level but none at the level of story, while they repeated many passages exactly. The crucial moment, then, is the one at which these poems existed as recognizably the *Iliad* and the *Odyssey*. From outside, it is impossible to know just how divergent songs that were recognized as "the same" could be, but not every song of Achilles' wrath was an *Iliad*, not every version of Odysseus's return an *Odyssey*. We cannot think of a performance as (proto-)*Iliad* or *Odyssey* unless it included the episodes that the relevant epic now includes, in the order in which they now stand.

One can imagine the basic textualization of the epics as happening in various ways. The fundamental question is whether each poem was created at one time by one person or through a gradual process. A single poet could have composed such a work by either writing or dictating it. Alternatively, he could have composed it in performance at an extraordinary occasion. A widely accepted theory of the origins of the epics sees them as originally performances at a festival (e.g., the Panionia) where celebrants came together from several cities.[4] A bard could have created a monumental epic for a stable, local audience listening to a long series of performances over many evenings. Any hypothesis that

---

2. See Smith 1991.

3. See Parry, Lord, and Bynum 1974, 13–32, for a comparison of Avdo's version of *The Wedding of Smailagic Meho* with a printed version of 1886.

4. See Wade-Gery 1952, 14–18.

excludes a deliberate textualization demands further consideration of how a reasonably stable transmission took place. Gregory Nagy has argued for a gradual process, in which Panhellenic diffusion led to a gradual stabilization of the poems, with an important transition toward stability under the Pisistratids. Others have placed even stronger emphasis on the "Pisistratid recension."[5]

These different hypotheses produce very different bard-audience relations. If the epics as we know them developed gradually, their versions of the stories established themselves as canonical bit by bit, and no bard confronted any special difficulty with presenting unfamiliar material to an unfamiliar audience. Equally, if a single bard composed for the benefit of a stable, local audience in a serial performance and never considered any broader public, he could rely on genuine intimacy with his public. If the epics' structures were designed to meet the needs of the Athenian Panathenaea, their creators knew their audience and patrons well. In contrast, a bard who composed for a Panhellenic festival audience—or who generated a written version intended for many reperformances—would have to address an audience existing only on this occasion. The task of allowing for audience expectations and prior knowledge would have been tricky. What are the connections between performances and audiences, on one side, and the epics, on the other?

A plausible reconstruction must acknowledge evidence that points in two directions. The poems are linguistically "older" than other Greek hexameter poetry. Dating on the basis of linguistic evidence is very uncertain, since different branches of the tradition and different subgenres may have balanced innovation and archaism differently. Dating on the basis of geographical references and material culture is also tricky: basic textualization did not necessarily end oral performance and minor change, so an isolated allusion may be a later addition to the text. Still, both linguistically and in their contents, the poems are not later than the middle of the seventh century. They are probably earlier—the *Iliad* perhaps from the eighth century, the *Odyssey* from the end of the eighth or the beginning of the seventh. These facts are hard to reconcile with a tradition still highly fluid until the Pisistratids in the later sixth century.

---

5. Nagy 1996a, 29–112; 1990b, 56–60. I am defending what Nagy (1996b, 92–93) calls the "big bang" theory of Homeric composition. Other recent defenders of the Pisistratid role are Jensen (1980), Stanley (1993, 280–93), and Seaford (1994, 144–54).

The poems were certainly not canonical in the earlier seventh century. A vessel from around 720 inscribed as "Nestor's cup" clearly refers to the vessel described at *Iliad* 11.632–35. Some Homeric descriptions of significant objects go back to the Bronze Age, but it is not certain that this is one of them, and the cup could well be a joke on the passage in the *Iliad*.[6] Ischia, where it was found, was a colony of Euboea, where Hesiod competed—it may have been a center of epic. The earliest Greek lyric is engaged with epic but not necessarily with our *Iliad* or *Odyssey*. Lyrics by Alcaeus (frag. 44) and Ibycus (5151 *PMGF*) are the earliest lyrics that seem to presuppose an *Iliad*. Alcaeus refers to Thetis's plea, while Ibycus reflects the Catalogue of Ships (but not necessarily the version adapted for our *Iliad*).[7] Although scenes from Trojan stories appear often in Greek art of the seventh century, specifically Homeric ones are rare compared to the Trojan Horse, for example.[8] Depictions of scenes that have parallels in the Homeric epics nonetheless do not represent exactly what the epics narrate.[9] The differences are not great enough to prove the existence of true narrative variants within the performance of the epics. Greek artists rarely followed literary sources scrupulously, and lyric was creating and diffusing new variants. The differences do, however, suggest that the Homeric poems were not dominant.

The claim that the poems are somehow Panhellenic is familiar and uncontroversial. They are remarkably free of local connections. The *Iliad* was probably composed in Asia Minor; the poet's knowledge of the geography there is more detailed than the poet's knowledge of other places. Scholars have often argued that the fight between Achilles and Aeneas (*Il.* 20.158–352) adapts a poem flattering Aeneadae, but as the poem stands, Achilles is winning when the god intervenes. The poem promises that Aeneas and his descendants will rule over the Trojans

---

6. Latacz (1996, 61–63) argues that the inscription presupposes widespread knowledge of the *Iliad*. However, he assumes that the Homeric were the only hexameter poems in wide circulation.

7. See Fowler 1987.

8. See Friis Johansen 1967. Kannicht (1982) suggests that the exceptional quality of the poems discouraged artists.

9. This point has been stressed by Lowenstam (1997). I suspect that most of his examples—the François vase, for example—depend on lyric narratives that are themselves deliberate variants on our epics (which professional poets would know in the sixth century), not on "traditions."

(20.307–8), without saying where their home will be. The poet offers Aeneas as founder or ancestor to whoever claims him.[10] M. L. West has suggested Euboea as the site of composition for the *Odyssey,* seeing a locally based joke in Alcinous's reference to the island as remote.[11] The *Odyssey* may give an etiology for the tripod dedications of the ninth and eighth centuries at Polis Bay in Ithaca, but it is just as likely that both the poem and the tripods reflect an association of the hero with the place.[12] The epics avoid locating themselves.

The descriptions of bardic activity within the epics themselves provide fundamental evidence for the background of their performance, although they are obviously idealized (songs are uniformly of high quality and well received) and adapted to their contexts. They may also be archaized (bards may have recited rather than sung when the *Iliad* was composed); but even as a mixed memory and fantasy of how things once were, they are revealing. The bards Phemius and Demodocus seem to be attached to the leading household in their communities, and they perform in the king's hall after meals. However, Demodocus does not live in Alcinous's house but must be fetched, and Democodus's role in the royal household may not be permanent or fixed. The bards not only sing heroic tales with musical accompaniment but provide music for dancing, and they appear in a list of artisans whom one might invite to one's community, in contrast to beggars (*Od.* 17.383–85). Their "official" audience thus consists of the elite males who gather regularly in the chief's house, but they have a "secondary" audience of servants and women, since Penelope can hear the song from her own apartment, while Arete is present during the performances. Demodocus also performs for the large crowd at the Phaeacian games, but for this occasion, he sings not the deeds of heroes but a comic song of sexual misdoings among the gods; we cannot know whether this implies that heroic song is inappropriate for a mass audience. Apparently, bards may travel but

---

10. Smith (1981) sees no etiological force here or at *Hymn to Aphrodite* 196–97; but both passages invite such use, without specifying it. *Od.* 7.80–81, where Athena heads home to the Athenian acropolis, has often been suspected; but at 8.361–62, Ares and Aphrodite flee to Thrace and Paphos, respectively. Having implicitly praised one place for its special connection with a god, the poet not much later mentions other places with their own patrons.

11. West 1988, 172. See also Garvie 1994, 231–32 (ad loc.).

12. Malkin (1998, 94–119) argues that the tripods reflect Odysseus's landing in the *Odyssey,* which he dates very early.

do not wander constantly from place to place. The performances in the epics do not last longer than a few hours. Evidently, the Homeric poems do not fit the kind of performance they depict.

Hesiod provides complementary evidence. Although he did not compose heroic narrative in the Homeric style, he says in the proem of the *Theogony* (99–100) that people forget their cares when a bard "hymns the famous deeds of former people and the blessed gods who hold Olympus." The genre we call Homeric hymns was used as a prelude to epic performance. The corpus attributed to Hesiod included heroic genealogy (the *Catalogue of Women*) and other clearly epic material (*Melampodia, Descent of Perithous*). In other words, although Hesiod's poetry is quite different from Homer's, Hesiod himself did not see a sharp generic distinction, nor did archaic and classical Greek audiences. Hesiod says that the heroes died either in Cadmaean Thebes, fighting for the herds of Oedipus, or at Troy, where they fought for Helen (*Works and Days* 161–65), and he also refers to the mustering at Aulis to give epic coloring to his journey to Calchis (*Works and Days* 651–53). He and his audience thus had a basic familiarity with epic stories.

Hesiod says that his ferry ride to Euboea, where he competed successfully in the funeral games of Amphidamas (*Works and Days* 650–57), was the only time he traveled by sea. His victory shows that he could entertain an unfamiliar audience, even though, if he really was a farmer, he could hardly have traveled much more by land than by water. Surely, many Ascraeans traveled no more widely than Hesiod, so their experience of poetic performance may well have been limited to a few performers. A member of the elite who patronized a performer doubtless knew that performer's repertory very well, but not the stories that bard did not sing.

The comparative evidence from other epic traditions does not provide any tidy parallels. Traditions of heroic song can generally be divided into one-story and multi-story traditions. In a multi-story tradition, each performance normally offers one story, clearly demarcated from others and having its own beginning and end. Each story may have its own variants, but in each performance, the singer performs an identifiable song (unless the singer, as sometimes happens, accidentally slips from one similar song into another). Although each song is distinct, the songs may form a loose cycle, and even if they do not, performers and audiences recognize the tradition as a genre. The Muslim Serbo-Croatian tradition is of this kind.

In a one-story tradition, a typical performance offers an episode from a whole story that is too long to be performed all at once. The whole story is often a *notional epic,* like Pabuji from Rajasthan, and even where the performer's repertory includes episodes from more than one such epic, the stories of each epic are fully distinct. Each epic is really a genre in itself. When a collector induces a single performer to perform the entire work at once, an *induced epic* is generated. John Smith induced a full performance of Pabuji, Biebuyck and Mateene induced a full performance of Mwindo, and 'Abd al-Rahman al-Abnoudy both invited full performances of the Sira Bani Hilali and popularized them over the radio.[13]

The *Iliad* and *Odyssey* fit neither type of story tradition precisely. Indeed, the Homeric epics are notoriously odd as possible oral compositions.[14] They are very long, too long for most performance situations. But despite their length, the epics seem clearly, in their present form, designed for continuous reception or at least for reception within the context of a whole they themselves define. Both epics are mere episodes in a much longer story, the Troy tale, which is itself incorporated into the overarching legendary history of the Greeks. The epics explicitly locate themselves within this larger frame. They belong to a multi-story tradition in which cycles of stories are well established. However, they are relatively self-contained. Most of their episodes do not work well if their implicit frame is the Trojan cycle as a whole, instead of the epics themselves. In the *Iliad,* some episodes could effectively be performed by themselves, such as book 10. The single combat between Ajax and Hector can take place only while Achilles is away, but otherwise it can stand alone. The funeral games of Patroclus could perhaps stand alone. Otherwise, most parts of the poem seem very weak when removed from the whole as the whole (approximately) now stands. Many sections could be modified to stand by themselves, but in their present form, the context they imply is the context of the *Iliad.* The same is true of the *Odyssey.* The Cyclops and Circe episodes could stand alone, although the first-person narration of their extant versions demands a frame. Perhaps the bow contest and slaying of the suitors could be performed by themselves. Many episodes, though, completely lose their point in a different context. The Telemachy works only in a richly expanded version of

---

13. See Smith 1991, 17–18; Biebuyck and Mateene 1969, 14; Connelly 1986, 48–49, 185–86.

14. There is a good discussion of the problem of reception in Ford 1997.

Odysseus's return. The spatial and chronological crosscutting of the narrative would make it hard to perform outside the *Odyssey*, since the main section ends at a point where none of the narrative issues has been resolved, with Telemachus asleep in Sparta.

Analysts generally postulated that each stage of the epics' composition involved some modification of the existing material, because most of what is before us clearly could not stand alone. That means not that single episodes could not be performed—they surely were, once the poems were composed—but that the whole of which such episodes were a part was not the epic tradition in general or the Troy story but the *Iliad* or *Odyssey*, at least as notional epics. The epics work, in many ways, as if they were the product of a continuous tradition of performance of a one-story tradition. At the same time, they very frequently refer to other stories—those of Heracles, Agamemnon, Jason—placing themselves firmly within a multistory tradition.

The epics do not break easily into episodes within the whole tradition, and each is also a unified composition. They yield more meaning in a continuous reception. Some repetitions, both of small groups of lines and of large-scale narrative patterns, are meaningful even though the passages are too widely separated to have been performed (or, nowadays, to be read) at the same sitting. Furthermore, the epics notoriously attempt to encapsulate much larger sections of the story than they actually narrate. The *Iliad* obviously wants to be *the* Trojan epic, even though it tells a section of the Troy story that could easily disappear completely without serious consequences for the tale of Troy as a whole; the *Odyssey* seeks to be *the* return story.[15] The epics achieve their grandiose goals through devices uncommon in oral compositions. The *Iliad* boldly transfers events from early in the Trojan War into its own narrative and frequently foreshadows events to come. The *Odyssey* includes events between the fall of Troy and its own action through extended character narratives. Only by combining the tales that Nestor and Menelaus tell Telemachus with the narrator's account and with Odysseus's own narrative can the hearer reconstruct the full story.[16]

Nagy attributes the first stage in stablilization, the creation of notional epics, to the process of diffusion. In Indian epic traditions, for example, there is a link between the spread of an epic beyond its original

---

15. See Kullmann 1960, 365–66; Griffin 1980, 1.
16. See Hölscher 1990, 98–102.

locality and the expansion of the story away from the hero's death to-
ward the hero's birth.[17] Local epics are death stories, tied to cult. With
diffusion comes a narrative development. If the epic is to achieve
regional status, the hero must also be identified with a Pan-Indian
figure, and a birth story is required. It is hard to say which comes first:
can a narrative only win an audience outside its ritual center by incor-
porating elements not appropriate to its original ritual function, or does
a wider audience expect and demand a story that begins with the hero's
birth? In either case, Greek stories, too, doubtless developed as they dif-
fused, losing local, idiosyncratic features. The nature of the Homeric tra-
dition shows that it experienced extensive diffusion and transformation
over a long period. Nagy suggests that wandering bards, encountering
different local versions, established Panhellenic versions by finding a
common denominator. This common denominator was the oldest ver-
sion.

Certainly, whenever many singers perform the same song and fre-
quently hear each other, their versions will tend to become similar. Vari-
ation is strongest at the point of transmission—when a new singer
learns a song—and is likeliest to persist when the singer is not "cor-
rected" by others. Hence, institutionalized, competitive performance
was an ideal medium for stabilizing songs, and regional festivals and
contests—such as Amphidamas's funeral games—could have helped
stabilize the tradition. Similarly, portions of the Hebrew Bible may have
formed through the Pan-Hebraic festivals in Jerusalem under the
monarchy.[18] However, such events were hardly frequent enough to
stabilize the Homeric epics at a time when local audiences pressured po-
ets to adapt their songs to local tastes. The Athenian tyrants could only
have established a competition in the performance of these particular
songs when they were already fairly stable, recognizably the same ba-
sic version of the same story.

The poetic language and the poetic gods were clearly both widely
diffused and widely accepted before the epics themselves. These spread
most easily because they did not belong to specific stories; poets who
learned any section of the repertory acquired them and could transmit
them. There are other signs of the influence of diffusion. One striking

---

17. See Blackburn et al. 1989, 15–32.
18. See Niditch 1996, 120–25. Niditch suggests that Levites could have been
performers and transmitters.

quality of Greek heroic story in general is its concentration on enterprises that bring together heroes from different parts of the Greek world: the hunt of the Calydonian boar, the voyage of the Argo, the Seven against Thebes, the Trojan War. Other stories center on heroes who wander widely, such as Heracles, and so could have many local connections. These show that performers had adapted these stories for broader appeal by offering audiences a variety of characters with whom to identify and including a variety of locales. No local favorite needed to be excluded. Hence it is difficult to make a sharp distinction between more and less Panhellenic compositions; the Panhellenic tradition could only be formed though endless exchange, as local stories did or did not win wide acceptance or interest and as localities did or did not accept versions and stories from elsewhere. As a hero became widely known, a locality might generate a story that linked the hero to it or that identified a local figure with the hero. Performers had to balance these various stories with the demands of narrative coherence. A given fixed text represents a moment in this ceaseless process of negotiation. The Homeric epics avoid adopting stories—whether local stories of this kind or Panhellenic variants—that do not cohere well with their plots and characters. So, for example, the *Odyssey* includes traditions about Odysseus in Thesprotia by basing lying tales on them, but it is very hard to imagine the Odysseus of the *Odyssey* marrying a Thesprotian princess, as he did in the *Telegony*. If *Iliad* 3.144, in which Helen has a handmaid whose name is *Aethra*, is not a later Athenian addition, Homer knows the story that Helen was abducted by Theseus; but perhaps this is an inadvertent reference to a story he did not mean to evoke, for he does not develop it, nor does it fit easily into the *Iliad.*

However, diffusion without institutionalized control does not automatically stabilize songs, if bards wander as well as come together. A community of performers exerts centralizing pressure; geographical dispersal creates centrifugal force. The most widely diffused of all Indian epic stories, the *Ramayana*, is probably also the most varied, despite the powerful authority of the Sanskrit written text. Indeed, precisely the familiarity and prestige of such universally known tales make them vehicles for expressing very different political, social, and personal positions.[19] Epics may be highly fixed within regions and performance groups but very distinct across these boundaries, like languages with

---

19. See Richman 1991.

distinct dialects. So Lorik-Canda has very different characteristics in Uttar Pradesh and Chattisgarh: in Uttar Pradesh, it is martial and has been appropriated by the Ahir caste in support of its ambitions; in Chattisgarh, it is primarily erotic, and performers and audiences vary in caste.[20] The Homeric epics show the process in action in the narratives that characters tell, which always adapt traditional material to a speaker's rhetorical purposes. For Homeric characters, the past is meaningful only as the present can use it.[21] As I will argue in the following chapter, Homer tries to distinguish his own narrative from such context-dependent products—but this is a mystification in the service of traditionality.

Certainly, the process of diffusion could have created cycles of tales, linking the many stories about different heroes into potentially extended narratives and probably extended performances. As bards encountered new stories, they surely tended to connect them in this way. The Troy story is the product of diffusion. The *Iliad* and *Odyssey*, however, are not just the natural outcome of this process. They are hegemonic, assimilating an immense amount of narrative material to challenge all other songs. They also reveal an aesthetic that is not found elsewhere in the tradition.[22] Moreover, from the evidence we have, we can conclude that the tradition was not of the kind in which stability would "naturally" arise; lyric, tragedy, and vase painting certainly present constant variation. Above all, the epics' structural complexity is not a possible result of diffusion.

This is not an argument against the epics' orality but an argument in favor of self-conscious artistic intervention. Various stories about these heroes did not just agglomerate into a cycle and eventually a notional epic. Somebody had the idea of making narratives with these peculiarities. The *Iliad* and, to a lesser extent, the *Odyssey* have other features, too, that distinguish them from other Greek epic poems. The *Iliad* poet dislikes magic, and even the *Odyssey* poet, who includes much fantastic content, confines it to Odysseus's narrative, setting it in a world distinct from that of the rest of the epic.[23] Then there is the convincing argument of W. M. Sale that the *Iliad* avoids the sharply hostile traditional epithets of the Trojans and that the epic language is weak in for-

20. See Blackburn et al. 1989, 33–59 (Flueckiger).
21. See Andersen 1990.
22. See Dowden 1996.
23. See Griffin 1977.

mulae for movement from Troy or for being in Troy. In other words, the full, sympathetic treatment of the Trojans in the *Iliad* is a relatively recent development in the tradition.[24] The most economical hypothesis connects these peculiarities: a poet (or possibly a small group of poets), perhaps under the influence of an exceptional patron, conceived the monumental epic that expanded a single episode, imagining an unusual style of expansion that could encompass the whole tale of Troy in one work. The *Iliad* was an inspired invention; the *Odyssey*, a slightly later one. This unitarian position requires not a single original genius but that the epics are the product of individual ideas and decisions. From everything we know of the tradition as a whole, it was not inevitable or even especially likely that these particular poems would emerge from it. The tradition was necessary but not sufficient.

For the most part, the poems do not advertise their unusual qualities. Only once does Homeric epic use a rhetoric of innovation, and then innovation and traditionality are inextricably joined. At *Odyssey* 1.351–52, Telemachus says,

τὴν γὰρ ἀοιδὴν μᾶλλον ἐπικλείουσ᾽ ἄνθρωποι,
ἥ τις ἀκουόντεσσι νεωτάτη ἀμφιπέλεται.

[For people most make famous the song that comes around as the newest to those who hear it.]

He is defending Phemius's selection of subject, the return from Troy: ὁ δ᾽ Ἀχαιῶν νόστον ἄειδε / λυγρόν, ὃν ἐκ Τροίης ἐπετείλατο Παλλὰς Ἀθήνη [He sang the unhappy return of the Achaeans, which Pallas Athena enjoined when they came from Troy] (1.326–27). The epic incorporates several returns—Menelaus's, Agamemnon's, Ajax's—as foil to its own subject, the return of Odysseus. Simultaneously, then, Telemachus says, as if the fact were obvious to all, that audiences prefer novelty in their songs, while the poet powerfully underscores the traditionality of his material, which has been a topic of song since the heroic age. He and probably his audience must therefore value a song for its antiquity. So far as the truth and authority of the song rest on this tradition going back to the contemporaries of the events, the poet implies a faithful and unchanging transmission. However, the poet can hardly have implied that

---

24. See Sale 1987, 1989.

his own song, being old, was not likely to be widely praised. According to Telemachus's statement, people make a particular song famous not because it concerns recent events but because the song itself is new. In this case, the song is the newest in the poet's repertory because its subject is so recent, but a new song need not tell a new story. The *Odyssey* is new in part because it so boldly assimilates other returns, implying that its own tale is best as its hero is best; the other heroes clearly do not match him.

In *Homeric Misdirection*, J. Morrison makes a powerful argument for the view that the Homeric epics are in some sense "new."[25] Morrison shows in detail how the Homeric narrator consistently offers false clues to the audience about how the story will turn out. These misdirections do not lose all purpose once the audience knows they are false, since they are still reminders of the alternate paths the story could have taken. Further, psychological experiments have proved that knowledge of the overall outcome of a story (e.g., the sinking of the *Titanic*) does not prevent its audience from experiencing suspense, with measurable physiological symptoms.[26] Still, the effort the *Iliad* puts into misleading the audience would be excessive if everyone knew exactly what would happen at every point. S. Douglas Olson has shown that the *Odyssey* uses similar narrative strategies.[27] The poems, therefore, must be new as well as old. They were not gradually created before audiences who heard the process; rather, they emerged as unique arrangements of mostly familiar material.

The theory of the Pisistratid recension, which associates the fixing of the poems with the establishment of rhapsodic competitions at the Panathenaea in the sixth century, has returned to fashion in a new form. While the Analytic model imagined that written texts were collected and shaped into the massive epics, recent scholarship postulates the festival as the occasion for the creation of a written text, an important force for stabilizing and diffusing a particular branch of tradition. It is difficult, though, to believe that textualization took place only in Athens under the Pisistratids.[28] If the epics became stable only in the middle to

---

25. See Morrison 1992b.
26. See Gerrig 1989.
27. Olson 1995, 145–48.
28. On the Pisistratid "recension," see Jensen 1980 (Jensen sees it as the occasion for dictation); Nagy 1992, 1996b; Stanley 1993, 279–96; Seaford 1994,

late sixth century, only special pleading explains the preservation of an older stage of epic language than appears in the major Homeric hymns and in the fragments of the Epic Cycle, as well as the stabilization of the material world of the poems.[29] The evidence implies that the hymns were performed by the same rhapsodes and on the same occasions as the epics. If the Homeric epics were being recomposed in performance in the fullest sense in the sixth century, they should have been subject to exactly the same linguistic pressures as the rest of the repertory.[30] Some deliberate archaizing is always possible, but the differences between Homeric epic and other hexameter poetry appear in a range of phenomena. The opening fragment of the *Cypria* could have been composed in Athens in the late sixth century, but the *Iliad* and *Odyssey* are very different.[31]

In any case, interest in Homer in the middle to late sixth century is evident not only in Attic vase painting but around the Greek world, which was not then under profound Athenian cultural influence as it would be a century later. The establishment of epic performance at the Panathenaea seems an attempt to appropriate an already prestigious, widely known text. (This does not mean that the Panathenaic text was not influential later or that our Homeric text does not betray Attic influence.) Evidently, the canonization of the epics and the growth of Panhellenic identity were reciprocal processes.

The remaining possibilities are festival performance, serial performance under local patronage, or composition using writing, whether by dictation or directly. These options are not entirely exclusive, since initial performance and transmission are separate stages. None of these possibilities is entirely without difficulties. The festival performer of these epics would have to have an extraordinary reputation (and extraordinary stamina; the later institutionalized performances used several performers in competition). The festival atmosphere would ensure a relatively inattentive audience. If the *Iliad* were performed at a festival over several nights, for example, as Oliver Taplin has suggested,[32] the audience would have had to sleep during the day, doing nothing else

---

148–54. Cook (1995) argues that the *Odyssey* is closely linked to Athenian cult, but he imagines a dictated text perhaps as early as the mid–seventh century.

29. For the relative chronology, see Janko 1982.

30. This argument is made in Haslam 1997, 80–84.

31. See Davies 1989, 3–4.

32. Taplin 1992, 22–31.

during that time, like the audience at Bayreuth. Festival performance of the epics is especially hard to imagine because so much Greek festival performance was competitive, whereas the length of the poems leaves no time for competitors. A festival performance makes sense only if Homer was known as a bard of quite extraordinary talent, so that the sponsors expected to win great prestige and the listeners were motivated to devote their time. Similarly, serial performance of a complex poem within a fluid tradition demands an exceptionally committed audience. Once a long poem has been textualized and has a fixed sequence of events, members of the audience can miss part of a serial performance without becoming confused. When the *Iliad* was new, however, while an occasionally inattentive listener could follow, someone who completely missed large sections would have been confused. Moreover, it would be surprising if a massive poem produced for a particular locality were so lacking in local reference of any kind.

If the epics are oral works of individual poets, how were they transmitted? G. S. Kirk has tried to define stages in oral epic traditions, distinguishing a reproductive period from a creative one.[33] Many singers of Novi Pazar sang their repertories with only slight variation (consider Lord's example of Zogic's reproduction of a narrative inconsistency after seventeen years).[34] Even at the point of transmission from singer to singer, variation was often slight; moreover, the singers did not compose new songs. Clearly, singers were more creative at an earlier period.

Two different issues to some extent run together in this discussion: variation within existing songs and the composition of entirely new songs. Bani Hilali in Egypt, for example, allows no deviation in plot, and its singers do not compose new epic material—it is very stable in both ways. Variation in performance is confined to the verbal/musical level. In the Finnish tradition, old songs were very stable, but singers also created new material.[35] In Indian ritually linked traditions, new songs may be created as local heroes are incorporated into cult, but these songs are extremely stable once they reach their limit of diffusion.

We really do not know how notional epics are formed and shift the balance in a particular song from innovation toward repetition. Various

---

33. Kirk 1962, 91–101.
34. Lord 1960, 94–95.
35. See Kiparsky 1976, 95–98.

factors obviously contribute to greater fixity. Ritual performances tend to be fixed as entertainments are not. Many oral epic traditions have developed in intimacy with written culture. The social function of epic performance must also be an important factor in determining how a particular milieu will resolve the tension between repetition and adaptation. This important aspect of oral epic tradition demands a rich comparative investigation. Intuitively, we expect a strong tendency toward fixity in the epic traditions of self-consciously marginalized peoples. The epic is a usable past because it is a reiteration of past glory to those whose way of life is under threat. Lord and Parry studied primarily the Muslim tradition of Bosnia, a tradition celebrating the period of the greatest expansion of the Ottoman Empire, thus a history in opposition to both Austria-Hungary and Serbian-dominated Yugoslavia. Its singers were largely illiterate in a world in which power required literacy. The performers of Egyptian epic are outsiders; the genre is excluded from the classical Arabic canon; its audiences are village people threatened by modernity. Within one culture, such a tradition may take on the task of (mostly) repeating the past, while other performance genres (e.g., personal anecdote) directly confront the problems of the present. These are conservative traditions.

Many traditions (even many that exist in symbiosis with literacy) are fluid, and the epic performances that produced the Homeric corpus are likely to have been very flexible. Throughout the archaic period, Greek epic was extremely creative in the composition of new songs and in extending the epic style to new subject matter—foundation epic and mock epic, for example. Lyric constantly re-created the old material, greatly varying its details. This is not surprising, for epic was a central cultural expression of a dynamic culture, with expanding economic, technical, political, and cultural horizons.

Given the exceptional nature of the poems, it is easiest to connect the immense labor of creation with the vast work of transmission: in whatever circumstances an original performance may have taken place, these poems were composed with the intention that they would be transmitted. They were new songs, intended to be remembered. As the poet must have decided to create them, someone had to decide to learn them or write them down. The idea of creating the *Iliad* perhaps came to Homer or to his patron along with the idea of writing it down, on the model of Near Eastern literature. The *Iliad*, in turn, inspired the *Odyssey*. Such a transcription was a guarantee of authenticity for performance

and a precious object.[36] It would not have been intended as an arche-
type for copying or as a control over each word in later performances,
but it gave its owner a claim of direct descent from the poet. In any case,
a single copy would not control the transmission in a culture where
word-for-word reproduction of literary texts was not an established
practice. The exact wording was a concern only when it had political or
other immediate relevance.

The ancient testimony about the Homeridae of Chios allows for a
reconstruction that fits the facts, though it is very speculative. The
Homeridae claimed to be descendants of Homer.[37]

> The Homeridae, they say, were descendants of Homer who sang his
> poetry by right of inheritance. Later Homeridae no longer traced
> their ancestry to Homer. Cinaethus and his followers became fa-
> mous and are said to have attributed their own verses to Homer.
> Cinaethus was a Chiot; he composed the *Hymn to Apollo* and at-
> tributed it to Homer. This Cinaethus was the first to recite the work
> of Homer at Syracuse, in the sixty-ninth Olympiad [504–500], as
> Hippostratus says [*FGrH* 568F5]. (Schol. Pindar *Nemean* 2.1c)

Given how often bards learn from their fathers, the guild may indeed
have arisen with an *Iliad* poet's (or poets') sons or his students, with the
Odyssey composed within their milieu. They "had" the text (whether in
writing or as oral tradition) and performed it. We hear of at least one
other collective body of rhapsodes named for a founding poet, the Creo-
phylidae. Creophylus of Samos was associated with the *Sack of Oechalia*,
a Heracles epic; according to the legend (*Oechaliae Halosis* T 3 Davies),
Homer "gave" him the poem as a reward for his hospitality toward the
poet (a similar tale has Homer "give" Stasinus the *Cypria* as a dowry
[*Cypria* T 1 Davies]). In a familiar epigram, Callimachus denies the at-
tribution (6 Pf.). According to Plutarch (*Lycurgus* 4), Lycurgus had the

---

36. Blackburn (1988, 28) describes how in bow-song performance, palm-leaf
manuscripts may be dictated to the performer but more often are simply dis-
played as a proof of authenticity.

37. Fehling (1979, 193–99) argues that the testimonies about Homeridae are
derived from two originally quite separate strands, one concerning a family in
Chios, the other a term meaning "rhapsode," so that the synthesis, a clan of
rhapsodes, is a fiction. But he ignores Cinaethus and argues from silence.

Creophylidae introduce Homer to Sparta, as the tradition says that Hipparchus obtained the Athenian Homer from them.

At a time when epic performance was popular, the Homeridae had a unique property in two prestigious poems (and I assume that the Creophylidae had the *Sack of Oechalia*). Guilds typically exist largely to preserve the value of their members' intellectual capital by keeping it scarce, and the *Iliad* and *Odyssey* combined are the length of many mature bards' complete repertory in many cultures. These are not poems that even a capable bard could sing competently after one hearing. The Homeridae, who were hardly numerous if they were in origin a descent group, could have refused to teach the epics to outsiders. The Homeric epics do not tell the episodes crucial to the overall story, which almost everyone must have known (the abduction of Helen, the Trojan horse), so the narrative material before textualization was not among the most diffused—except for certain episodes of the *Odyssey* that were very widely familiar, if not in the exact form in which they appear in the poem (Polyphemus, Circe). With such a limited cadre of performers, these epics would initially have been less widely familiar than others. At the same time, compositions by members of the group could be attributed to the authoritative ancestor and share in his prestige.

Scholars have tended to assume that a guild could not try to assert this kind of control or would not wish to.[38] It is not the case, however, that performers in oral epic traditions cannot see their works as intellectual property. There is an excellent parallel from the medieval French tradition, in the proem of *La bataille Loquifer.*

> This song was made a long while ago. In truth I will tell you it was a hundred and fifty years back in the past. Graindor de Brie who composed the poem because it was so good took such great care of it that he never instructed or taught anyone how to sing it. He obtained and won with it great wealth in Sicily where he used to go about. When he died he gave it to his son. King William flattered

---

38. Burkert (1972) remarks that oral poets do not see their works as property; Stanley (1993, 279) comments on "the unlikelihood that a guild of oral poets would so easily and so totally accept the textualization of a heritage over which they might risk losing control." Textualization, though, could be a way of asserting control. For other examples of ownership of oral poetry, see Finnegan 1977, 203–5.

him so much that he got the song out of him and put it and sealed it up in a book. He [the son of Graindor de Brie] when he knew it grieved deeply over it. He never recovered his health as long as he lived. (1–13)[39]

Similarly, another chanson de geste, *La destruction de Romme,* claims:

He who composed the song for long kept it to himself. He would indeed never take any wealth for it—neither mule nor horse nor mantle nor rich fur—nor was it ever sung by him in a great court. (16–19)

The composer of *La destruction de Romme* avoided singing it in great courts, because there he could be pressured to transmit it. Hesiod says, in a line that sounds proverbial, that beggar φθονέει beggar, and bard φθονέαι bard (*Works and Days* 26). In context, the verb φθονέει must mean "envy" (since Hesiod is assimilating the saying to his positive treatment of competition), but it regularly applies both to resenting another's possession of a good that one lacks (envy) and to not wanting another to have a good that one possesses (begrudging). Proverbially, neither bards nor beggars like to share.

Of course, such a monopoly could not last. Even from the start, the Homeridae owned only these texts, not the stories constituting them. Other bards could learn at least part of the epic simply by hearing it; disloyal members might teach it; powerful patrons might insist on having portions taught. Likewise, economic pressures change. With the popularity of such poets as Stesichorus, producing epic-style stories in lyric form, rhapsodic performances may themselves have lost favor for a while. It may have made sense to be less exclusive to maintain popular interest in the epic product as a whole.[40] By the late sixth century, the Homeridae probably no longer had control over the Homeric poems and were embroiled in polemic over their authority and that of others.

---

39. The translation and that of the extract from *La destruction de Romme,* which follows, are those of Ross 1980, 96–99.

40. Burkert (1987; cf. 1979, 56) sees the late sixth century as a period of revival for Homeric epic, with rhapsodes in competition with Stesichorean lyric performance (he also associates this revival with the abandonment of composition-in-performance).

There were accusations, as the scholium to Pindar shows, over which texts were actually the work of the now legendary Homer and over the purity of their transmission. The Old French tradition is rich in polemic about the incompetence of those who perform songs without knowing them properly and so ruin them. The scholium's reference to claims that the Homeridae corrupted the Homeric tradition suggests a similar atmosphere by the time of Cinaethus, even as formal institutionalized rhapsodic competitions rendered the epics truly canonical. (The statement that Cinaethus introduced Homer at Syracuse in the sixty-ninth Olympiad probably indicates the first record of such an event there.)[41]

As in many epic traditions worldwide, basic textualization did not mean that oral performance or recomposition in performance stopped completely. Both performers and audiences had expectations based in the oral register, and such recomposition continued to generate small-scale variation (*mouvance*) of the kind richly attested in the quotations and Ptolemaic papyri.[42] The variation of the classical and early Hellenistic period, though, is trivial; while there are many additional lines, the variants rarely change the story.[43] At least from the sixth century onward, the never-ending work of reinventing the past to make it usable in the present belonged to other epics, to other genres (lyric and tragedy), and to rhapsodes in their role as interpreters. Regular, institutionalized competitions in the performance of preexisting texts surely increased the level of polemic about their purity and authority.

If the implied audience of the epics is not confined to a group for whom the poet had often performed, the categories of narrative material multiply, to include what everyone had heard before, what some individuals had heard but others had not, what nobody in this audience had heard but other Greek audiences had heard, what no Greek audi-

---

41. See Nagy 1990b, 23. The bibliography on Cinaethus is large: see Wade-Gery 1952, 21; Sealey 1957; Burkert 1979; Janko 1982, 113–15, Dihle 1970, 114–19.

42. *Mouvance* is Zumthor's term (1990). Haslam 1997 is an excellent survey of the ancient variants.

43. This is the obstacle to arguments like that of de Vet (1996), who suggests ongoing interplay between written texts and full oral recomposition on the Balinese model. The only real evidence for significant narrative variation comes from vase painting (see Lowenstam 1997), where the influence of lyric versions is likely; and in any case, artists do not scrupulously illustrate textual/performance sources, as the vases related to tragedy demonstrate. Variation in such transitional texts is common: for Anglo-Saxon examples, see O'Keefe 1990.

ence had heard, and what no audience had ever heard. The poet—like the dhalang—did not always know exactly what stories the audience (or most of it) had heard before. The audience cared deeply about the traditionality of the epics. Traditionality, however, left considerable scope for "innovation" (borrowing from unfamiliar narrative strands, mixing different strands), since the traditional content was rich, varied, and flexible, and since the poets knew it more thoroughly than their audiences did. Poets begin as exceptionally attentive listeners, and the better trained they become, the more skilled they are at appreciating, criticizing, and appropriating what other poets do differently.

While the unfamiliar audience made the poet's work harder in some ways, it opened possibilities in other ways, since the poet was not bound by direct experience of the wants of a particular audience. He had to create his audience. In modern fiction, there is often a considerable gap between the *narrative audience* and the *authorial audience.* The narrative audience is the audience that "goes along" with the fiction as if it were true; the *authorial audience* appreciates the narrative's artistic qualities and recognizes it as a construct.[44] The two audiences may differ considerably in knowledge. In a novel, expository technique does not always directly reflect the authorial audience. In *Nineteen Eighty-Four,* for example, the narrator addresses a narrative audience already familiar with the imaginary world: he does not tell us what telescreens are or explain the identity of Big Brother. Of course, the authorial audience is not supposed to know these things; we figure them out. Scholars tend to assume that the narrative and authorial audiences of Homeric epic are always very close to each other. The epics would thus be transparent to their audiences. When the narrator refers to some "fact" of the heroic world as known, the audience must have known it already. However, even if bards aimed at such transparency, it would be difficult to achieve with an audience whose experiences were varied and not well-known to the bard. Once we dispute this assumption of transparency, we need to ask how the poems construct the narrative audience.

The gaps and difficulties in Odysseus's lies his argue strongly against transparency. Odysseus spontaneously creates and varies his lies to fit their specific occasions. Only an audience that has heard an *Odyssey* almost exactly like this one has heard these particular fictions. They therefore reveal how the poet works when his freedom to invent

44. See Rabinowitz 1987.

is greatest and when he is least likely to rely on an audience's familiarity with the stories. If the rule of transparency holds, Odysseus's lies should be completely understandable, since the audience cannot use its traditional knowledge to fill in the gaps. In his first tale (*Od.* 13.256–86), told to the disguised Athena, Odysseus is seeking to explain why he is alone with a pile of treasure in a place he does not know and to warn the stranger not to attempt to steal the treasure from him.[45] He therefore says that he fled his Cretan home after a homicide.

> . . . because I killed the dear son of Idomeneus, Orsilochus the swift-footed, who defeated all grain-eating men on broad Crete with his swift feet, because he wanted to deprive me of my booty from Troy, all of it, for which I suffered many pains in my mind, experiencing both war and cruel waves, because I did not serve as subordinate to his father, doing him service at Troy, but went as leader of other companions. I threw a bronze-tipped spear into him as he was on his way home from the country, lying in ambush near the road with a companion. A very dark night covered the sky, and nobody observed us; I was unseen when I killed him. But when I had killed him with sharp bronze, I went straight to their ship and entreated the lordly Phoenicians, and I gave them satisfying booty.

This story is full of small, odd gaps. For example, just how did Orsilochus attempt to deprive the speaker of his booty, especially of all of it? Moreover, it would surely be very difficult for the speaker to convey his goods to the ship in the dark of night with only one helper (and what happened to him?). However, if he is to escape, the murder must go undetected for a while, and that is easiest to believe if it took place at night and if few men were involved. The details of the story both explain how the speaker could be in his present situation and warn the auditor, and these purposes take precedence over internal logic.

Similarly, in his lie to Eumaeus, Odysseus claims that a Phoenician enticed Odysseus to go to Phoenicia with him; after Odysseus had stayed there a year, his host asked him to accompany cargo to Libya, with the intention of selling Odysseus into slavery (*Od.* 14.288–98). Although Odysseus knew he was being tricked, he went along, because he had no choice. But why does the false host wait a year, except that

---

45. See Erbse 1972, 154–55.

Odysseus needs to fill the years since the Trojan War? He spends seven years in Egypt to parallel the seven years spent with Calypso, and he spends a year with the Phoenician to parallel the year with Circe. The listener needs less knowledge of particular epic "facts" than the ability to distinguish details meaningful within the story from those whose meaning requires a broader context. In character narrative, the competent listener pays more attention to the speaker's purposes and less to the story itself.

The Homeric poems presuppose an audience for whom narrative competence can in large part replace specific knowledge. They are not aimed at an audience without experience of the epic tradition. They assume familiarity with the epic language and style, the basic outlines of the most important stories, and narrative conventions. However, they do not presuppose that everyone in the authorial audience has detailed knowledge of each and every tale the poet has heard. Those who are not knowledgeable connoisseurs of epic must efficiently use the information the narrator provides to bridge the gaps in the story—and must recognize that not all gaps need to be bridged. As a general principle, audiences are likeliest to know characters who play an important part in more than one story. Thus, audiences heard of Agamemnon both as leader of the Trojan expedition and as the man murdered on his return. They might have heard songs about Achilles' love affair on Scyrus; his wounding of Telephus; his killings of Troilus, Hector, and Memnon; and his death at Apollo's hands. Their memories were available if the bard chose to activate them, but he could not always be certain how many hearers could remember a particular tale.

Homeric Rhetorics:
Traditionality and Disinterest

Homeric epic relies on rhetorics of traditionality and disinterestedness. The epics remind the audience that earlier audiences heard these same stories, and they emphasize their own repetition of the familiar. At the same time, the rhetoric of disinterestedness implies that epic song, despite its traditional content, depends for its transmission not on oral tradition but on the Muse, who instructs the poet anew at each performance. Each rendition echoes earlier performances but is independent of them. Identifying tradition—what people say—as a source of authority for ordinary speech but not for themselves, the epics mark the narratives of sung performances as a special form distinct from the narratives of those who are not bards. Although these two rhetorical positions appear to contradict each other, they do not. The Muse independently guarantees each performance, so each performance repeats what others have performed before without ever depending on it. Together, the two rhetorical positions define epic narrative as a peculiarly authoritative speech act. It exists outside the social pressures that constrain ordinary human speech, and its distance from the everyday guarantees its truth.

As M. Finkelberg has argued, Homeric language associates truthful narrative, in both bardic performance and ordinary speech, with chronological sequence and point-by-point telling. Speakers are asked or promise to recount either "the truth" (ἀλήθεια) or "in order" (κατὰ κόσμον), with no difference in meaning.[1] Greeks of the Geometric and Archaic periods can hardly have believed that all such narratives were necessarily truthful, but such narratives claimed truth. They offered information, which was or was not in accordance with the facts. Hence, where the poet repeats "core" traditional material, such as catalogues,

---

1. See Finkelberg 1998, 131–60. I do not, however, accept Finkelberg's interpretation of *Od.* 4.239 (where I think ἐοικότα means "appropriate") or of Hesiod's Muses.

in the point-by-point style, he invokes the Muse as guarantor of accuracy. Goal-directed narratives—paradigms and self-seeking tales—often use ring-composition and give far more attention to some details than others; these techniques transmit their messages. Homer's overall rhetorical strategies confront not just the danger that someone will disagree with a particular item of information about the heroic past but the worry that a hearer may find the poem's emphases and judgments—explicit or implicit—misleading or unfair. His best defenses against such objections are the traditionality of his poem and the impartiality of the immortal Muse.

Implicitly, the epics appeal to traditionality at every moment, through their poetic dialect, formulaic language, and hexameter meter.[2] The rhythm is traditional in the strongest sense, and its use for literary oracles and the wisdom of archaic philosophers proves that it carries authority. Other features of the language are often objectively traditional, and even recent innovations within the *Kunstsprache* may well have been subjectively traditional. For a listener who recognizes some linguistic features and some phrases from earlier performances, other, less familiar forms and expressions that are different from everyday speech may have the effect of archaism, whether they really are old or not.

As Egbert Bakker has demonstrated, noun-epithet phrases powerfully present a character (hero, heroine, or god) at the moment he or she becomes the focus of action.[3] Within narrative, they help the narrator guide the audience's attention. Speech introductions, though, are especially privileged sites for whole-line formulae that incorporate noun-epithet phrases. These serve the rhetoric of traditionality especially powerfully. Speeches are both a particularly flexible part of the genre (though probably a very old part) and the moment at which the narrative most vividly approaches the world it represents—the heroes are most "present" when they speak.[4] Most of the mythological invention that scholars have identified appears within speeches, for the ability to find appropriate narrative to support an argument is an important part of the skill of the Homeric speaker. Linguistically, the language of

---

2. See Kahane 1997, 111–13.

3. Bakker 1997, 167–73.

4. See Bakker 1997, 167–73. Kelly (1990) argues that since speeches have a higher rate of correption than narrative, they are more archaic, but no single test is valid; for the free composition of speeches, see Martin 1989, 45.

speeches is more innovative— "newer"—than that of narrative. Tradition, as generic rule, makes speeches less "traditional." Hence, the poet introduces speeches by first emphasizing a character's traditionality. Thus, a speech, although the audience may never have heard it before, will bring to life some aspect of the traditional personality that an introduction has invoked. The speech also becomes part of the inherited past; it has what A. Kahane has called a "semblance of fixity."[5]

Patronymics also serve traditionality. By linking characters to ancestors, patronymics imply that the narrative has temporal depth. Whether or not a particular father or grandfather is himself a traditional subject of epic story, each patronymic implies the existence of stories from farther back in time than the main action. The patronymic implies that the characters themselves carry the memory of earlier heroic deeds—an implication that the *Iliad,* especially, often actualizes as the characters speak of earlier heroes. Patronymics are more frequent in the *Iliad* than in the *Odyssey.*[6] The poet is interested in the genealogies and names of heroes more than in those of the gods, perhaps because the gods require no rhetorical support for their traditionality.[7]

Both epics begin with a device familiar from ancient hymns, in which a relative clause expands an opening term, "anger" and "[the] man." The syntax itself implies that these subjects, like the gods and their deeds, exist before the act of narration. The performer calls on the Muse to narrate an already available story. That the *Odyssey* does not name the hero in the proem further marks the traditionality of the story, since the audience is surely expected to identify the hero through the information the proem provides about him. Laying even more stress on the story's traditionality is the conclusion of the proem with the words εἰπὲ καὶ ἡμῖν, "tell us also." There are two possible interpretations of the sentence. Either the poet asks the Muse not to keep her knowledge to herself but to share it, or the poet knows that the Muse has told this same story to others and asks her to do so again. The second possibility is likelier, because the poet has already summarized important details of the tale: Odysseus tried to save his men but could not because they ate the cattle of Helius. To be sure, it is not impossible for the Muse to

---

5. Kahane 1997, 112. Bakker (1997, 27) speaks of "phrases with *traditional intent.*"

6. See West, *Od. Comm.,* 1:77 (on 1.30).

7. See Higbie 1995, 23–25.

help the poet even in asking her for help. Still, the proem is especially
effective if the summary alludes to previous tellings: the poet already
knows enough to ask for this specific tale, a narrative of Odysseus's re-
turn that will include the death of his companions. The help of the Muse
will turn this summary into the full story. (That does not mean that there
is a sharp division between the proem and the rest of the song, as if the
Muse assumed control once invoked.[8]) Even if we understand the con-
cluding line of the proem to mean that the poet asks the Muse to share
her knowledge, the emphatic καὶ ἡμῖν implies that the story is already
there in the Muse's mind. If it is available now, it has surely been avail-
able to other servants of the Muse in the past.

The poet unites himself with the audience, emphasizing the collec-
tive aspect of the performance.[9] The resulting "we" has no particular
definition but includes the entire audience (real or authorial). The
rhetorical position of the poems is thus inclusive—everybody may join
the authorial audience, while all who join have the same knowledge of
the tradition. The *Iliad* similarly underscores its traditionality in the be-
ginning of the narrative proper, after the proem (*Il.* 1.8), through the
question τίς τ' ἄρ σφῶε θεῶν ἔριδι συνέηκε μάχεσθαι [Which of the gods,
then, hurled them into strife so as to fight?]. The poet can ask such a
question because there is an answer (which he immediately gives)—
Apollo.

Passages containing references to fate also emphasize the narra-
tive's traditionality, since "fate" on the level of characters is "traditional
story" for the audience.[10] This is particularly clear at *Iliad* 2.155–56,
when the Achaeans rush for the ships in response to Agamemnon's test-
ing speech.

Ἔνθα κεν Ἀργείοισιν ὑπέρμορα νόστος ἐτύχθη,
εἰ μὴ Ἀθηναίην Ἥρη πρὸς μῦθον ἔειπεν . . .

[Then the Argives would have had a return home contrary to fate,
had Hera not addressed Athena . . .]

---

8. See Lenz 1980.

9. The Serbo-Croatian *pripjev* does this too. See Foley 1991, 68–72 (on the
creation of a timeless space for the performance), 214–23 (on Anglo-Saxon
epic—the traditionality is even more strongly marked here).

10. On these passages, see Kullmann 1956; de Jong 1987a, 68–78; Morrison
1992a; Morrison 1997, 284–85; Lang 1989; Louden 1993; Nesselrath 1992.

The capture of Troy must have been firmly fixed in the "canon of facts," so that every hearer realizes that a return at this point would be contrary to the tradition. For the characters within the poem, including the gods, this necessity becomes "fate." The narrator also uses the "if not" formula for other events that would violate the canonical tradition, without explicitly invoking fate—when Menelaus almost fights Hector at 7.104–8 (since he would have died) and when Patroclus threatens to take Troy (16.198–701). Even if these passages in some ways challenge the tradition by claiming that what happened was not inevitable, Homer emphasizes his fidelity to the tradition.

Such counterfactual passages, however, are not confined to sequences that threaten the center of the canon. They also appear when the threat affects the plan of Zeus in the poem (*Il.* 17.319–25)—that is, the plot of the *Iliad*, which is only a retardation of the Trojan story as a whole. The averted counterfactual may even be an event apparently without long-term consequences, as when Apollo knocks Diomedes' whip from his hand during the chariot race (23.383–84); Diomedes wins anyway. By extension, these events, too, partake of the rhetoric of traditionality. Whether or not this performance was the first time members of the audience heard these stories, Homer's emphasis that the events of the stories almost did not happen "correctly" implies that the events he narrates are correct.

In another aspect of traditionalizing rhetoric, characters within the poems speak of the songs that will commemorate the action. Helen claims in the *Iliad* (6.356–58) that the gods caused the war to provide material for future songs. Clytemnestra, according to the dead Agamemnon, will be the subject of "hateful song" (στυγερὴ ... ἀοιδή, *Od.* 24.200), whereas the gods will create a lovely song for Penelope (*Od.* 24.197–98). The effect is not that of self-reflexivity in a novel. Since the present performance is unlikely to have been the first time most people in the audience had heard of Helen, Clytemnestra, or Penelope, such allusions point not only to the present performance but to its place in a chain of songs and stories. Similarly, characters often reflect on the *kleos* that will survive them. Achilles contemplates his two fates: by staying at Troy, he guarantees his early death, but his fame will be everlasting (*Il.* 9.412–16). Although the present occasion is only one of those that commemorate Achilles, the present song, commemorating that choice itself, sufficiently demonstrates that his fame endures.

Not every reference a character makes to his own future *kleos* need be strongly traditional, for if some are, the traditionality effect is guaranteed. Hector imagines how a monument for the warrior he hopes to kill in single combat will cause those who see it to praise himself (*Il.* 7.85–90). Nobody is killed, so this tomb never exists. Nonetheless, when Hector imagines his fame as people continue to speak of his deeds, his fame is placed in the context not only of the present performance but of all other times at which people might speak of Hector. Indeed, the traditionality effect is especially powerful because the passage reminds the audience that the tradition about Hector, as this poem recollects it, is far richer and more nuanced than he imagines. Its authority appears to be without limit.

Simultaneously, Homeric epic claims to be disinterested. Inside the world of the Homeric characters, truth as adherence to fact is not always important, because the characters are far more concerned with the purposes and effects of speech. Speech is, as Richard Martin has shown, a competitive performance.[11] It is also persuasive, manipulative, and goal directed, a form of action. So both Homer and his characters evaluate speech and its referential component primarily in relation to the goal speaking serves. Speakers may be more or less open about the ends that they seek, and these ends may be more or less benign from the recipient's point of view. Sometimes speakers aim at a competitive advantage over others, either openly (e.g., in threats and boasts), or manipulatively. The poets have a whole-line formula, ὅς σφιν ἐϋφρονέων ἀγορήσατο καὶ μετέειπεν [wishing them well, he spoke to the assembly and said] (occurring nine times in the *Iliad,* six times in the *Odyssey*), employed when a speaker intervenes to warn against a danger to the group or to promote its unity. The poet frames such speeches, for they are not the norm.

The Homeric poems claim to tell stories that serve no immediate end, so the poems give the listener no reason to worry about whether the stories are literally true. The audience has no motive to compare the present version with alternate versions. Most Homeric speech is aimed at controlling action, but poetry claims no purpose beyond its own enjoyment. Hence, although members of their audience may request or object to a particular song, the singers depicted in the poems do not adapt their narratives for individual audiences. Songs therefore have a credibility superior to storytelling in other situations. Song in the poems is entertainment, not "serious" speech—although it may have rich sig-

---

11. Martin 1989.

nificance in contexts wider than the performance occasion.[12] In the *Theogony* (99–101), Hesiod praises the Muses for relieving audiences of care, as they forget their troubles when they listen to either of two genres, hymns to the gods or the "famous deeds of the people of former times," the κλεῖα προτέρων ἀνθρώπων. Another form of this phrase, κλέα ἀνδρῶν (deeds of men) appears in Homeric epic: this is what Achilles sings to himself (*Il.* 9.189) and what the Muse rouses Demodocus to sing in his first song, on the quarrel of Odysseus and Achilles (*Od.* 8.73). In the *Iliad*, Phoenix uses the same phrase to characterize his story of Meleager (9.524–25). His knowledge depends not on poetry but on personal memory (9.527–28); the phrase therefore denotes not strictly a genre of song but whatever is known about the heroes of the past. Only as song, however, does narrative about the past lead to forgetfulness of the present; Phoenix, like other Homeric narrators, tells his story with a view to the present.

Gregory Nagy has argued that Greek poetry's claims to truth function on a local/Panhellenic axis.[13] Poets claim the authority of Panhellenic truths and values while dismissing alternative versions as local and therefore false. Yet it is hard to imagine that a real concept of "Panhellenic" was available to Homer or Hesiod. Local elements in poetry, however, are often self-serving: a poet could emphasize a particular cult or hero or place a legendary event at a site eager for the resulting prestige, whether as a local patriot or to flatter a patron. So the author of the *Homeric Hymn to Dionysus*, rejecting all local claims to be the birthplace of the god, places the birth far from people (1–9). The *Odyssey* similarly places Odysseus's adventures in a magical realm, relegating to Odysseus's lies and to other songs the real places (apart from Ithaca) that claimed Odyssean associations.[14]

The proem to the Catalogue of Ships (*Il.* 2.484–86) firmly distinguishes the actual knowledge of the Muses (which the poet asks them to transmit directly to him) from the mere report available without them: ἡμεῖς δὲ κλέος οἶον ἀκούομεν οὐδέ τι ἴδμεν (2.486). The poet thereby denies that he depends on human report.[15] The passage being

---

12. See Walsh 1984, 15–17.

13. Nagy 1990b, 52–81, especially 68–69.

14. On Odysseus's importance for ethnographic definition and self-definition, see Malkin 1998.

15. Pucci (1998, 36–39) analyzes the anxieties revealed by the invocation.

introduced is an immense catalogue, clearly based on a catalogue composed for a different context. The catalogue is the one passage in the entire Homeric corpus that is most certainly a product of memorization of a fixed text (though not necessarily a written one). From a naturalistic perspective, therefore, the modern reader is here tempted to dissolve the distinction between "oral tradition" (*kleos*) and the Muses, since what the poet needs here is the ability to remember what the tradition has taught him. The Muses are, after all, daughters of Memory. Why, then, does the poet insist on the distinction?

The Catalogue of Ships, which describes who was at Troy and with how many ships, is particularly dangerous for the poet. Such "factual" material claims literal truth, especially because information of this kind is politically relevant. Genealogies and catalogues are maps of the past, and since they are areas of contention, it is especially important that they be accurate. Moreover, the catalogue concludes with some firm statements of value: after Achilles, Ajax was the best hero, while Eumelus had the best horses (2.761–70). Such claims are potentially contentious (Ajax and Odysseus disastrously disagreed about who was best after Achilles). The passage, then, is an implicit defense against anyone who wants the catalogue to be different. The poet does not imply here that human report is wrong, but he needs the Muse to guarantee the passage. Except for the proem, all the invocations of the Muses in the *Iliad*, precede superlatives and are closely related to other rhetorical questions that precede superlatives.[16] Superlatives likewise frequently trigger references to (nonbardic) oral tradition in character speeches.[17] Claims that a hero did something first or that someone is best demand authority, because they are claims that someone might challenge.

Indeed, some of the character speeches deny precisely the authority that oral tradition asserts. For example, Penelope complains that people wrongly say that Antinous is the best man in Ithaca (*Od.* 16.418–20). The invocations do not just emphasize the superlatives but mark points of danger (or pretended danger) for the poet, where members of the audience might object. The Muses mediate between the particular occasion and the demands of the past. As daughters of Memory, they represent the singer's accumulated experience. However, because they are independent of mortal tradition, they confer on the poet an authority independent of

---

16. See de Jong 1987a, 49–51.
17. See de Jong 1987a, 238.

earlier experience. As in the proem to the *Odyssey*, the poet identifies with his audience, as if, without the Muses' help, he had no better access to human report than they. This identification with the audience makes it clear that the distinction here is not between poetic/nonpoetic tradition but between access to real knowledge through the Muses and any "mere" tradition.[18]

Andrew Ford has stressed how Homeric representations of poetry suppress the real process of transmission, even as the *Odyssey* portrays the oral tradition as it is created.[19] When the ambassadors find Achilles singing the κλέα ἀνδρῶν [deeds of heroes] at *Il.* 9.186–89, the poet expands by narrating how he acquired his lyre, not by describing how he learned to use it. Phemius, in particular, boasts of being αὐτοδίδακτος (self-taught), even though his patronymic, *Terpiades* (*Od.* 22.330), hints that his father was also a bard; a god has planted all kinds of songs in his mind (*Od.* 22.347–48).[20] Nowhere does the narrator or any character acknowledge that bards learn their repertory from other bards. Songs, to be sure, have fame of their own and may rise or fall in popularity (*Od.* 1.351, 8.74), and this aspect of the reception of the song is naturalistic. The song itself, though, is just there, "surrounding" (ἀμφιπέληται, *Od.* 1.352) those who hear it.

Poets do not learn their stories from other poets, and they are also quite distinct from narrators who are not engaged in formal bardic performance. The epics identify the oral tradition with such narrative. "Ordinary" narrative derives its authority either from personal experience or from human report. Human report, in turn, may have its ultimate origin in Zeus, but its genealogy is vague. Epic performers, in contrast, are informed directly by the Muse and do not depend on ordinary sources. This divine source for bardic knowledge results in only one significant

---

18. For the Muse as doublet of the poet and on the poet's identification with the audience, see Calame 1995, 60–64. See also Segal 1992.

19. Ford 1992, 90–130. Cf. Mackie 1997 on Odyssean song as "news."

20. Fernández-Galiano (*Od. Comm.*, 3:279–80) denies that αὐτοδίδακτος really means "self-taught," on the odd ground that Odysseus, who had no teachers himself, would be unimpressed. He argues that Phemius claims exactly what I argue Homer suppresses, "an innate capacity to *apply* the traditional repertory of inherited poetic craft to the particular case relevant to the audience of the moment." Would such a claim not make Odysseus likelier to kill him, as he has just killed the priest who, he insists, has doubtless prayed for Odysseus's death (*Od.* 22.321–25)?

practical difference between bardic narratives and those of less-author-
itative characters—the bard's freedom to report the doings of the gods.
Nonetheless, the Homeric narrator maintains the distinction. Narrative
outside the frame of epic performance normally either answers a re-
quest for information or serves an explicit paradigmatic function. It is
occasional and specifically motivated, serving a specific communicative
need within the social relationship of speaker and hearer(s). Bardic nar-
rative, by contrast, ordinarily does not seek to manipulate its audience;
it is essentially disinterested. Although the bard's song may on a par-
ticular occasion have special significance for the audience or some mem-
bers of the audience, the singer does not intend these effects. Both blind-
ness of Demodocus within the epic and the tradition of Homer's
blindness probably represent the singer's remoteness from social cues.[21]

   These two distinctions are closely related. Narrative within the epic
world is a continuum. At one extreme lie bardic performances, based on
information provided by the Muses, potentially meaningful far beyond
their immediate contexts, but with the details of content not specific to
particular occasions, even if a member of the audience has requested the
subject of the song. At the other extreme are the false tales that have in
the past deceived Penelope and Eumaeus (*Od.* 14.379–85), invented sto-
ries that served only the greed of those who told them. In between are
the lying tales of Odysseus and the various paradigmatic and autobio-
graphical tales that fill the two epics, which their narrators have ac-
quired from personal experience or oral tradition and adapted to their
immediate needs.

   Both the *Iliad* and the *Odyssey* often identify the source of narrative
authority for character-narrators.[22] Many, of course, speak directly
about personal experience: in the *Odyssey*, Odysseus does so in the
Apologos and in his lying tales, and Nestor, Menelaus, and Helen do so
in the narratives they deliver to Telemachus. Nestor's narratives in the
Iliad tell his own deeds, not those of another.

   Contrast nonautobiographical narratives. In the *Iliad*, when Phoenix
tells the story of Meleager, he first speaks of having "heard" (ἐπευθόμεθα,
9.524) of how earlier heroes were placated with gifts. The first-person

---

21. See Peradotto 1997, 29.
   22. Olson (1995, 1–23, with especially good comments at 13 on how narra-
tors establish authority) discusses oral tradition in the *Odyssey*. See also Ford
1992, 101–10.

plural marks the shared transmission. When he tells the story of Meleager in some detail, however, he seems to claim some personal knowledge: μέμνημαι τόδε ἔργον ἐγὼ πάλαι, οὔ τι νέον γε [I remember this event from long ago—it is certainly not recent] (9.527). Pisistratus defers to Menelaus's personal knowledge of Antilochus's excellence to confirm what people say, since he himself did not know his older brother (*Od.* 4.200–202). Agamemnon tries to rouse Diomedes by insisting that Tydeus was always among the forefighters.

> ὡς φάσαν οἵ μιν ἴδοντο πονεύμενον· οὐ γὰρ ἔγωγε
> ἤντησ' οὐδὲ ἴδον· περὶ δ' ἄλλων φασὶ γενέσθαι.
>
> (*Il.* 4.374–75)

[So they said who saw him in action. For I never met him or saw him. But they say that he was superior to others.]

When Diomedes himself cites his father's might as the basis of his own authority at *Iliad* 14.110–27, he recites his genealogy, following his assertion that Tydeus was the best spearfighter among the Achaeans with the words τὰ δὲ μέλλετ' ἀκούεμεν, εἰ ἐτεόν περ [You surely know whether it is true] (14.125).

Reciters of genealogies often stress the likelihood that the hearer is already familiar with the information. When Glaucus agrees to provide his ancestry to Diomedes, he adds, πολλοὶ δέ μιν ἄνδρες ἴσασιν [And many men know it] (*Il.* 6.151). While this remark may be intended snidely, as a hint that Diomedes ought to know Glaucus's ancestry as well as others do (Richard Martin calls it a "veiled insult"),[23] the parallels show that Glaucus may also be insisting that the genealogy is accurate, since it is widely known. Aeneas insists that he and Achilles know each others' parentage through report.

> ἴδμεν δ' ἀλλήλων γενεήν, ἴδμεν δὲ τοκῆας,
> πρόκλυτ' ἀκούοντες ἔπεα θνητῶν ἀνθρώπων·
> ὄψει δ' οὔτ' ἄρ πω σὺ ἐμοὺς ἴδες οὔτ' ἄρ' ἐγὼ σούς.
> φασὶ σὲ μὲν Πηλῆος ἀμύμονος ἔκγονον εἶναι . . .
>
> (*Il.* 20.203–6)

---

23. Martin 1989, 128.

[We know each others' ancestry, we know each others' parents, since we hear the famed tales of mortal men, though you have never seen mine with your eyes, nor I yours. They say you are the offspring of blameless Peleus . . .]

Like Agamemnon, Aeneas here lays an apparently superfluous emphasis on his never having seen the addressee's parents. Asteropaeus refers to report for his parentage itself, saying that the River Axius begot "famous" Pelegon τὸν δ' ἐμέ φασι γείνασθαι [and they say he begot me] (*Il.* 21.159–160).

Flyting can take the form of denying the plausibility of such familiar genealogical information. Tlepolemus claims that Sarpedon does not behave like a son of Zeus.

ψευδόμενοι δέ σέ φασι Διὸς γόνον αἰγιόχοιο
εἶναι, ἐπεὶ πολλὸν κείνων ἐπιδεύεαι ἀνδρῶν
οἳ Διὸς ἐξεγένοντο ἐπὶ προτέρων ἀνθρώπων.

(*Il.* 5.635–37)

[They lie when they say that you are the child of aegis-carrying Zeus, since you are far inferior to those heroes who were born of Zeus in the time of earlier people.]

His example of such a hero is, naturally, his own father, Heracles: ἀλλ' οἷόν τινά φασι βίην Ἡρακλείην / εἶναι [but such as they say mighty Heracles was] (5.638–39). He cites specifically Heracles' sack of Troy. Sarpedon, though, counters by saying that Heracles was able to destroy Troy only because Laomedon had acted foolishly in mistreating Heracles after Heracles had benefited him (5.648–51). He, too, is well informed about Trojan history, and he disagrees with Tlepolemus's version, just as Tlepolemus disputed Sarpedon's genealogical just claims.

To be sure, not every citation of genealogical or other information footnotes the oral tradition. Homeric speakers refer explicitly to oral tradition as a source of knowledge only when the reference is rhetorically useful. In the *Odyssey*, Nestor knows about the suitors from the oral tradition but does not mention them until Telemachus does (3.211–13). His (partial) knowledge allows him both to ask why Telemachus has allowed this situation to come about and to suggest that he could change it. Both Athena-Mentes and Nestor tell Telemachus that he must already

have heard about Orestes' killing of Aegisthus (1.298–99, 3.193–94), be-
cause the paradigm is all the more effective that way. By taking
vengeance, Orestes has won fame that has reached even faraway Ithaca.

This oral tradition is clearly not the same as the epic tradition it-
self.[24] Although Glaucus's recitation of his genealogy to Diomedes is
epic performance in that he is an epic character and although it is clearly
an oral performance within the mimetic world, it is not epic perform-
ance within the mimetic world. Indeed, since such verbal performances
are genres of discourse, the audience must have recognized them as epic
adaptations of independent forms.[25] Diomedes does not sing about his
ancestors.

The Muses are therefore only one method of access to knowledge
beyond that naturalistically available to human beings. This method is
not automatically superior to others, despite the polemic tone of the
proem to the Catalogue of Ships. Odysseus praises Demodocus for
singing about events in Troy as if he had been present at them or had
heard them ("from an eyewitness" is implied): ὥς τέ που ἢ αὐτὸς παρεὼν
ἢ ἄλλου ἀκούσας (Od. 8.491). He has learned, Odysseus thinks, from the
Muse or Apollo (8.488). The praise itself indicates that not all bards
would do as well and thus that bardic knowledge, being dependent on
the gods' love for a particular performer, is not always so complete. In
any case, even Demodocus's knowledge is not better than Odysseus's.
It is not perhaps surprising that Odysseus regards his own eyewitness
knowledge as a standard for evaluating the bard's performance, but the
standard even includes a rendition at second hand. This potential su-
periority of nonpoetic oral tradition to the poetic, as long as the line of
transmission is very close, may seem to contradict the Iliad's disparage-
ment of kleos. The oral tradition of the Trojan War, however, is far more
remote than even a second-hand report from the perspective of the
Odyssey and its audience. If the events are far away in time, direct access
through the Muses is better. Bardic performance offers the possibility of
unmediated and independent access to otherwise inaccessible knowl-

---

24. Nagy (1974, 248) calls kleos "the formal word" for epic song. To be sure,
κλέα ἀνδρῶν is the regular term for the contents of heroic song; but epic per-
formance is not the only medium for kleos. Similarly, Nagy (1979, 271) identifies
the oral tradition with poetry, connecting the "I did not myself see" topos with
the theme of the blind poet.

25. See Martin 1989, 42–47.

edge. Odysseus's praise, after all, emphasizes that the Muses or Apollo can replace human knowledge.

Furthermore, both Odysseus as eyewitness narrator (*Od.* 11.328–29) and the *Iliad* poet (*Il.* 2.488–92) acknowledge that a complete catalogue of heroes or heroines is not physically possible.[26] Praise of a poetic account may imply that it is genuinely complete (*Od.* 8.490), but this is a hyberbole—stories could always be fuller, and the poet does not hesitate to add details in later passages to what appeared to be a full account.[27] For the performing bard, however, the Muses, who know the complete account, are always present; only the individual performance is confined. Odysseus, in contrast, is a mortal. Those heroines whom he does not name could be lost to memory in the oral tradition if he never tells about them. So the individual performer, on each occasion, is imagined as selecting from the entire memory of the Muses, rather than from oral tradition, which has inevitably already winnowed what any individual can hear and learn. This is, however, recognized hyberbole. The Homeric narrator himself does not hesitate to add details later to an apparently full narrative.

The gap between bardic knowledge and oral tradition is remarkable. Not only do poets not learn from other poets, but they do not learn from anyone except the gods.[28] Despite the gap between oral tradition and bardic knowledge, however, performers within the epics do not actually stray beyond what oral tradition could plausibly tell them about human affairs. In the *Odyssey*, nobody asks Phemius to report on the whereabouts of Odysseus. Demodocus can sing about Odysseus's deeds at Troy, which took place in the presence of the army, but he has evidently not sung of Odysseus's post-Trojan adventures. The Ithacan books could hardly exist if the Muse told Phemius Odysseus's location, and the Apologos would be silly if the Phaeacians had heard all this material before. Nonetheless, there is a practical reality here. The Homeric bard is not clairvoyant. It may not be a meaningless formulaic variation that Hesiod claims that the Muses gave him song ἵνα κλείοιμι τά τ᾿ ἐσσόμενα πρό τ᾿ ἐόντα [so that I might make famous things to be and things past] (*Theog.*

---

26. Ford (1992, 67–87) discusses the problem of selection.

27. For such "retrospective gaps," see Scodel 1999, 59–60.

28. Finkelberg (1990) argues that the Muses allow more creativity to the individual performer than does South Slavic epic, in which only the tradition sanctions content.

32), omitting the present. The present is not open to bardic intrusion. In-
deed, all three times that the Homeric poet attributes information to oral
tradition in his own voice, using the φασί formula that is so common in
character speeches, concern the present, not the past. At *Iliad* 2.783, "they
say" that Typhoeus's bed is at Arimoi; at 17.674–75, "they say" that the
eagle has the sharpest vision of all birds. Both these examples occur
within similes, where the narrator's authority over the past is least at
stake. At *Odyssey* 6.42–43, the poet attributes to oral tradition the belief
that Olympus is a secure and blissful home for the gods. Elsewhere, the
narrator speaks about Olympus on the Muse's authority; the formula
"they say" evokes oral tradition not because the poet needs its authority
for this information but to bring the hearer closer to the poem's world.

The singers know events on Olympus in detail. Demodocus can
sing about events at which only gods were present, just as the great epics
themselves regularly present Olympian scenes. By contrast, though
Odysseus slips into omniscience at various points in the Apologos, he
is generally careful not to show excessive knowledge of divine matters:
he explains that Calypso told him of Helius's complaint to Zeus (*Od.*
12.374–90, especially 389–90). Usually, he follows the standard rules that
govern human speech about the gods.[29] We can perhaps assume that
Ariadne would have been able to guess and so tell Odysseus of the mys-
terious role of Dionysus in her death (*Od.* 11.324–25), just as Achilles can
assume that Apollo has caused the plague at *Iliad* 1.64 and just as the
Calydonian boar shows that Artemis is angry in the Meleager story (*Il.*
9.535–40). Agamemnon's speech of apology at *Iliad* 19.78–144 tests the
limits of a mortal speaker. Telling how Hera tricked Zeus at the birth of
Heracles, Agamemnon includes speeches of both Hera and Zeus.[30] The
story is treated as so familiar that Agamemnon need provide no au-
thority for telling it.[31] However, he may also be asserting his own au-
thority by asserting unusual narrative power, to emphasize his status in
a situation that threatens his prestige.

The representations of bardic knowledge in the poems are thus
largely a mystification, but they are a completely transparent one. In a
demystified account, we would say that bards adapt oral tradition—

---

29. Jörgenson 1904 is the standard analysis of these rules.

30. Page (1959, 313) heaps scorn on the passage ("the laws of the Epic art lie
in fragments at our feet").

31. Schol. bT on 19.101 already has this explanation.

both the stories people tell and the songs they have heard—by including supernatural forces. Precisely because oral tradition does not usually attempt to describe the part played by divine powers (except when the gods act openly or mortals can infer their involvement), bards freely go beyond the spoken tradition when singing about the gods. Otherwise, however, even as the bards recount those stories that have achieved wide popularity and as the epic's very form is a constant reminder of its traditionality, Homer never overtly acknowledges any connection between oral tradition and song.

Most nonbardic narrative is sharply goal directed. Odysseus's lies are blatantly manipulative, but so are "true" narratives. Battlefield genealogies seek to intimidate; mythical paradigms exhort to appropriate behavior. Although narrative may also serve as entertainment, as do the narratives Menelaus and Helen tell Telemachus (*Od.* 4.234–89), even such narratives are usually self-interested. Helen and Menelaus ostensibly speak to praise Odysseus for the benefit of his son, but Helen's tale is self-justifying, Menelaus's a rejection of her self-justification. At the extreme, such storytelling becomes *ainos,* like Odysseus's story to Eumaeus about the ambush at Troy, a scarcely veiled request for an extra blanket that provides Odysseus with a test of Eumaeus's hospitality (*Od.* 14. 459–506).

Narrators who do not tell their stories to test or manipulate their audiences are typically responding to straightforward requests for information. Telemachus asks Nestor and Menelaus about his father (*Od.* 3.98–101 = 4.326–31); their stories answer this request. The oral tradition thus depends on what is useful for particular individuals. Stories that respond to curiosity about the teller come closest to bardic narratives. The Apologos responds to Alcinous's direct request to Odysseus to identify himself, so that he can be taken home (*Od.* 8.550–56); to tell the story of his travels and those he met wandering (8.572–76); and to explain why he has wept at songs about Troy (8.577–86). One motive for the request for autobiography is therefore completely practical, while another is personal curiosity: Alcinous expects the narrative to explain Odysseus's odd behavior. The length of the narrative is thus justified by the fullness of the request. Odysseus's narrative is, in any case, gently manipulative, and his voice is distinct from that of the external narrator, more emotional, more given to explicit judgment.[32] He begins by im-

---

32. See de Jong 1992.

plicitly apologizing for refusing to marry Nausicaa, by celebrating the love of one's native place and stressing how he rejected two goddesses. His narrative encourages the Phaeacians to take him home and thus avoid being bad hosts.[33] He flatters Arete by giving considerable time to cataloguing the heroines in the underworld.[34] The central moral is one the external narrator obviously endorses, and the Phaeacians endorse it, too—they have already promised Odysseus his return when he tells his tale. Allusions to various details scattered throughout the *Odyssey* prove that Odysseus is a reliable narrator. The narrative is obviously very successful, since Arete urges that the Phaeacians not hasten to send him away and that he receive more gifts, since he is so impressive a guest-friend and is in need [οὕτω χρηΐζοντι] (*Od.* 11.336–41).

When Alcinous endorses this proposal, Odysseus offers to remain for as long as a year, if this would mean receiving more gifts (*Od.* 11.358–61). This frank greed is unbardlike, yet it is to this remark that Alcinous reacts when he praises Odysseus and compares him to a bard.

ὦ Ὀδυσεῦ, τὸ μὲν οὔ τί σ' ἐΐσκομεν εἰσορόωντες
ἠπεροπῆά τ' ἔμεν καὶ ἐπίκλοπον, οἷά τε πολλοὺς
βόσκει γαῖα μέλαινα πολυσπερέας ἀνθρώπους
ψεύδεά τ' ἀρτύνοντας, ὅθεν κέ τις οὐδὲ ἴδοιτο·
σοὶ δ' ἔπι μὲν μορφὴ ἐπέων, ἔνι δὲ φρένες ἐσθλαί,
μῦθον δ' ὡς ὅτ' ἀοιδὸς ἐπισταμένως κατέλεξας . . .

(*Od.* 11.363–68)

[Odysseus, in no way as we look at you do we reckon that you are a trickster and a cheat, as the black earth feeds many people who are all over the world and invent lies whose source one could not find at all. But the proper form of words lies upon you, and a good mind is within, and you have told your tale through competently, like a bard . . .]

Odysseus is bardlike because his tale is arranged chronologically and fittingly rather than with a view to persuasion. Alcinous may be understood to have taken Odysseus's remarks as ironic: in offering to remain for a year for the sake of gain, Odysseus has implied that the audience's

---

33. Most 1989.
34. See Doherty 1995, 93–99.

request that he wait puts him in the position of a begging storyteller, someone who might tell lies for profit. By comparing him to a bard and simultaneously asking him to talk about his companions from Troy (11.371–72), Alcinous insists that he does not place Odysseus in this category.

Similarly, Odysseus asks Eumaeus to tell the story of how he was enslaved (*Od.* 15.381–88), and Eumaeus agrees, since he has been asked, the night is long, and people enjoy speaking even of their troubles, when these are over (15.390–402). Odysseus introduces his request for more information by showing himself moved by the pathos of Eumaeus's early separation from his home and parents (15.381–82). Odysseus surely knows the story already but elaborately affects ignorance, asking whether Eumaeus's city was sacked or whether he was captured in a cattle raid (15.381–88). After Eumaeus tells his story, he acknowledges Eumaeus's misfortune and expresses sympathy, using the same formulae Eumaeus used in response to his own (false) story (15.486–87 are almost identical to 14.361–62). Yet he claims that Eumaeus's story has a relatively happy ending, while his own condition is worse (15.491–92): there is an implicit competition in pathetic storytelling, a competition that only makes sense because the winner is entitled to the most pity.

Such interest in the narrator is foreign to poetic narrative. At epic performances, audiences feel either unalloyed pleasure (the Phaeacians) or pain because they are personally involved (Odysseus, Penelope). Some critics have thought that the Phaeacians' cheerful response to epic is peculiar to this exceptionally privileged community.[35] Yet the speech in which Telemachus rebukes his mother for interfering with Phemius's performance indicates that such painless enjoyment is the norm: the bard must be allowed to delight (τέρπειν, *Od.* 1.347) his audience as his mind directs him. Telemachus weeps when reminded of his father at *Odyssey* 4.185, so he is not insensible on all occasions. He can speak as he does because delight and performance are closely linked. Nobody shows the slightest curiosity about the bards themselves apart from their professional function, and the bards do not sing to achieve immediate personal ends. Apparently, Achilles sings only for his own pleasure (*Il.* 9.189–91); Patroclus waits in silence for him to finish but is not said to be listening.[36] Nobody in the poems recites nonpoetic narrative

---

35. See Walsh 1984, 1–6.
36. Segal (1994, 115) rightly emphasizes the middle voice in *Il.* 9.186.

to himself or herself for pleasure (nearest to doing so is Penelope, who tells the story of the daughters of Pandareus while praying to Artemis at *Od.* 20.66–78). To be sure, all songs potentially serve the cause of social control, simply by reminding their hearers that others will remember and judge their actions. Specific songs, however, do not serve immediate practical purposes. Despite the warlike content of heroic song, it is associated with peace.[37] The embassy finds Achilles singing the famous deeds of heroes; apparently he sings because his anger makes action impossible (*Il.* 9.186–89). Odysseus says that listening to an excellent bard like Demodocus is the "most delightful fulfillment" (*Od.* 9.5), associating the performance occasion with a contented populace and an abundant feast. Epic singing thus belongs to situations in which there is no need for action.

This is quite clear in the case of Demodocus's two songs about Troy, for the topic is remote from most of the audience. The quarrel between Odysseus and Achilles (8.75–82) is relevant to the context in which Demodocus sings it, but not in ways the singer can intend. Up to this point, the *Odyssey* has not displayed Odysseus's fierce temper, but this aspect of his character will soon be prominent in his anger with Laodamas (8.152–57) and in the ensuing quarrel with Euryalus. The song also prepares for the thematically important contrast between Achilles and Odysseus as candidates for "best of the Achaeans" (and between songs about these heroes as candidates for the greatest of poems), a contrast the Nekyia will develop.[38] The internal audience cannot, however, appreciate these resonances. Demodocus's song of the Trojan horse certainly is performed in response to Odysseus's request and serves to prepare the audience for Odysseus's own narrative. It can serve Odysseus's needs precisely because Demodocus is not singing with the purpose of praising a known patron. Demodocus has no ax to grind; his praise of Odysseus therefore rings true.[39]

Phemius sings among the suitors of the bitter return of the Achaeans: ὁ δ᾽ Ἀχαιῶν νόστον ἄειδε / λυγρόν, ὃν ἐκ Τροίης ἐπετείλατο Παλλὰς

---

37. Inspiring warriors is a function of epic in many cultures: see Zumthor 1990, 85.

38. This contrast is the subject of A. Edwards 1985.

39. Ahl and Roisman (1996, 74–75, 81–82) suggest that Demodocus may have recognized Odysseus, but I find coincidence not only truer to the text but poetically more meaningful.

Ἀθήνη [He sang the unhappy return of the Achaeans, which Pallas Athena enjoined when they came from Troy] (*Od.* 1.326–27). J. Svenbro has argued that Phemius selected this theme to please the suitors and that indeed the "real" subject is the death of Odysseus.[40] One may well guess that the topic would please the suitors, but the point needs careful qualification. Since the song names Athena, the song's subject is presumably either the celebrated storm that drowned many and sent Odysseus off course or possibly the death of Agamemnon, which Athena caused by inciting the quarrel that led Agamemnon and Menelaus to go home separately rather than together (*Od.* 3.132–36). Penelope says that the bard knows "many other enchantments of mortals, deeds of gods and men, which bards make famous" (1.337–38), so this choice of subject is unnecessary. Unless we assume that the bard has ignored most of his repertory since the suitors arrived, Phemius regularly sings a variety of material, even though he has evidently sung this theme before, since Penelope says that it "always" causes her pain.[41] Penelope, in directing her complaint to the bard, does not blame pressure from the suitors for the bard's choice. The song hurts her, because grief has come to her more than to anyone (με μάλιστα, 1.342). Her very complaint thereby acknowledges that her grief, though extreme, is by no means unique. Alcinous thinks that Odysseus may have wept at hearing songs about Troy because he lost an in-law or a good friend there (*Od.* 8.577–86)—that is, he assumes that for someone grieving for a friend who died at Troy, any song about the war would cause pain.

Telemachus's response also points away from the song's being distorted to please the suitors.

> οὔ νύ ἀοιδοὶ
> αἴτιοι, ἀλλά ποθι Ζεὺς αἴτιος, ὅς τε δίδωσιν
> ἀνδράσιν ἀλφηστῇσιν, ὅπως ἐθέλῃσιν, ἑκάστῳ.
> τούτῳ δ᾽ οὐ νέμεσις Δαναῶν κακὸν οἶτον ἀείδειν.
> τὴν γὰρ ἀοιδὴν μᾶλλον ἐπικλείουσ᾽ ἄνθρωποι,
> ἥ τις ἀκουόντεσσι νεωτάτη ἀμφιπέλεται.

---

40. Svenbro 1976, 24–31. Pucci (1987, 195–208, 228–35) does not follow Svenbro but still treats Phemius as singing "false" songs.

41. "Always" here probably means "whenever I hear it"; otherwise, Penelope's use is an example of the common hyperbolic "always" and "never" of Homeric speakers (see MacLeod 1982, 96, on *Il.* 24.62–63, 72–73).

σοὶ δ᾽ ἐπιτολμάτω κραδίη καὶ θυμὸς ἀκούειν·
οὐ γὰρ Ὀδυσσεὺς οἶος ἀπώλεσε νόστιμον ἦμαρ
ἐν Τροίη, πολλοὶ δὲ καὶ ἄλλοι φῶτες ὄλοντο.

(*Od.* 1.347–55)

[The bards are not to blame, but somehow to blame is Zeus, who gives to barley-eating people, to each as he wishes. For the bard to sing the miserable fate of the Danaans is not cause for just anger. For people most make the song famous that comes around as the newest to those who hear it. Let your heart and mind endure to hear it, since Odysseus was not the only one who lost his day of return at Troy, but many other men died.]

First, Telemachus insists that Zeus is to blame, not the bards, implying that the song is true and therefore belongs in the repertory. When he justifies the song as newest, he judges it not as it affects a particular audience, whether Penelope or the suitors, but more generally, in terms of what "people" like. He thus implicitly denies that this topic serves the interests of the suitors.[42] Finally, he answers Penelope's assertion that her grief is beyond that of others, by using a traditional formula of consolation—Odysseus was not the only one who died in the Trojan campaign. If the song were actually about Odysseus, neither Penelope's praise of Odysseus nor Telemachus's exhortation would make sense, as both do if the song reminds Penelope of Odysseus but is not about him. Telemachus is urging her to take a different message from the song.

Songs, therefore, are by no means without moral implications, but these are not explicit or self-interested. Phemius does not tell his audience how to respond, and his song is capable of multiple uses.[43] Indeed, the summary of the song can be turned directly against the suitors, since it is a tale of divine vengeance. Athena gave the Achaeans a bitter return because they had offended her, and the suitors, too, will soon suffer under Athena's direction. The song can help justify the suitors (by hinting

---

42. Nagy (1990b, 69) suggests that "new" here means exactly what I argue is suppressed: the application of traditional material to the present situation. The topic is not yet traditional for the internal audience, however. On the *Odyssey's* "newness," see chapter 2.

43. As Edmunds (1997, 419–20) points out, ordinary character narratives often have meanings beyond those intended by the speaker; these other meanings often reflect ironically on the speaker.

that Odysseus, like so many others, doubtless died) or warn them (by
implying that the gods do concern themselves with mortals, who had
best therefore follow social norms). The suitors force Phemius to sing
but never praise his singing, while both Penelope and Telemachus do.[44]
While it is typical of the suitors that they do not behave graciously or
recognize what is socially appropriate, their failure to praise the bard
may also mark their failure to listen properly.

The song of Ares and Aphrodite is, like Phemius's song, a contro-
versial case. Some interpreters have seen a parallel in the quarrel be-
tween Ares and Hephaestus (one physically attractive and swift, the
other ugly and crippled) to the dispute between Euryalus and Odysseus
(one good-looking but foolish, the other unprepossessing to look at but
with qualities that do not appear on the surface).[45] The song could ap-
ply to the immediate situation, particularly in its hint that appropriate
compensation can heal even the worst of quarrels. Still, there are
difficulties with interpreting the song as a direct and intentional com-
ment on the quarrel. Surely it would hardly be courteous to compare an
honored guest to a cuckold, even if the cuckold receives compensation.
Hephaestus appears ridiculous; he is angry and vexed (ἀκάχημαι, Od.
8.314), while the other gods are laughing (8.326).[46] If Odysseus under-
stood the song as a comment on himself, he would surely be angered
further, not appeased. Moreover, Odysseus is not physically unprepos-
sessing. Laodamas has invited Odysseus to compete, probably intend-
ing no insult but, rather, in the belief that he looks like an athlete (8.145).
Alcinous surely does not consider him unattractive when he considers
him as a possible husband for his daughter (7.312), and Arete praises his
looks (11.336–37). Only after Odysseus has indignantly refused to com-
pete does Euryalus claim that he looks like a merchant, not an athletic
aristocrat (8.159–64).[47] In throwing the discus, Odysseus has not shown
himself to be crafty like Hephaestus but has triumphed by physical
prowess. The Phaeacians do not yet know his identity, so they have no
reason to connect Hephaestus's cunning with the stranger's. Further-

44. See Rüter 1969, 233.
45. Bliss 1968; Braswell 1982.
46. Brown (1989) argues convincingly that this laughter is directed at Ares
and Aphrodite and represents a mechanism of social control, like a shivaree.
Even though the gods are not laughing at him, however, Hephaestus himself
does not find the matter funny.
47. See Garvie 1994, 264 (on Od. 8.133–57), 268–69 (on 8.158–64).

more, Alcinous's order to Euryalus to give Odysseus a gift responds not directly to the song, but to Odysseus's praise of the performance (8.382–84).

Indeed, the song seems so clearly linked to the main plot of the *Odyssey* that it would be a distraction for the external audience to apply it too closely to its immediate context. As a song about adultery and cunning, it foreshadows Odysseus's success over the suitors.[48] It could misdirect the external audience, inviting them to imagine that even after adultery has been committed, compensation could control a husband's anger—and that therefore compensation could settle Odysseus's quarrel with the suitors (as Eurymachus indeed will briefly hope it may, at 22.55–59). Within the whole plot as it stands, the song shows, as do so many divine scenes in the *Iliad*, that the lives of the gods are simply not serious as human lives are.

All these possible implications, however, are available only to the external audience, not to the Phaeacians or Demodocus. The song is certainly relevant to Odysseus but is not intended to be. The only song directed at a specific audience is that of the Sirens. The Sirens' song represents a sort of antisong, which can define normal song by what it is not. They address Odysseus by name as his ship approaches (*Od.* 12.184) and offer to sing precisely what might most interest him from their all-inclusive repertory.

ἴδμεν γάρ τοι πάνθ᾽ ὅσ᾽ ἐνὶ Τροίῃ εὐρείῃ
Ἀργεῖοι Τρῶές τε θεῶν ἰότητι μόγησαν·
ἴδμεν δ᾽ ὅσσα γένηται ἐπὶ χθονὶ πουλυβοτείρῃ.

(12.189–91)

[For we know everything that the Argives and Trojans suffered in broad Troy by the will of the gods. We know everything that happens on the earth that feeds many.]

Their knowledge of Odysseus's identity confirms this claim. Goddesses themselves, they apparently do not require the help of the Muses to sing. Of course, those who listen to them without precautions die. They thus bring together the extreme ends of the narrative continuum. Like the de-

---

48. On connections between the song and the Ithacan plot, see Burkert 1960; Newton 1987; Olson 1989.

vious liars, they match their song precisely to a specific audience to
profit by manipulating the hearer. Yet they have the full knowledge of
remote events characteristic of true bards. Only because they are god-
desses is this possible, because for a mortal singer, the Muses guarantee
not only that the song is accurate but that it is innocent. Independence
from oral tradition and repetition of traditional story serve the same
purpose, a narrative without ulterior motives.

The audience of epic performance, therefore, can apparently eval-
uate the main narrative by the pleasure it provides, without worrying
about being manipulated. This unsuspicious reception is possible only
because the Homeric tradition so rigorously defines its subject matter as
the heroes of the past. Despite its representations of bards who sing of
their contemporaries, Homeric epic does not praise the living.[49] The
narrative's claim of "truth" emphasizes literal, historical accuracy only
in catalogues. More often, it implicitly promises that it rewards great
deeds with merited praise.[50] The Homeric strategy is also closely tied to
the practice of recomposition-in-performance and to the consequent
ephemerality of most variation. Traditional referentiality adds signifi-
cance to each performance, but the referent is imprecise and un-
bounded. The fiction of independence could not be sustained if other
versions were directly available for comparison, and even in an oral
context, it demanded the audience's co-operation in "forgetting" con-
tradictions.

The history of the political use of Homer shows how a particular
poem, a detail in it, or, indeed, the tradition could please or offend a polis
as a whole. The Megarians accused the Athenians of interpolation (see
Strabo 9.394; cf. Aristotle *Rhetoric* A 15.1375b29–30), and Cleisthenes of
Sicyon forbade rhapsodic performances entirely (see Herodotus 5.67.1).
The pressures these stories imply must have existed before either individ-
ual compositions or the canon as a whole took shape. Yet what is truly re-
markable is the success of the tradition in achieving wide authority across
boundaries. The Megarians claimed interpolation, not pro-Athenian bias,
on Homer's part, and they argued about authenticity: the archaic Homer
may have been multiform, but each version claimed to be correct.

---

49. See Nagy 1990b, 147–50.

50. See Pratt 1993, 37–42. Walsh (1984, 20) makes a distinction between po-
etry that is true but remote and poetry with a point, but he sees both as possi-
bilities within Homer.

For Svenbro, the Muse hypostasizes social control; for Nagy, her "message is equated with that of creative tradition."[51] I suggest that the Muse represents an attempt to finesse the impossible complexity of potential claims. The care with which Homer presents bardic performance as uncontaminated and free, even as he shows the forces that would realistically limit its freedom, reflects a serious anxiety. Each performance had to negotiate its way through competing pressures. The fiction of independence offered space to maneuver. The Muse protects the poet from anxieties about his own memory and the tradition; she guarantees that he remains within the tradition and so permits him to select among variants, adapting as he must. If she is helping him, he cannot be making incorrect choices. Simultaneously, she protects the poet from excessive demands from the audience; if the source of the song is supernatural, he cannot modify it to please the most powerful members of the audience or its largest segment. The fiction of independence could make some real independence possible. For the audience, it was worthwhile even for patrons to accept the bards' fiction of complete independence, since only by believing that they did not tell the bard what to sing could they receive the song as confirmation of their beliefs instead of as a reflection of their own power.

The epic's distancing of itself from oral tradition does not undercut its rhetoric of traditionality. On the contrary, if no performance actually depends on any other, then when the audience recognizes repetitions from earlier occasions, the similarities are especially powerful markers of stability and truth. By presenting themselves as disinterested, performers discourage the audience from looking for the details that gave one performance a different message from another. By separating their own narrative from its tradition, they place it all under the sign of traditionality. Since the poet could not be certain exactly what was "traditional" for his audience, he carefully pointed to the traditional and disinterested nature of the whole.

---

51. Svenbro 1976, 16–35; Nagy 1979, 16.

Homeric Exposition

Rhetoric and Strategies

The poet confronting a large and unfamiliar audience faced difficulties with exposition as well as with authority. If he did not know exactly what songs they had heard before and in what version, he did not know what they already knew. Since only stories of the origin of the world (Genesis, Hesiod's *Theogony*) can begin at the beginning, narratives must use characters, places, and worlds as if they already existed when the story begins, and they must somehow inform the audience about the contextual world of the story, its furniture and properties.[1] In the realist novel, we often find summaries and descriptions, at the beginning or deferred. Modern drama leans on the program, from which the audience learns time, setting, and the names and basic relationships of characters. In many oral epics, characters and situations have a rich existence before the story begins, in all the tales told before. In most traditions, performers need not meticulously explain such background: the audience knows it already, each song is self-contained, or the story is not the most important element in the performance.[2] But once the poet is not intimately familiar with the audience, the objectively traditional status of a character does not entail audience familiarity with all that character's exploits. If the poet fails to provide necessary information, listeners will be unable to follow. At the same time, he (or, rarely, she) needs to avoid boring members of the audience or talking down to them. The poet also needs to make sure that the audience "forgets" traditional stories that contradict the one he tells, unless he is confident that his own version will prevail and wants to use alternative versions as foil. There

---

1. The fullest treatment of exposition is Sternberg 1978.
2. Songs in the South Slavic tradition are independent enough not to require extensive explanation (especially because the audience knows the thematic patterns in play). In Pabuji, the story is relatively unimportant (see Smith 1991, 39–40).

are thus several related questions. What overall rhetorical positions does the poet take toward this unfamiliar audience? How much shared knowledge does he assume in actual practice? What are the poet's strategies for giving information to the audience?

Some epic traditions allow bards to begin performances by explaining background that members of the audience may not know, as 'Adwallah frequently did (see the chapter "What Are We Talking about When We Talk about Tradition?" earlier in this book). Homeric epic, however, does not openly admit that anyone in the audience might lack knowledge. It is a sustaining fiction that before the performance starts, the poet and audience are in the same position of having heard the tradition (*kleos*, "what is heard") but lacking precise knowledge. Even when the poet has called on the Muses, the tone of the narrative ordinarily implies as little as possible about what the audience does or does not know already.

When the epic occasionally assumes a didactic voice, it does not serve expository purposes. The famous passages that tell the gods' special names for things (*Il.* 1.403–4, 2.813–14, 14.290–91, 20.74; *Od.* 10.305, 12.61) are displays of poetic power. Even these passages do not always imply that the hearer does not know the names already, since Achilles mentions both the divine and human names of Briareos/Aegaeon to Thetis in a story about her own rescue of Zeus (*Il.* 1.403–4). Circe mentions the Clashing Rocks (*Od.* 12.61) only to refer to how the Argo, "known to all," passed through them.

Character-narrators have more freedom to use the informative voice than the poet does, since one character frequently conveys previously unfamiliar information to another. Thus, more often than the primary narrator, character-narrators use the *topographical introduction* ("there is a certain place called . . ."), which implies that the hearer might not know the information already. Eumaeus, who has no reason to think that the beggar has heard his autobiography, introduces his story with the words "There is a certain island called Syrie—maybe you've heard of it" [Νῆσός τις Συρίη κικλήσκεται, εἴ που ἀκούεις] (*Od.* 15.403). Homer himself uses this means of effecting a transition at *Iliad* 2.811 (where it is combined with a divine name) and 13.32 and at *Odyssey* 4.844 and 13.96, while characters use it at *Iliad* 11.711 and 722 and at *Odyssey* 3.293, 4.354, 15.403, and 19.172. Such passages do not provide information irrelevant now but useful later, as modern exposition does, nor do they compensate for possible ignorance in the audience. Instead, they create *reality effect,* locating the action precisely in a landscape. For the hearer, it is unimportant whether the landscape is real or imagined, traditional or invented. When the *Odyssey* tells us that the Ethiopians fall into two distinct groups (1.23–24), the information is truly irrelevant, whether in this context or in the poem as a whole. What does matter is that Poseidon is on vacation far away. Such passages are thus not very useful for broader narrative purposes.

The poet's rhetoric of inclusion, by pretending that everyone knows the inherited stories thoroughly, is an essential aspect of his rhetoric of traditionality. It asks the hearer unfamiliar with a particular item to assume that others in the audience are familiar with it. The rhetoric of inclusion allows the poet to avoid sharp distinctions between obscure or even invented epic material and the objectively traditional and widely known. He does not want to distinguish different groups within the audience, some knowing more and some less. If he acknowledged differences of knowledge, he would be in danger of acknowledging also different preferences or the validity of alternate versions and of diminishing the authority of his version. The poet unifies the audience by never admitting that it is not united already. At the same time, he actually takes for granted only a basic familiarity with the background of his story and his characters.

Fortunately, this rhetorical assumption of shared prior knowledge does not force the narrator to skip significant actions because people know them. The poet's task is to tell the story fully and vividly, with the precision the Muse offers. Homeric narrative is thus full and easy to follow. Background is the problem, since the dominant rhetoric of inclusion forbids the poet to explain too much too overtly. The poet avoids the explicit exposition familiar to modern readers from the nineteenth-century novel, where the narrator provides background that may not be needed until much later. The rhetoric of inclusion complicates the task of making the song truly inclusive.

The poet has several strategies for informing his audience while pretending that no information is required. Often, he naturalizes exposition, so that he does not openly provide information. He does not describe his characters but has them explain themselves to each other. Such naturalized exposition must often be delayed, however, since the poet must create occasions for the characters to tell their stories. Also, since characters present the information from their own, self-interested points of view, the hearer must take care in evaluating it.

The poet explains the motives of both gods and mortals, especially when these are not obvious from their actions: Hera, he says, sends Athena to stop Achilles from killing Agamemnon is because she cares for both heroes (*Il.* 1.195–96), and it is out of brotherly understanding that Menelaus comes to Agamemnon's feast without being summoned (*Il.* 2.409). Such explanations of the characters' immediate motives are part of the telling of the tale, not the kind of explanation that would violate the norms of inclusion.

When a narrative moment is especially significant, the epic emphasizes it by expansion.[3] It is possible to be brief and a good speaker in the Homeric world, as is Menelaus (*Il.* 3.213–15), but a great orator, such as Odysseus, usually has words like snowflakes (3.222). The poet can use such expansive moments to inform the audience, because providing information is only one function of narrative in the world depicted in the epics and is not the most important function. Characters regularly tell each other stories they already know. For rhetorical purposes, they "remind" each other.[4] The assembly of the gods that opens the *Odyssey* offers a striking example. Zeus, having "remembered" Aegisthus and his death at the hands of Orestes, gives a summary of Agamemnon's death and Orestes' vengeance. The summary is brief but very clear—especially with the help of the narrator's preface (1.29–30, 35–43). The gods, of course, know this story, but Zeus tells it because it illustrates the point he wishes to make. Athena's response includes a genealogy of Calypso that expands on the power of her father, Atlas (1.51–54), and on the situation of Odysseus (1.55–59), which the narrator has already mentioned (1.13–15). Athena's speech is an overt attempt to convince Zeus to act, in which Athena gives details because they contribute to the persuasive effect. His reply insists that he has not "forgotten" (λαθοίμην, 1.65) Odysseus. His explanation of his failure to help Odysseus earlier includes a full genealogy of Polyphemus (1.70–73).[5] None of this information-laden speech implies ignorance on the part of the hearers. Good speech makes the most relevant facts salient and so inspires proper action. Poetry differs from other narrative in not direct-

---

3. See Austin 1966.

4. See Martin 1989, 77–88.

5. This peculiar genealogy (the monstrous and mortal Cyclops is the child of Poseidon and a nymph) is unlikely to be objectively traditional; see Danek 1998, 46.

ing its audience to act. It reminds its audience to help them select from memory the most significant facts for this moment. Each "reminding" may also be a hint that inappropriate material should be forgotten. However, the poet can only use reminding as a means of exposition when the information is relevant to the context at hand; there are limits on reminding.

A brief introduction amplifying a character's name (often with a relative pronoun) can function almost as an expanded epithet. Just as epithets can be repeated without any implication that the audience does not know them (because they honor the hero or god and make the character more fully present), so introductions remind the audience of what especially matters about the character at this point. The poet routinely pauses and expands to mark the significance of the coming action, while reminding his audience of the most relevant facts about the character.

Scholars have already pointed out that the external narrator's occasional formal introductions of characters and places usually help the audience evaluate a character or place and prepare for the episode at hand.[6] The function of introductions of characters can actually be specified more precisely. They appear immediately before the character's speech or entrance (usually, but not always, the first), before an internal audience. The information the narrator provides allows the external audience to evaluate not only the speech itself but the response of the internal audience. Nearly always, the internal audience knows or should know the information the introduction provides, so the introduction is quasi-focalized, allowing the external audience to become an idealized member of the internal audience.

Sometimes the introduction goes beyond information available to the internal audience. The *Odyssey*, for example, tells the external audience that one of Aegyptius's sons had been eaten by the Cyclops (2.19–20). The Ithacans at the assembly do not know this, but they do presumably know that Antiphus, who went to Troy with Odysseus, has been gone so long that he is probably dead, while another son, Eurynomus, is a suitor. Aegyptius has no reason to feel goodwill toward Telemachus, so when he blesses whoever has summoned the assembly, the effect is particularly powerful. Because the information in these in-

---

6. See Edwards, *Il. Comm.*, (5:176 on 18.249–53); de Jong 1987a, 199; Richardson 1990, 36–42 (contrasting Homer's limited use of introductions with their frequency in Icelandic saga).

troductions serves to evaluate both what the character does or says and how others respond to it, it does not violate the boundaries of reminding. The introduction of Theoclymenus (*Od.* 15.224–56) is unusual in providing information apparently never learned by Telemachus, although he receives Theoclymenus as a suppliant and a guest. This information is certainly helpful to the hearer in realizing that Telemachus behaves not only correctly but wisely in helping this prophet. From everything the audience might possibly know about a character, the narrator selects the details that are relevant in this context.[7]

The introductions are especially associated with failed interventions. The introduced speeches "misfire" and do not have their intended effect. The introduction allows the audience to judge this failure. For example, when Hector finds Andromache after his search for her, the narrator tells us that she is the daughter of Eetion from Thebe (*Il.* 6.395–97). The introduction prepares for her plea to Hector to be more careful of his life, a plea based on Andromache's complete dependence on him, since her natal kin are all dead (6.413–28). Her plea does not succeed. In another example, the introduction of the beggar Irus at his first entrance at *Odyssey* 18.1–7 stresses his gluttony and his physical weakness, despite a strong appearance. As events unfold, this knowledge enables the listener to judge not only Irus himself but Odysseus and the suitors.

Catalogues also permit the main narrator to introduce characters. Expanded entries occur not only in the big catalogues of Achaeans and Trojans but also in "minicatalogues," such as the list of leaders of the Myrmidons at *Iliad* 16.168–97. However, the poet cannot use introductions freely. Except in catalogues, fighters in battle normally only receive introductions of more than a line as victims.

The apparently anomalous introduction of Euphorbus as he stabs Patroclus (*Il.* 16.807–11) belongs in this last category, since Euphorbus dies very soon after this killing.

> . . . a Dardanian hero, Euphorbus, son of Panthous, who excelled everyone his own age with the spear, with horse driving, and with his swift feet. Indeed, he had once passed twenty men and their teams, coming first with his chariot, when he was first learning war.[8]

---

7. See Danek 1998, 293–97.

8. This translation and Janko's in *Il. Comm.*, 4:414–15 (on 16.808–81) follow the vulgate reading ποτέ rather than Aristarchus's τότε.

Euphorbus is a peculiar character, and this introduction probably provides genuinely unfamiliar information. He has not appeared or been mentioned before, and Menelaus will kill him within a few minutes in both story time and narrative time. There is no sign of him elsewhere in the tradition. He appears to exist only to diminish Hector's glory in killing Patroclus and perhaps so that the Achaeans who defend Patroclus's body may take some vengeance for him before Achilles returns. Scholars disagree intensely about how philhellenic the poet is.[9] He is hardly anti-Trojan in his depiction of the Trojans and their institutions.[10] However, there is little doubt that battle narrative privileges the Achaean side. For example, far more Trojans die than Greeks, even though the poem concerns a period of Greek defeat; no Trojan ever wins in a second try after both sides fail with their initial spear casts.[11] The death of Euphorbus is typical, resembling the deaths of those who wound the Achaean leaders in the wounding of the chiefs in book 11; they do so ingloriously and are quickly killed.

Euphorbus also appears to be a doublet of Paris, who, in the tradition, kills Achilles ingloriously, with an arrow shot (see *Il.* 22.359–60). Euphorbus's name suggests that he is a shepherd; he is both a Dardanian and a member of the Trojan elite; he excels in sports (in the later tradition, Paris, exposed and reared as a herdsman, defeats all his brothers in athletics); and when he dies, "his hair, like that of the Graces, was wet with blood, and his locks were bound tightly with gold and silver" (17.51–52)—he is pretty, like Paris.[12]

Euphorbus is probably a contextually bound character. Whether invented by the *Iliad* poet or not, he belongs to this story only, and anyone who has never heard the story of the death of Patroclus has never heard of him. His similarity to Paris is not just the result of the poet's compositional method. Since the death of Patroclus should make the audience think of the death of Achilles, the poet highlights the similarities. He therefore introduces Euphorbus not only so that Patroclus will not die at the hands of a nobody but to help the audience make the connection with Achilles' death.

The gods do not receive narratorial introductions. This is both an

---

9. See van der Valk 1953.
10. See Mackie 1996, 7–9, 161–63 (but without Sale 1987, 1989).
11. See Armstrong 1969; Fenik 1968, 7.
12. See Mühlestein 1987, 78–89.

expositional and a generic limit. Everyone knows the gods and their at-
tributes (which their epithets repeatedly bring to mind), and because
they are never in danger of being ignored, the narrator need not remind
the audience of them. Generically, the mechanics of the narratorial in-
troduction, the amplifying relative clause, resembles the opening of a
hymnal narrative. Homer perhaps avoids using it for gods because it
would imply that formal praise of the god should follow and because
failing to fulfill such an implicit promise could offend the god and con-
fuse the audience. The exception is Leucothea (*Od.* 5.333–35), a deified
mortal. She is introduced according to the usual pattern of the "misfired"
speech; Odysseus does not trust her and decides to use her magical veil
only when his ship breaks apart.

In the *Odyssey*, both Eurycleia (1.429–33) and Nausicaa's nurse,
Eurymedusa (7.13–12), receive extended introductions, and so does
Melantho (18.321–25). Melantho's introduction fits the pattern, coming
just before her speech of abuse, but both of the other women are intro-
duced as they perform chores. Low-status characters perhaps belong at
the opposite end of the continuum from the gods. The rhetoric of tradi-
tionality makes it especially difficult even to remind an audience about
the gods, whom everyone should be prepared to remember adequately.
In contrast, the audience is especially likely to need reminding about the
names and origins of servant women, who lack heroic actions to keep
them in memory. Eurycleia's introduction is especially impressive, in-
cluding not only her patronymic but her father's—and the patronymic
is unique, the grandfather's name archaic. At issue is not just social sta-
tus but location in the tradition. The gods appear in all stories, so any
audience, whatever its traditional experience, knows them. Slaves are
single-story characters, so extra reminding is needed. Yet while Eu-
rycleia receives an extended introduction, her doublet, Eurynome, is not
introduced; similarly, the swineherd Eumaeus tells his story in detail,
while his shadow, Philoetius, remains obscure.[13] The introductions are
rhetorical, not practical, so they effectively serve more than the charac-
ter introduced.

Similarly, the main heroes appear in many stories.[14] Their intro-

---

13. On these doublets, see Fenik 1974, 172–74, 189–92.

14. Reinhardt (1961, 22) associates introductions with new, invented charac-
ters, but this is at best a tendency, not a rule. However, he asks a question I have
pursued: does Homer present "the new as familiar"?

ductions remind the audience of the heroes' attributes that matter in the current context. Very minor heroes introduced at their moment of death are contextually bound, belonging only to the stories in which they appear. The brief obituary biographies that characters receive at death primarily create pathos but also ensure that the audience is not less knowledgeable than the characters. The narrator most often extends these biographies when they are quasi-focalized, enabling the external audience to share the killer's knowledge of the victim. Thus, the narrator tells about Othryoneus's offer to perform a heroic feat as bride price for Cassandra, because Idomeneus mocks him for it after killing him (*Il.* 13.361–82);[15] the narrator tells the story of Lycaon at some length, because Achilles recognizes his victim (*Il.* 21.34–35). Sometimes, however, the narrator provides an extended introduction for precisely the opposite reason, as with Iphidamas (*Il.* 11.221–47)—Agamemnon has known his last two pairs of victims, but he does not recognize Iphidamas.

The quasi-focalized introductions of places work similarly. When a character arrives in a new location, the narrator may pause for a description of what the character sees; such descriptions can provide useful expository information along with their other functions, since they are not strictly focalized. Telemachus, for example, arrives at Pylos to find Nestor, his family, and his people sacrificing to Poseidon on the beach (*Od.* 3.4–9, 31–39). The sequence allows the poet both to mark the order and security of Pylian life in contrast to the social disorder of Ithaca and to make Pisistratus step forward from a striking tableau.

At *Odyssey* 5.29–42, Zeus announces that he will send Odysseus to the Phaeacians in Scheria, "who are near to the gods" [οἳ ἀγχίθεοι γεγάασιν]. They will honor him like a god and send him home with many gifts. When Athena first arrives at the city of the Phaeacians, they receive an extended introduction that provides important information about them: their city is far from men; they colonized Scheria after leaving Hypereia because of the Cyclopes; they have a walled city, temples, and apportioned fields (they are civilized); their king is Alcinous (*Od.* 6.3–12). The poet also briefly identifies Nausicaa when Athena approaches her (6.15–17). Athena, of course, knows all this—the narrator thus gives the audience Athena's view. Athena herself then provides Odysseus with a genealogy of Alcinous and Arete (7.54–66).

---

15. The narrator need not explain how Idomeneus is so well informed (cf. Bassett 1938, 130–33).

These introductions thus have their own conventions and do not violate traditionality and inclusion. What the poet says in such an introduction is not necessarily supposed to be new to the audience. The introductions still contribute to exposition. Once we abandon the assumption that the narrator always expects everyone in the audience to know every detail that he appears to expect them to know, it is impossible to be certain exactly how much prior knowledge the Homeric epics expect of their audiences. Indeed, the line between informing and reminding is not always clear. Nonetheless, it is possible to define certain parameters. That a character receives an introduction does not prove that he or she is unfamiliar to the audience. However, the length with which the narrator introduces the Phaeacians and their royal family before Odysseus actually encounters them suggests that Homer did not want to rely on his audience's knowing about them. They do not appear in other epic stories. (That does not, of course, imply that the *Odyssey* poet invented them.)

What Does the *Iliad* Assume?

Some oral traditions allow quite extended passages the audience cannot fully understand (as I have shown in the first chapter). However, in no oral tradition (and in no literary tradition before postmodernism) do narrators tell incomprehensible stories, so where the narrator fails to provide information that is crucial to following the plot, we can assume that the narrator assumes this knowledge in the audience. It is therefore possible to estimate how much prior knowledge the poet takes for granted. Such a study can only estimate, since good listening can often replace prior knowledge. Skilled narratees can draw inferences and wait for delayed exposition. Members of the audience whose prior knowledge was less could partially compensate through heightened attention.

Let us look at the opening of the *Iliad*, taking a deliberately naive attitude and assuming a priori that the audience knows the names and main attributes of the Olympian gods. The entire opening action, until the Catalogue of Ships, concentrates narrowly on a few characters: the gods, Chryses, Agamemnon, Achilles, Patroclus, Nestor, Odysseus, Calchas, and Thersites. Ajax and Idomeneus are mentioned in passing. How does the poet manage exposition?

We hear that the anger of Achilles began with strife between him and the son of Atreus, then that Apollo, in anger with the king, had caused the plague, because the son of Atreus had dishonored his priest. So far, the narrative goes backward in time; from this point, it moves forward, as Chryses addresses the whole army but especially the "two sons of Atreus" (1.17–21).

> Sons of Atreus and other Achaeans who wear fine leg armor, may the gods whose homes are on Olympus grant to you that you sack Priam's town and reach home safely. But release my dear daughter to me and accept this recompense, avoiding the anger of the son of Zeus, Apollo, who shoots from far away.

The crowd shouts its approval, but Agamemnon angrily refuses.

We can see immediately that the narrator certainly takes for granted that the audience knows about the Trojan War: book 1 offers no explanation of the setting at all. Troy is "Priam's city" at line 19, "Ilios" at 71, "Troy" first at 129. The audience must know who Priam is, too, since his name is used to identify something else. Certainly an efficient modern reader can infer from the prayer that Priam is the king of a city and that the Achaeans are besieging it. For a listener, however, this seems too much to comprehend at once, especially since the audience needs to follow important action.

It seems also almost essential that an auditor know who Agamemnon is. The proem calls him "son of Atreus, lord of men" (1.7), and the lines immediately following the proem say that Apollo was angry with "the king" because "the son of Atreus" had dishonored his priest (1.9–12). Chryses then beseeches the sons of Atreus in the dual, and not until 1.24 is Agamemnon named (along with the patronymic). Someone who does not know Agamemnon's status or his relationship to Menelaus would have to infer a great deal astutely and quickly. This is improbable, though not perhaps impossible. (Again, modern readers do it successfully, but they can pause to think.) The scene surely works better if we also already know that Agamemnon is the convenor of the army and holds a recognized overall authority. Otherwise, the failure of Menelaus to speak might puzzle an audience and distract from the real issue here.

Chryses himself receives no introduction. First, the narrator tells us that Agamemnon had dishonored "that Chryses, a priest" (1.11); then, he describes how Chryses came to the camp, "with the fillets of Apollo in his hand along with a golden scepter."[16] However, the external audience does not need to know Chryses: like the Greeks, the external audience initially recognizes the priest from his attributes, which he confirms by warning his internal audience of the wrath of Apollo. The sequence puts the external audience in a position close to that of the internal audience. Agamemnon's reply acknowledges Chryses' special status without deferring to it, and Chryses then expands on it in his prayer, where he reminds Apollo of how he built a roofed temple (1.35–42).

Chryses' speech merits attention, especially since it is the first supplication (or quasi supplication) in the epic. Successful and unsuccessful supplications are important both structurally and thematically.[17] Chryses addresses both sons of Atreus, presumably because, even as an outsider, he knows them as the leaders of the expedition. He apparently does not know that his daughter has actually been awarded to Agamemnon, since he speaks to the army generally and its leaders in particular, using plural verbs throughout. Given the tact of his speech, we would expect him to address Agamemnon directly if he knew of the award. Because he does not know that his daughter already belongs to an individual, he cannot tailor his request to that person, as successful speakers do.

Before Chryses speaks, the entire audience knows that Agamemnon will be the one who rejects the priest and causes Apollo's anger, since the poet has said so already. The poet has not, however, said anything about the daughter's present status or how she came to be captured. Does he expect the audience to know this? If anyone in the audience does not already know that Chryseis belongs to Agamemnon, his or her knowledge is not superior to Chryses'. Only Agamemnon's reply provides this important detail. This speech works very cleverly for the audience that does not yet know that Chryseis is Agamemnon's own prize. Agamemnon's rage is evident before we learn about his personal motive.

---

16. Contrary to the usual Homeric practice, Chryses receives the definite article when first mentioned, which implies that he is familiar. The article may belong to the rhetoric of beginning. While the audience may or may not know Chryses already, the poet has just asked who began the quarrel; working backward, the poet asked himself whom Agamemnon dishonored: he selected "*that* man, Chryses, the priest," from the characters in his memory.

17. See Whitman 1958, 259–60; MacLeod 1982, 33–34.

> Old man, let me not find you by the hollow ships, either delaying
> now or coming back once again—in that case, the scepter and rib-
> bons of the gods may not help you. I will not ransom her. Before
> that happens, old age will reach her in our house, in Argos, far from
> her native country, as she goes back and forth at the loom and
> comes into my bed. So go and do not provoke me, so that you can
> go home safely. (1.24–32)

Agamemnon uses the first-person singular at line 29, refuting Chryses'
second-person plural at 20. He clearly regards the decision about ran-
som as his and no one else's. Yet at line 30, he speaks of "our" house;
only at 31 does he speak of "my bed." Suppose the woman had be-
longed to one of the other leaders? Would Agamemnon still have
replied, since Chryses addressed him? (Would it be proper for him to
reply?) The coincidence that the prize belongs to the commander allows
the narrator to delay a few lines further before clarifying the situation.

   While we cannot prove anything about the original audience, the
narrative provides special rewards to someone who does not know the
details of this particular story. Evidently, Agamemnon is furious be-
cause Chryses' ignorance of the exact situation leads him to address the
whole army and because the army has responded, telling Agamemnon
what he should do with his own prize. Because Chryses' request is cour-
teous despite its warning of Apollo's possible anger, Agamemnon's fury
is surprising. To be sure, the hearer who does know the situation can ap-
preciate from the start how Chryses' ignorance dooms his request, tact-
ful as he tries to be.

   The narrator withholds details of Chryseis' capture until after the
quarrel. At a minimum, therefore, the audience must be able to infer that
the Achaeans have opportunities to capture such high-status women in
the course of the war. This would be easier if everyone knew that the
war lasted a long time and included successful raids on cities of Trojan
allies. At 1.365–69, though, Achilles explains his unhappiness to his
mother by renarrating the story so far. However, he begins with the cap-
ture of Thebe, Eetion's city.[18] In the distribution of booty, the Achaeans
gave Agamemnon Chryseis.

---

18. de Jong (1985) argues that Achilles knows more than he naturalistically
could when he narrates Chryses' prayer and Apollo's response; but I do not
think that he exceeds the limits of believable inference.

We went to Thebe, holy city of Eetion, and we sacked it and brought everything here. The Achaeans divided everything among themselves appropriately, and they selected beautiful-cheeked Chryseis for the son of Atreus.

This is typically delayed *naturalized exposition*.

Commentators, including the scholia, find it troublesome that Chryseis is not at home when she is captured; taken at Thebe, she returns to Chryse. Later expositors said that she was visiting Thebe for a religious ritual (Sch. bT 1.366).[19] However, a form of traditional referentiality is at work here: this is a ransom story, and a woman who is to be ransomed after the sack of a town must have a home elsewhere; otherwise, there will be no survivors to ransom her. Most often, the woman was married, as were Andromache's mother and Andromache herself. Andromache's mother returned to her natal family after the same raid of Thebe and died in her father's house (6.425–30), and Andromache's pathetic address to Hector has a very practical component: if the Achaeans take Troy, Andromache will be a slave forever, because her natal family is already gone. Briseis, Achilles' concubine, turns out to have been married (19.291–96), but the audience learns this fact only from her lament over Patroclus; she apparently married within her own town, since her three brothers died too, so nobody was left to ransom her.[20] An audience experienced in epic would not trouble itself over why Chryseis was at Thebe, because women were frequently captured in towns other than the homes of their natal families. Since Chryseis' father is a priest, he would perhaps have been spared even if his town had been sacked, but then his daughter would never have been taken captive. If the story took any interest in Chryseis herself, as it does not, the narrator would explain her situation. To make her a widow, though, would detract (slightly) from the emotional power of Agamemnon's ugly words to her father when he insists, "old age will reach her . . . in Argos, far from her native country, as she goes back and forth at the loom and comes into my bed" (1.30–31). The story that she was visiting

---

19. Kirk (*Il. Comm.*, 1:91 [on 1.366–92]) thinks the story in the scholia may be a later invention, but says, "our poet must have known something about Khruseis' visit."

20. Wilamowitz-Moellendorff (1884, 410–11) argues that Briseis originally belonged to Lesbian saga; the argument is developed by Reinhardt (1961, 12–17).

Thebe may be a later invention inspired by precisely the sense that this captive should be a virgin.

I have already suggested that Achilles' recapitulation may have a practical function in compensating for the very rapid movement of the beginning of the *Iliad*. Achilles echoes the language of the main narrator until he mentions his own first speech in the assembly. From there on, the action is severely telescoped, and from this point, the speech functions less as exposition than as a portrayal of character. Achilles is insightful where he himself is not involved, so he has no difficulty inferring how Chryses prayed to Apollo and was heard (although Homer generally tends to blur the distinctions between what the audience knows and what the characters know).[21] But Achilles either does not realize or does not want to say how his own invective against Agamemnon further angered the king and caused him to take his disastrous action against Achilles. Simply hearing the story in Achilles' voice, in a form so close to the narrator's, invites the audience to sympathize with Achilles, but the narrator simultaneously distinguishes his own version from that of Achilles.[22]

If an auditor can efficiently combine everything he or she hears in book 1, the auditor needs remarkably little prior knowledge about Achilles (despite his objectively traditional status). The opening line of the book joins his name and patronymic and, by announcing that his anger is the subject of the song, makes it clear that "Achilles, son of Peleus," is an important hero. This announcement also warns the auditor to pay close attention to Achilles. As the book's quarrel between Achilles and Agamemnon begins, Achilles points out that the Trojans have not plundered his cattle or horses or destroyed his crops back in fertile Phthia (lines 154–57): he thus incidentally informs the audience where he lives. Agamemnon says at line 178 that Achilles' might is the gift of a god, and he tells Achilles to go rule the Myrmidons (lines 179–80). At line 244, Achilles calls himself "best of the Achaeans," and at 280, Nestor says that he is mighty and the son of a goddess (but that Agamemnon rules more men; see line 281). Finally, at line 352, his prayer to his mother implies that he is fated to have a short life—a theme that the narrative will emphasize repeatedly. In effect, the narrative of

---

21. See MacLeod 1982, 279 (on *Il.* 24.203–5).

22. For the speech as a way of attracting sympathy to Achilles, see Wyatt 1988.

the first book tells us everything we need to know about Achilles: that he is the son of Peleus and the sea goddess Thetis, that he is an exceptionally powerful fighter, that he comes from Phthia and leads a people called Myrmidons, and that he is fated not to live long. Of course, there is a great deal more that one could know about Achilles, and the narrator will provide some of it later; but the story can be followed perfectly well with what he provides.

As for other characters, the narrator formally introduces Calchas. The introduction stresses that Calchas has played an important role earlier in the story:

> . . . Calchas, son of Thestor, by far the best of bird seers, who knew the present, the future, and the past, who had guided the Achaeans' ship to Troy through his prophetic skill, which Phoebus Apollo gave him. In goodwill to them he spoke publicly and said . . . (1.69–72)

The name *Thestor* appears as a patronymic elsewhere and may not be objectively traditional. Exactly how Calchas's skill guided the Achaeans to Troy is unclear: the main options are that Homer has in mind the story that the Achaeans first attacked the wrong place and had to sail again; that he is alluding to the important portent that Calchas interpreted at Aulis, which Odysseus narrates in book 2; or that he has the sacrifice of Iphigenia in mind.[23] None of these options precisely fits the context. For the narrative at hand, though, a precise reference is unimportant, since all that matters is that Calchas's abilities are beyond question.

Agamemnon's reply likewise stresses the past.

> Prophet of evil, never yet have you prophesied anything positive for me. You always like to prophesy what is bad, but you have never yet spoken or fulfilled any good word. (1.106–8)

Since antiquity, readers have disagreed about whether these lines allude to the sacrifice of Iphigenia. The Homeric poems never mention the sacrifice, and in the *Iliad*, Agamemnon has a living daughter named Iphianassa (9.145). Not only is the sacrifice not part of the recognized

---

23. See Kirk, *Il. Comm.*, 1:61 (on 71). Kullmann (1960, 198) sees it as an unmistakable allusion to the sacrifice.

antecedents of the action, but it is probably inconsistent with the *Iliad* (and it is inconsistent with its ethos).[24] Still, the story of the sacrifice is a parallel for the present situation. Agamemnon offended a god, leading to a disaster for the army as a whole, and as a result, he was forced to give up something he valued. When Agamemnon says that he prefers Chryseis to his wife Clytemnestra (1.113–15), his lack of respect for his wife fits well within the narrative that begins with the sacrifice and ends with his death.

The parallel is tricky, however, because it can easily tip the listener's emotional response inappropriately. One one hand, remembering the sacrifice could create too much sympathy for Agamemnon, since the prophet's words really caused him suffering on that occasion. On the other hand, precisely because Agamemnon was then a relatively innocent victim, his behavior now could seem grotesque: a man who has been forced to kill a daughter should not have been cruel to a man trying to ransom his daughter, a man who has caused disaster to his army by a foolish boast that angered Artemis should have known better than to antagonize a priest of Apollo, and a man who has had to kill his own child should be better able to evaluate his loss of a prize. The audience, therefore, probably should not remember the story, at least not in detail. Agamemnon's words should not be taken as the literal truth, since the poet has already emphasized how angry he is and since angry speakers use hyperbole of this kind. The audience also knows that Calchas's account of Apollo's anger is accurate and that he is not angering Agamemnon because he enjoys it. Although these lines, especially combined with the poet's own introduction of the prophet, imply that he has played an important role in earlier parts of the story, they do not demand that the audience use their prior knowledge to reconstruct the exact references. The poet probably had the sacrifice in mind as he generated angry words for Agamemnon, but the audience need not follow the allusion.

The poet, then, does not rely on prior knowledge of Calchas but tells the audience everything necessary for understanding his role. The poet does, however, surround this figure with vague references to past events that he does not narrate. There is no particular narrative profit in specifying how Calchas "led" the ships to Troy or which earlier prophecies of Calchas offended Agamemnon; the function of these allusions

---

24. See Seaford 1994, 11–13.

lies in the difference between them. The narrator mentions an important service the prophet performed, while the angry king complains that the prophet has always caused trouble; the introduction thus belongs to the "misfire" pattern.

Nestor also receives a brief formal introduction when he first speaks (1.247–52). The narrator provides three crucial items of information about him: that he rules Pylos, that he is very old, and that he is a superior speaker who aims at the common good. His first speech includes an exemplum that reiterates exactly these points. He stresses that he is older than those he addresses and that he fought along with great heroes of the past; he insists that those great men listened to his advice; and he mentions that those same heroes summoned him from Pylos (1.269–70). Nestor's speech demands that the younger heroes show deference to him, and the narrator endorses this claim by showing deference himself through his introduction. Although Agamemnon attempts to show appropriate respect, he does not control himself as Nestor recommends; the introduction that reminds the audience of Nestor's claims to attention prepares them to disapprove of Agamemnon's failure to respond correctly.

The Odysseus of the first book is relatively colorless; Agamemnon gives him the task of returning Chryseis, and he performs it competently. This Odysseus requires no prior knowledge, because any hero might do what he does (as Agamemnon himself says at 1.145–47). Still, some familiarity with the character pays a narrative dividend here. Initially, Agamemnon threatens to take the prize of Achilles, Ajax, or Odysseus (1.137–38). Since Achilles argues with him, soon only Achilles' prize is in question; Achilles' character is implicitly contrasted with the characters of Ajax and Odysseus. The selection of the hero who will return Chryseis tweaks the same technique. While Agamemnon offers a catalogue of possible leaders, including Ajax, Idomeneus, Odysseus, and Achilles (1.145–47), Odysseus is the diplomat among the heroes, the one best suited for this job, and at 1.311, without any narrating of Agamemnon's actual command, he goes. The poet does not narrate the choice of Odysseus, because the omission itself marks the action: the listener should recognize that Agamemnon *of course* chose Odysseus. Nonetheless, anyone relatively unfamiliar with Odysseus can follow the story without difficulty and soon retrospectively understands why he was appropriate for this mission.

Within the *Iliad*, an aspect of Odysseus's traditional character is realized when he intervenes to stop the flight to the ships. Significantly, the poet introduces Odysseus at 2.169 with an infrequent and appropriate epithet, Διὶ μῆτιν ἀτάλαντος (which occurs three times in book 2, once at 10.137, and twice in the vocative for Hector). Athena addresses him with a whole-line vocative formula, which by itself provides a summary of essential information: διογενὲς Λαερτιάδη, πολυμήχαν᾽ Ὀδυσσεῦ [Zeus-descended son of Laertes, Odysseus the contriver] (2.173); a moment later, he tosses his cloak to his attending herald, Eurybates the Ithacan (2.184).[25] The poet has thus effectively informed—or reminded—his audience of Odysseus's parentage, home, and most famous characteristic, his ability to find ways and means. The poet proceeds to display Odysseus's other outstanding characteristic, his ability to take energetic action on behalf of the community, by having him halt the panic and subdue Thersites. The praise of the army following this episode (2.272–77) defines Odysseus further: he has many past accomplishments in both war and council. So the narrator provides adequate information about Odysseus.

When Odysseus answers Thersites, he accompanies his threat with a wish should he not fulfill it: "may I not be called the father of Telemachus" (2.260). The line is comprehensible, though barely, without prior knowledge: Odysseus evidently has a son named Telemachus, and he mentions him in a counterassertion of his virility, because Thersites has called the Greeks "Achaean women, no longer Achaean men" (2.235). However, this reference to Telemachus clearly has more power for a listener who knows the story of Odysseus's return. Odysseus again calls himself "father of Telemachus" in his angry response to Agamemnon's rebuke during the Epipolesis (4.353–55)—a speech where Agamemnon calls Odysseus "excelling in evil tricks." In book 4, Odysseus seems to evoke the story of his initial reluctance to join the Trojan expedition and feigned madness. Palamedes used Telemachus to trick Odysseus into revealing his sanity (see the first chapter). The narrator surely knows these stories and uses them to create his Odysseus. However, the Odysseus of the *Iliad* is not a trickster (except perhaps when he deceives Dolon at 10.383) but a loyal helper of Agamemnon. Agamemnon is deliberately provoking Odysseus, and his words are not

---

25. The epithet is necessary, since Agamemnon also has a herald named Eurybates (see Kirk, *Il. Comm.*, 1:134 [on 2.184]). This herald is described at *Odyssey* 19.246 and is probably objectively traditional.

supposed to be literally true. The poet thus evokes Odysseus's less no-
ble side, though only vaguely, and the audience is not supposed to re-
member in detail but only, perhaps, to be aware that in some stories,
Odysseus's craftiness is self-serving.

The poet's exposition of the character of Patroclus is another spe-
cial case. Patroclus first appears at 1.307, named only by patronymic, as
Achilles returns to his encampment "with the son of Menoetius and his
companions." Achilles addresses Patroclus by name (but without
patronymic) at 1.337, and Patroclus obeys his "dear companion" at
1.347. Kirk comments that the use of the patronymic "suggests (proves,
indeed, unless it be the result of minor oral insouciance) that the audi-
ence was already familiar with him."[26] Indeed, Patroclus's name and
patronymic do not appear in unmistakable contiguity until 9.202. How-
ever, an audience familiar with the narrative conventions could assume
that a person named in the formula "with X and his companions" is the
dearest companion of the subject of the sentence. A hearer could easily
infer, when Patroclus appears in this role as the heralds remove Briseis,
that Patroclus and Menoetiades are the same person.

Controversy has surrounded Patroclus. Neo-Analysts especially
have argued that he was invented for the *Iliad* on the model of An-
tilochus, the friend for whom Achilles takes vengeance in the *Aethiopis*.[27]
That his story depends in part on the story of Antilochus is very likely,
but it depends just as much on the story of Achilles' death, to which it
alludes explicitly, inviting the hearer to see the similarities. Patroclus
first enters battle as a substitute Achilles, in a folklore motif; then he dies
a death modeled on Achilles' death; then he is avenged on the model of
Antilochus. Patroclus may or may not have an objectively traditional
story, but his function, as the friend who dies and is revenged at the cost
of the hero's life, is fully traditional. The poet probably expects his au-
dience to recognize the pattern as it develops. Although the poet gives

---

26. Kirk, *Il. Comm.*, 1:84 (on 307). Reinhardt (1961, 21) makes this point
against those, such as Schadewaldt (1966, 20), who see Patroclus as Homer's in-
vention.

27. Howald (1924, 41) first argued that the relationship between the names
Kleopatre, the name of Meleager's wife in the paradigm at 9.561, and *Patroklos*
indicates that the character Patroklos was invented by Homer. Many scholars,
such as von Scheliha (1943, 236–51), have followed Howald on this. Janko (*Il.
Comm.*, 4:313–14) suggests that Patroclus is an old character whose role Homer
has expanded.

Patroclus a biography that tells of more than his death, Patroclus's part is always minor, subordinate to Achilles. Patroclus is never extensively developed outside this particular story.

Thersites receives the most elaborate introduction of any character in the *Iliad* (2.212–21) but has no patronymic or toponym. Thersites comes from nowhere. In unusual language, the narrator elaborately describes Thersites' nasty appearance and uncontrolled, abusive speech. This is not just a conventional introduction emphasizing the importance of the character's intervention. Because the language and contents of the introduction are not customary, they do not belong entirely within the expansion aesthetic of reminding. Neither is the speech a "misfire" of the common kind, since Odysseus's harsh response to the speech is in precise accord with its negative introduction. This does not in itself prove that Thersites is objectively untraditional, though it supports a claim that the poet did not expect universal knowledge of the character—at least not in this form—in his audience. Thersites appears only in this scene; the action itself guarantees that he will no longer intrude. More important, he is portrayed as an intrusion. The description of Thersites violates the rhetorics of traditionality and inclusion, because he is completely unworthy of praise and therefore of memory. Even if the audience knows about Thersites already, the poet can pretend that it does not. Thersites is a foil for the army's praise of Odysseus, whose achievements are already "traditional" (i.e., established in social memory) during his lifetime.

The narrator seems deliberately to confine himself to this group in the first section of book 2, which concludes at the Catalogue of Ships. Other than Thersites, the speakers and actors in the council and assembly of book 2 are characters who already participated in the earlier scenes; even when Odysseus recalls Aulis, he speaks of Calchas's prophecy (2.299–300). Agamemnon summons his council for breakfast at 2.404–9: present are Nestor, Idomeneus, both Ajaxes, Diomedes (identified by patronymic only), Odysseus, and Menelaus (who comes uninvited). Only Nestor speaks, however. The narrator avoids overwhelming the audience with characters until the Catalogue of Ships allows him to introduce everyone. There are passing references to Ajax and Idomeneus, but there is no need for the audience to know precisely who these heroes are.

The Catalogue of Ships introduces Diomedes but does not include his patronymic (although it provides that of his companion Sthenelus)—

at least not in the manuscripts (the *Contest of Homer and Hesiod* gives it a plus verse, 2.563a). The narrator, though, has already referred to the hero by patronymic alone. While an uninformed hearer could probably combine the first references to Patroclus by patronymic with his name, nothing in the Catalogue of Ships identifies this hero with the "son of Tydeus" for a hearer lacking prior knowledge. The poet expects the audience to know who Tydeus's son is.

Diomedes and his father were important figures in the Theban story and so are likely to have been widely known. At 4.365–67, during the Epipolesis, Agamemnon sees Diomedes and Sthenelus standing by their chariots. Both characters are identified by name and patronymic, and Agamemnon proceeds to rebuke Diomedes by telling a long anecdote about the heroism of Tydeus. Sthenelus then tries to refute Agamemnon by reminding him that the expedition of the Seven against Thebes failed and that the expedition of the Epigoni succeeded. The reminder alerts the audience to the salient characteristic of Diomedes in this poem: the divine support he receives. Here, once again, background is eventually clarified—before Diomedes takes an important part in the action. The narrator provides exposition for poorly informed listeners and perhaps surprises some. Diomedes is more important than the opening sections lead the hearer to expect, and the poet ignores darker sides of his traditional character.[28]

The opening of the *Iliad* does not introduce the Trojan side. The auditor must know who Priam is. Nestor imagines how Priam, his sons, and the other Trojans would rejoice to hear of the quarrel at 1.255–58. Similarly, the audience would have difficulty without prior knowledge of Helen. Hera addresses Athena, who repeats her words to Odysseus.

κὰδ δέ κεν εὐχωλὴν Πριάμῳ καὶ Τρωσὶ λίποιεν
Ἀργείην Ἑλένην, ἧς εἵνεκα πολλοὶ Ἀχαιῶν
ἐν Τροίῃ ἀπόλοντο φίλης ἀπὸ πατρίδος αἴης·

$$(2.160-62 = 176-78)$$

[And leave as a boast for Priam and the Trojans Argive Helen, for whose sake many of the Achaeans have perished at Troy, far from their dear native soil.]

---

28. Bassett (1938, 216–17) provides an excellent discussion of why the poet keeps Diomedes "in reserve."

On the other hand, Nestor speaks as if the Achaeans should strive to rape the wives of the Trojans to avenge a Helen taken by force (2.355–56), and the narrator reuses 2.356 at 2.590 to describe the feelings of Menelaus. This surely represents character focalization, but it also misleads the audience into imagining that the Helen of this song is an innocent victim. The *Iliad* presupposes familiarity with the character but not with a canonical form. The auditor who knows many variants about Helen—some exculpating her, others blaming her—is ideal. So is the auditor who knows that her abduction by Paris caused the war but who has no specific version of the tale in mind. The Teichoscopia at 3.146–244 not only informs the hearer about the Achaeans but also provides further background about the war (in the story of Menelaus's and Odysseus's visit to Troy), and it introduces a group of important Trojans (whose families provide many of the victims in the later fighting).[29]

The narrator obviously takes familiarity with Alexander/Paris for granted. His first appearance in the poem is a distinctly satirical description: wearing a leopard skin, he challenges the Achaeans but panics the moment he sees Menelaus, who hopes for vengeance on "the wrongdoer" (ἀλείτην, 3.16–37). Finally, Achilles refers to the Achaeans who will die at the hands of "manslaughtering Hector" because of Agamemnon's insult (1.242–44). Hector first appears in person when Iris addresses herself to him at the Trojan assembly (2.802), and the Trojan Catalogue formally introduces him as the leading Trojan commander, with a patronymic (2.816–17). Prior familiarity with Hector is therefore helpful but not indispensable.

In sum, the *Iliad* relies on its audience to know the basic background of the Trojan War, including the identities and functions of Agamemnon, Menelaus, Helen, Paris, and Priam. Only that much is strictly necessary. The poet evidently expects his audience to be familiar with Odysseus, but he does not demand this knowledge. We may well believe that everyone would have known Nestor and Achilles, but the narrative does not exploit such prior knowledge. The story is easier to follow if the auditor knows at least the names of Ajax, Idomeneus, and Diomedes and ideally somewhat more. Such information is richly provided by the Catalogue of Ships and then by the Epipolesis and the Teichoscopia, one providing "objective" information about where the leaders come from and the size of their contingents, the others providing "subjective" in-

---

29. See Bassett 1938, 118–19.

formation about the leaders' relations with Agamemnon and their spe-
cial characteristics as heroes. The Catalogue of Ships provides clarifi-
cation and many introductions. It carefully distinguishes Locrian from
Salaminian Ajax, and it introduces lesser heroes, such as Meriones, Tle-
polemus, and Polypoetes.

Of course, the Catalogue of Ships does not introduce the *Iliad* as
much as it does the story of the Trojan War. It makes an important
contribution to the rhetoric of traditionality by including heroes who
are already dead (e.g., Protesilaus) or who are absent but will be im-
portant later (e.g., Philoctetes) and by naming heroes who are obscure
within the *Iliad*. The Trojan Catalogue identifies Aeneas, Sarpedon,
Asius, and Glaucus. The handling of Sarpedon is perhaps typical. The
catalogue gives him place of origin but no patronymic (2.876–77). He
next appears on the battlefield, rebuking Hector. When Sarpedon has
his first major encounter, his opponent, Tlepolemus, denies that Sarpe-
don can really be a son of Zeus (5.635–37)—thereby conveying the im-
portant information that Sarpedon is Zeus's son. The exposition is nat-
uralized, and Sarpedon's defeat of Tlepolemus confirms Sarpedon's
divine parentage.

In general, heroes who first appear in battle are only gradually in-
troduced, but this delay creates no difficulty. Antilochus, for example,
makes his first appearance as the first Greek in the poem to kill a Trojan,
at 4.457. (Oddly, he was not present when Nestor marshaled his troops
at 4.295–96.) At 5.565, he finally receives his patronymic. Many charac-
ters receive minimal identification. Helenus has a patronymic and is
"best of bird seers" at 6.76, when he first appears—but he gives a piece
of ritual advice here, so his authority to speak in this way expects
grounding. Deiphobus receives his patronymic (the most important
identifier for sons of Priam) in his first appearance, at 12.94–95.

Polydamas first appears, at 11.57, as simply a leader of the Trojans,
beside Hector and Aeneas. At 12.60, he approaches Hector and gives his
first speech of advice, and at 12.88, he is again simply a leader. At
12.211–14, he begins his second attempt at advising Hector with a re-
minder of the past.

> Hector, you always rebuke me in assemblies somehow, although I
> give good advice, since it is not at all appropriate for a common
> man to speak outside of bounds, neither in council nor ever in war,
> but always to increase your power.

This opening is characteristic naturalized exposition, preparing the audience for Hector's ferocious rejection of Polydamas's speech (he threatens to kill Polydamas) and, indeed, for a previously undisclosed aspect of Hector's character: thus far, Hector has accepted the advice of both Helenus and Polydamas, but his refusal to listen will become more important as the tale progresses. At 13.756, Polydamas receives a patronymic. As son of Panthous, he is hardly a representative of the common people—the audience could hardly think he was, since he appears repeatedly in lists of the Trojan leaders in battle. His sarcastic self-description to Hector is a quotation of what Hector says in his anger. Polydamas finally receives an honorific introduction before his great speech at 18.249–52, when it is appropriate to remind the audience of how his words should be received (this speech is of course a "misfire").

The poet's exposition of Teucer is more difficult to follow than others. His name does not appear in the Catalogue of Ships, and he is not mentioned by name in the Epipolesis, although the "two Ajaxes" there are surely Ajax and Teucer (4.273–91). He suddenly appears at 6.31, killing a Trojan. This is normal and unproblematic. However, he reappears at 8.266–68 in his most characteristic pose, darting out from behind Ajax's shield to shoot his arrows, then ducking again under its protection. This unusual behavior would puzzle a listener who did not know that Ajax and Teucer were brothers. As so often occurs, however, the listener who does not understand soon receives explanation: At 8.280–85, Agamemnon encourages Teucer by urging him to give glory to his father, Telamon, who cared for him even though he was a bastard.

The *Odyssey*

The *Odyssey*'s technique is similar to the *Iliad*'s. In general, the exposition is less difficult because so much of the plot depends on traveling. There is thus great opportunity for both informative descriptions (as the traveler arrives at an unfamiliar location) and embedded character narratives. Telemachus, for example, travels to hear about his father. This situation permits the poet, through Nestor, Helen, and Menelaus, to provide an immense amount of background.

Again, the poet presupposes familiarity with the Trojan War in general. The *Odyssey* clearly expects everyone to know that Greeks captured Troy and, at least very roughly, where Troy is. Line 2 of the proem, "wandered after he sacked the holy citadel of Troy," would simply be too hard to understand otherwise, and proems, as pointers to the tale to come, need to be clear. Furthermore, when the narrative proper begins, the narrator says that everyone who has escaped war and the sea was home already (1. 11–12); thus, he presupposes some familiarity with these others—the basic knowledge that many heroes died or were delayed while returning from Troy. The poem also presupposes a basic familiarity with its hero, since it notoriously delays giving his name until line 21. This looks like a riddle. We learn that the poem is to be about a man who wandered after sacking Troy: Odysseus was not the only hero to have a difficult return, so this does not identify him. If πολύτροπος in the opening line means "wily," we have a strong hint, but this meaning is not certain. Also, although Odysseus is the only mortal to receive this epithet in the surviving epic tradition, it appears only twice, so it is hard to be certain that its association with Odysseus would be universally familiar.[30] Next, we learn that the hero did not save his companions, who ate the cattle of Helius (1.8–9). This clearly identifies Odysseus for anyone who knows his adventures. It also answers briefly the question of why Odysseus is alone when the narrative starts. We then learn that the hero was the very last to return home and that he was held captive by a goddess who wanted him as a husband; that the home to which the gods fated his return was Ithaca, where further troubles still awaited him; and that among the gods, Poseidon alone did not pity him. Finally, we learn his name. For someone who knows at least some of these details about the story of Odysseus, there is narrative pleasure in becoming more and more certain that he must be the hero. An auditor who knew none of this could not combine and absorb it while still reaching out for the all-important name. Evidently, the poet expects everyone to know some details about Odysseus.

There are other interesting points about the expository technique here. First, the poet explains immediately that Odysseus longed for his return and his wife but that Calypso held Odysseus because she desired him to be her husband (1.13–15). Since the audience will not actually learn in detail about the relationship between Calypso and Odysseus until after the Telemachy, in book 5, this helpfully removes worry about the hero: his situation is static and secure, allowing the audience to concentrate on his family. Second, Zeus carefully explains the cause of Poseidon's anger at 1.68–75, with the genealogy of Polyphemus. In other

---

30. See S. West, *Od. Comm.*, 1:69 (on 1.1).

words, Poseidon's anger is not taken for granted; the narrator carefully
motivates it naturalistically (Zeus must remind Athena to explain his
apparent indifference). This anger is an important cause of action. The
anger of three different gods moves the action, since Athena's anger led
to the storm that sent Odysseus and others off course, Poseidon's has
prevented Athena from helping him, and Helius's has caused the loss
of his final ship. Although Athena's anger is needed for the plot, its
cause is not relevant for Odysseus's story, and the poet does not em-
phasize it, while he carefully stresses the separate causes of the anger of
Poseidon and Helius.[31]

The difficult return of Odysseus was clearly objectively traditional,
and the opening of the poem shows that the poet treats it as known.[32]
Indeed, the Cyclops and Circe episodes are the two Homeric episodes
frequent among the earliest Greek representations of mythology.[33] The
folktales and travelers' tales that are the basis of the Apologos were doubt-
less popular in oral tradition outside the epic that absorbed them. Fur-
thermore, in the Cyclops episode, Odysseus's narrative—or Homer's—
is careless in the way of oral performers in other traditions: notoriously,
Odysseus fails to remind the audience that the Cyclops is one-eyed,
even though this detail is crucial to the story as he tells it.[34] The Phaea-
cians are well informed about Cyclopes already (6.5–6), and Alcinous
has mentioned them to Odysseus as "wild races" close to the gods
(7.205–6). As narrator, Odysseus is thus not incompetent in failing to tell
them about the single eye—and if Homer is not very careless, he, too,
relies here on foreknowledge. For at least some of the adventures, the
poet assumes that the audience has heard stories much like these before.
At the same time, the very popularity of these tales probably ensured
that they circulated in varying versions, with varying emphases. Simi-

---

31. Critics who find the preface inconsistent with the adventures of
Odysseus include Fenik (1974, 208–27) and Clay (1983); arguing for theological
coherence are Olson (1995, 205–27), Segal (1994, 195–227), and Louden (1999,
69–103). Kullmann (1985) sees the entire poem as motivated by issues of justice,
in sharp contrast to the *Iliad*.

32. Louden (1999, 69–90) argues that the verb πλάγθη ("wander," *Od.* 1.2)
functions in traditional referentiality to evoke an entire narrative pattern.

33. On early illustrations of the scene, see Touchefeu-Meynier 1968, 10–21;
Fittschen 1969, 193–94.

34. See Page 1955, 14.

lar stories were told of other heroes.[35] Other stories, too, were told about
Odysseus.[36] The *Odyssey* organizes the central adventures in a tidy, for-
mal structure (short, short, long).[37] It develops an overarching set of
themes (good and bad hospitality, self-control and gluttony) that the ad-
ventures can hardly have had in all other contexts.[38] From the start, the
poet emphasizes the two stages that will be crucial in his version and
differentiates the two angry gods.

At 1.93, Athena announces that she will rouse Odysseus's son (1.88–89);
when Telemachus then sees Athena-Mentes at the door, he is day-
dreaming about his father's return, but he is angered that a guest has
had to wait (1.113–20). The narrator thus establishes the basic outlines
of Telemachus's character for even an auditor who did not know the
name of Odysseus's son. Athena-Mentes names Penelope as Tele-
machus's mother (1.223); the narrator gives Penelope her patronymic at
1.329. The major characters are thus securely identified.

At 1.93, Athena first tells Zeus that she will send Telemachus "to
Sparta and sandy Pylos"; when she suggests the trip to Telemachus him-
self, she is more precise, telling him to visit Nestor at Pylos and
Menelaus, last of the Achaeans to return, at Sparta (1.284–86). The hearer
who knows something about Nestor and Menelaus is clearly at an ad-
vantage. But no specific knowledge of their natures or deeds—from the
Iliad, for example—is required. Telemachus refers to Nestor's age at
3.24; Nestor's long speech at 3.102–200 effectively reminds the hearer of
the main losses of the Trojan War and of Nestor's chief role as advisor.
Similarly, Menelaus and Helen reveal themselves.

As in the *Iliad*, characters in the *Odyssey* receive formal introduc-
tions when the poet needs to prepare the audience to understand their
words or actions in context. Halitherses, who receives two introduc-
tions, is an example. When Halitherses speaks in the Ithacan assembly,
interpreting the bird omen that Zeus has just sent, the poet provides not
only a patronymic but the information that he was an expert in bird

---

35. Some episodes probably belonged originally to the Argonaut legends, as
has been famously argued by Meuli (1921).

36. There were probably adventures on the Greek mainland, which leave
traces in Odysseus's lies, as in 19.283–99 (see Wilamowitz-Moellendorff 1884,
173–98).

37. See Woodhouse 1930, 43–44.

38. See Most 1989.

signs (2.157–59). When Halitherses appears again, in the assembly of the suitors' families, the narrator again provides Halitherses' patronymic but this time adds that "he alone saw past and future" (24.452)—emphasizing, as is appropriate, that Halitherses is a wise man, not just a technical specialist. On this occasion, this rebukes the Ithacans for blaming Odysseus instead of themselves for the suitors' deaths, reminding them that both he and Mentor had warned them. Even if the listener remembers the first assembly in detail, the reminder is still thematically important, since the Ithacans would be morally in a much stronger position had they not been warned. So much has happened since the first assembly, however, that the reminder may also be practically useful. Both Halitherses' speeches are "misfires."

The poet introduces the "good" suitor, Amphinomus. The technique used for his introduction is that of the *Iliad*. Amphinomus first appears at 16.351, when he sees the failed ambush return. The poet formally introduces him shortly thereafter (16.394–99) and says that he has good sense, as he speaks to urge the suitors not to try to kill Telemachus without divine approval. The suitor Leodes receives a formal introduction before he tries to string the bow and fails (21.144–47). As many introductions, the narrator's statement here that Leodes felt disgust for the improper behavior of the other suitors and rebuked them prepares for his speech to fail. However, the introduction prepares primarily for Leodes' death, since he will unsuccessfully supplicate Odysseus at 22.310–25 on the grounds that he behaved properly to the women in the house. The broader expository function of the introduction is thus more obvious than usual.

The leading suitors, Antinous and Eurymachus, have patronymics at their first appearances (1.383, 399); they do not receive introductions and do not need any. Telemachus addresses the suitors as a group, and these two speak in response; the same two speak for the suitors in the Ithacan assembly. They quickly introduce themselves, and no prior familiarity with them is needed. Later, Penelope rebukes Antinous by describing how Odysseus helped Antinous's father (16.424–30), and Eurymachus himself mentions how Odysseus was kind to him when he was a small child (16.442–44). This delayed and naturalized exposition, coming right after the suitors have discussed the murder of Telemachus, makes their ingratitude especially striking.

The presentation of the suitors as a group is interesting. They are essential to the story of Odysseus's return, and it is hard to imagine that they are not objectively traditional. The poet uses his regular technique of delayed explanation and does not assume that everyone knows the story. Athena announces at 1.88–92 that she will go to Ithaca to rouse Odysseus's son, so that he will summon an assembly "and give notice to all the suitors, who constantly slaughter his sheep one after the other and his shamble-footed, twisted-horned cows." This is all the audience hears explicitly of the situation in Ithaca until Athena arrives. At 1.106, Athena "finds" the suitors outside in the courtyard, playing the board game *pessoi*. At 114–18, we hear that Telemachus is among the suitors, dreaming that his father will return, drive them out, and be restored to his rank and property. We then hear about the suitors' feasting. As Phemius begins to sing, Telemachus prefaces the standard questions to a stranger by a bitter remark on how carefree "these men" are and how frightened they would be if Odysseus returned (1.159–68). At 1.222–29, Athena asks about the feast and the noisy crowd: it is not an *eranos* (to which guests contribute), and the feasters are showing very bad manners (she incidentally names Penelope as Telemachus's mother at 1.223). In response, Telemachus explains:

> All the best men who have power in the islands, on Doulichium, Same, and wooded Zacynthus, and those who rule in rugged Ithaca, these are courting my mother and wearing away my household. She neither rejects a hateful marriage nor is able to make an end. They eat and destroy my household. And soon they will destroy me too. (1.245–51)

Telemachus very precisely tells both "Mentes" and the audience who the suitors are. Despite this narrative's gaps, a competent listener could surely follow it without prior knowledge until Telemachus explains it.[39] Mentes-Athena is only playing her part by asking so obvious a question, and Telemachus replies briefly and straightforwardly.

Odysseus tells his adventures to an audience familiar with the Trojan War (which he therefore does not narrate) but not acquainted with what has happened to him since. When Odysseus tells the Phaeacians his name, patronymic, and place of origin, he also announces, "I am famous among all men for my wiles, and my fame reaches heaven" (9.19–20): he thereby makes the traditionality of his deeds at Troy ex-

---

39. See Sternberg 1978, 58–62.

plicit for both the internal and external audiences. What follows belongs to a slightly different convention. Odysseus is an internal narrator, and despite whatever Homer's audience knows already, the Phaeacians have never heard these tales before. No rhetoric of traditionality need apply. He can therefore introduce the peoples whom he visits, and he provides formal introductions at the start of many of the adventures. Yet the introductions that Odysseus provides are largely irrelevant to the ensuing tale—the incestuous marriages of Aeolus's children (10.1–12), the social arrangement of Cyclopes (9.106–15), and the effect of meteorological peculiarity on the economy of the Laestrygonians (10.81–86) play no part in Odysseus's encounters with these groups. The most important fact about Cyclopes, that they lack ships, is not part of the formal introduction; Odysseus mentions it at 9.125–29 to explain why Goat Island is uninhabited.

Circe provides relevant introductions to the last groups of adventures at 12.38–110 (reiterating Tiresias's for Thrinacia at 11.106–11). Within the story, these adventures require that Odysseus know what is ahead—since he could not otherwise act wisely and survive—and allow the poet to escape some of the limits of first-person narrative. Narratologically, necessary exposition is here doubly naturalized, as the audience learns who and what the Sirens are when Odysseus tells the Phaeacians what Circe told him. Such exposition not only compensates for what the audience might not know but also protects against variant expectations.

Although the story of the hero who puts out the eye of the giant was surely traditional for Homer's audience, tales they might have heard probably told of Cyclopes who were quite unlike these.[40] Hence the adventures show a mixture of careful exposition (because the audience needs to locate itself within the right tradition, even when the poet is confident that everyone is familiar with the basic story) and occasional carelessness (because once the story is under way, the poet is unusually certain of the audience's previous knowledge).

Theoclymenus is an exception to the narrator's usual practices. He receives an extraordinarily long introduction at 15.223–56, a genealogy through several generations that connects him to his ancestor Melampus, whose story is briefly told. Just as Theoclymenus is fleeing Argos because he has committed homicide, his ancestor Melampus left Pylos, where he formerly lived.

---

40. See Mondi 1983.

So then he came to a foreign community, fleeing his native country
and great-minded Neleus, the most arrogant of living men, who kept
a great deal of his property away from him by force for a whole year.
And during that time, he was imprisoned in the house of Phylacus
in harsh bonds, suffering painful miseries, because of the daughter
of Neleus and the heavy *atê* that the Fury, the dread goddess, had put
into his mind. But he escaped death and drove the bellowing cattle
to Pylos from Phylace, and he paid back godlike Neleus's cruel deed,
and he brought the woman to his brother's house. But he went to a
foreign community, horse-pasturing Argos . . . (15.227–39)

The genealogy continues, including Amphiaraus, whom Zeus and Apollo
loved but who died at Thebes "because of gifts to a woman" (15.244–47);
Cleitus, who was abducted by the dawn goddess (15.250–51); and Theo-
clymenus's own father, Polyphides, who was the best of prophets after
the death of Amphiaraus and went to live in Hyperesia owing to a quar-
rel with his father (15.252–55).

This introduction uses an extreme form of the abbreviated style
typical of embedded character narratives, in which the information is so
compressed and allusively presented that it is not fully understandable
without prior knowledge.[41] However, full understanding is probably
not necessary. The two main points about the family are clear enough
even if the details of the tales remain perplexing: first, this is a very dis-
tinguished clan of prophets, so any predictions Theoclymenus makes
are very trustworthy; second, this is a quarrelsome and difficult family.

The narrator needs to emphasize Theoclymenus's prophetic inher-
itance, precisely because his role in the poem is to deliver prophecies
that are not received with the authority they would have were his iden-
tity known. The poet could have naturalized the exposition by allowing
Telemachus to learn his suppliant's identity in due course, but he does
not, because Theoclymenus will give a prediction of Odysseus's return
that Penelope will not credit. Were Theoclymenus recognized as a dis-
tinguished and disinterested prophet, Penelope would be foolish not to
believe him.[42] Indeed, Theoclymenus represents yet another variant of
the disguise theme of the Ithacan books.[43] Throughout, the characters—

---

41. See Friedrich 1975, 54–55.
42. See Erbse 1972, 42–54.
43. The richest treatment of this theme is Murnaghan 1987.

Eumaeus, the suitors, the servants, Penelope—are judged, by both Odysseus and the audience, on how they treat Odysseus before he reveals himself. In contrast, Odysseus quickly reveals himself to Telemachus. Theoclymenus tests Telemachus instead. Thus, the narrator ignores his usual practice of introducing characters only as the internal audience knows them, because the unusual ignorance of internal audiences is thematically important and because this is his best chance to involve Telemachus in the theme.

The genealogy also stresses the tendency of the family to wander and to get itself into trouble as a gloss on the situation at hand. Instead of telling his host his name and country, Theoclymenus asks Telemachus his (15.260–64). Exile for homicide is common in the poems, but nowhere else is the killer actually pursued outside his own community. Theoclymenus is in a desperate situation, and his family seems to have accumulated both friends and enemies. Since Melampus took revenge on Neleus, Nestor would be unlikely to help him; this fact matters, as the exact nature of the revenge and of Neleus's wrongdoing does not. The genealogy helps explain why Theoclymenus commits an apparent social solecism in asking about Telemachus's home and parents: he needs to know whether this young stranger can help him and whether he is likely to want to help him.[44] The story of Melampus, which concludes with a successful marriage and revenge, also echoes that of Odysseus.[45]

Conclusion

Neither the *Iliad* nor the *Odyssey* relies on extensive, detailed prior knowledge of the characters and stories for its main plot. Both certainly demand that their audiences be familiar with the basic saga of Troy. The *Iliad* presupposes that the audience knows the theft of Helen and thus the central cast of Helen, Paris, Menelaus, Agamemnon, and Priam. The poet expects his audience to know Diomedes as son of Tydeus and thus to know the outline of the story of the Seven against Thebes and the Epigoni. The story

---

44. Page (1955, 86) is particularly harsh on Theoclymenus here. For interpretations in broader contexts, see Erbse 1972, 43–45; Katz 1991, 120–28.

45. Danek (1998, 294–96) argues that while the Melampus story must already have existed in epic form (following Heubeck 1954, 19–22, 29–32), certain details have been adapted, while Theoclymenus's connection to the family and personal history are invented.

of Achilles and Patroclus, however, is not part of the essential framework of the Trojan tale, and the *Iliad* does not presuppose familiarity with it. Similarly, the *Odyssey* assumes familiarity with its hero and with some of the events of his return, but it does not assume that its listener has heard a full-scale version of the struggle with the suitors. However, the poet has a range of devices—catalogue, naturalized exposition, quasi-focalized introductions—to guide relatively inexperienced listeners along this particular path of story. Byways, the subject of the next chapter, are a different matter.

Abbreviated Narrative

The main narrative of both the *Iliad* and the *Odyssey* expects a general, fundamental knowledge of earlier epic stories but does not rely on the audience to know many details. The poet tells his audience what it needs to know as the need arises, and the attentive listener can easily follow without extensive prior knowledge. However, this is not always true of digressions, or *abbreviated narratives.* A fundamental category of narratology is *duration,* the ratio between the action and the discourse, a continuum with full dramatization at one extreme and minimal summary at the other.[1] While Homeric narrative varies greatly in duration, there is a sharp distinction between the main narrative, generally full, and subordinate narratives, much less detailed. Because the rhetoric of traditionality implies that all these stories have a life independent of this telling, a brief narration functions as an abbreviation. Every tale is potentially an independent, full-length performance. The absence or very sparing use of direct speech is typical of such narration. Most, though not all, abbreviated narratives are embedded character narratives (N2 in de Jong's notation).[2] Although a character narrative and a bard's summarized song have different sources of authority, both are abbreviated. Abbreviated narrative is distinct from the summaries that close dramatized scenes. Such summary tends to be formulaic and extremely curt, as in "so they continued fighting like blazing fire." Abbreviated narrative tells stories that are remote from the action at hand, either completely independent or temporally removed. The epics are full of such passages.

Two subcategories of abbreviated narratives parallel the distinction between poetry and oral tradition. In the first, the poet himself is the abbreviator: this category includes digressions in the narrator's own voice, such as the narrative included in character introductions and in the obituary stories about dying warriors. Summaries of bardic performances

---

1. See Genette 1980, 86–88.
2. De Jong 1987a.

belong in this category, since, like the main narrative, they are inspired by the Muse and are independent of occasion. Even the second song of Demodocus, for example, although it includes a dramatized scene (*Od.* 8.305–66), is probably abbreviated, for Demodocus's performance should take longer than the version Homer provides, which is less than one hundred lines long. In character narratives, in contrast, the character summarizes the story for particular purposes, then the poet quotes the summary. The hearer needs to interpret the two kinds slightly differently. Both are contextually determined, but the poet's context is the audience's need to understand the immediate narrative, while a character's narratives inform or persuade others. The listener must make basic sense of both kinds of abbreviated narrative in the same way.

Abbreviated narratives share with special intensity in the rhetoric of traditionality. The narrator leaves gaps and shortens stories so much that they are not fully comprehensible without prior knowledge. Such abbreviation implies that the story already exists and that the listener has heard it before. Allusion always depends on earlier experience. Character narratives have a double source of traditionality, since the frame makes them already traditional and in circulation in the remote past of the action. Since they are socially embedded, however, their tellers may take exclusive, rather than inclusive, rhetorical positions. Paradoxically, just as characters can be more informative than the poet because they know what their hearers do not already know, they can also be less informative. Characters may rely on the prior knowledge of their audiences to an extent that the main narrator does not.

Sometimes speakers explicitly define the audience they address. Phoenix, for example, says that he will tell the story of Meleager to the group in Achilles' tent "since you are all friends" (*Il.* 9.528). Such a defined audience is especially fitting for the αἶνος ("fable" or "riddle"— Greek uses a single word for both), since the audience must find the equivalencies between the characters of the tale and the situation in the world.[3] Hesiod addresses the fable of the hawk and the nightingale to the kings, "who are wise themselves" (*Works and Days* 202), as if special wisdom were required to understand it. Some such stories are explicitly reminders, and their audiences have not just intelligence or goodwill but full knowledge, as when Achilles briefly repeats to Thetis a story he has often heard her tell of how she saved Zeus from a rebellion (*Il.*

---

3. The word αἶνοζ also denotes praise; see Nagy 1979, 235–41.

1.396–406). Naturally, he does not explain why the gods rebelled but concentrates on the points of the tale that prove Zeus's indebtedness to Thetis.

Since Homeric characters, like the poets, are reminders, they can legitimately narrate more fully than a modern audience expects in a "realistic" narrative, even when the internal audience should already know much of what the characters tell (Achilles tells Thetis more of her story than is realistically required). Indeed, the reminding aesthetic is at its most explicit as a frame for contextually bound paradigms. Odysseus and Nestor, addressing Achilles and Patroclus, respectively, conclude their accounts of the parting words of the heroes' fathers with ὣς ἐπέτελλ' ὁ γέρων, σὺ δὲ λήθεαι [so the old man commanded, but you are forgetful] (9.259 = 11.790). The contents of these parting speeches are contextually bound: Achilles is angry, so his father warned him to control his anger; Patroclus needs to advise Achilles, so his father told him to be Achilles' adviser. We may recall how Sophocles invents for Telamon a farewell speech that is equally contextually fixed (*Ajax* 764–65). The departure scene clearly allows a father to make any necessary and appropriate remarks. In other poems where the plot demanded that Peleus must have said something else, he doubtless said something else. Yet here the speakers rebuke their audiences for failing to remember. They place these "inventions" simultaneously in the characters' memories and the audience's.

Exclusionary language, however, at least within early hexameter poetry, is a rhetorical position, not an accurate statement of who belongs in the authorial audience. Although Hesiod implies that only wise kings will understand his fable, the audience of the *Works and Days* as a whole is not so limited; the exclusionary rhetoric actually tells the authorial audience to view the kings' "wisdom" ironically. Since the main exposition of the Homeric poems is inclusionary and makes the poems accessible even to listeners without extensive prior knowledge, it would be peculiar if abbreviated narratives were truly exclusionary in style. For the main narrative, inclusiveness demands transparency: everyone has to be able to follow the story. In digressive, abbreviated narratives, however, transparency may not be required.

Indeed, although the reminding aesthetic allows the poet to be clearer than naturalism would dictate, abbreviated material can be far more difficult to understand than the main narrative. In subordinate narratives, the poet often uses a compressed, allusive style. This style most often raises difficult questions about tradition and innovation. Scholars frequently assume that if a narrative is so compressed that it is difficult to understand, it must be a shortened version of a longer, clearer story; the scholars then build further arguments on this understanding. D. Page, for instance, examines the problem of why Agamemnon, according to Nestor, left a bard to protect his wife when he sailed to Troy.[4] Aegisthus marooned the singer on a desert island before finally seducing Clytemnestra (*Od.* 3.267–71). Because the tale is so abbreviated, Page believes it must represent a longer, older story; he then argues that the role of the bard is an archaism, reflecting the ancient union of poetry and prophecy. If there was no older, traditional story of the bard's failure to prevent the seduction of Clytemnestra, his argument about the bard is much weaker.

Abbreviated narratives claim to be and may often actually be compressed or short versions of tales that circulated in fuller form. But, this may not always be so. The tools of analogy and recombination that created the main stories of the tradition can still operate. Even objectively traditional material may not have been familiar to everyone. The poet may have learned a story that told more about Agamemnon's bard, but that does not mean that everyone in his audience knew such a tale. The story is effective as it is, despite its obscurities. Clytemnestra's guilt is mitigated because she resisted Aegisthus as long as the bard was with her. The detail perhaps reminds the hearer of Penelope's isolation. The murder of the bard further blackens Aegisthus, who resembles the suitors. The bard is thematically appropriate because his songs preserve social memory, whether or not Agamemnon's choice of guardian is plausible as a social reality. The critic asks, why a bard was left with Clytemnestra and why Hera, Athena, and Poseidon rebelled against Zeus, but these are not contextually relevant questions.

Compression can itself be a creative force. In condensing allusions, the speaker molds the story into the form that suits his or her purposes, whether these are the poet's narrative needs or a character's persuasive requirements. When Glaucus's Bellerophon obeys obscure "portents of the gods" and so succeeds (*Il.* 6.183), his experience thereby contributes to Glaucus's own subtle argument that human success is not predictable.[5] Whatever portents occurred in longer versions, precise omens would not

---

4. See Page 1972.
5. See Scodel 1992b.

have been as germane, since Glaucus does not have any comparable omens in the present. There is always likely to be a complex interaction between the poet's memory of tales and the purposes they serve.[6]

The transparency of abbreviated narratives varies. In the *Odyssey*, the main foil for the story of Odysseus is that of Agamemnon and his family, and this tale reappears with different emphases and details over and over. Prior familiarity with it is not essential, though it is useful.[7] Menelaus is also a foil, and he tells his own story clearly and with considerable detail. Nestor, too, narrates his own return with full clarity.

Locrian Ajax, in contrast, serves as a minor foil in subordinate narratives. Phemius's song before Telemachus and the suitors concerns the bitter return of the Achaeans, which Pallas Athena caused (1.326–27). The cause of her anger is not important in this context, for the summary of the song does not mention it; the suitors fail to recognize what the song could teach them, the importance of avoiding the gods' anger. Later, Nestor tells Telemachus that Zeus caused a bitter return.

> Then Zeus planned in his mind a bitter return for the Argives, since they were not all by any means wise or just. Therefore, many of them met a cruel fate as the result of the destructive anger of the owl-eyed daughter of the mighty father. She caused strife between the two sons of Atreus . . . (3.132–36)

Nestor's story explains in considerable detail why and how some of the Achaeans, including himself, reached home before the great storm, while others, including Odysseus and Menelaus, did not. But Nestor does not explain the cause of Athena's anger and Zeus's vengeance any more clearly than Glaucus describes the "portents" Bellerophon followed. Finally, Menelaus repeats to Telemachus what Proteus told him.

> Ajax was lost along with his long-oared ships. At first, Poseidon brought him close to the great Geraean rocks and saved him from the sea. He would have escaped death, though Athena hated him,

---

6. Andersen (1987) discusses the interaction between their functions for the characters and their broader functions for poet and audience (cf. Edmunds 1997, 419–20).

7. The most extensive treatments of these parallels are those of Olson (1995, 24–42) and Katz (1991, 41–53).

had he not spoken a boastful word and been overcome by *atê*. He said that he had escaped the broad expanse of the sea against the gods' will. Poseidon heard him when he spoke boastfully. Immediately, he took his trident in his mighty hands and struck the Geraean rock and split it apart. Part of it remained there, but the fragment where Ajax was sitting when he was overwhelmed by *atê* fell into the sea. It carried him over the boundless, wave-filled sea. So he died there, since he drank saltwater. (4.499–511)

Together, these passages certainly imply the story—familiar from the *Iliou Persis* and later sources—that Locrian Ajax raped Cassandra in Athena's temple and that her anger spread to the other Greeks because they condoned his sacrilege. Otherwise, the poem gives no cause for Athena's anger, although the storm that drives Odysseus off course at Cape Malea—the same storm that Ajax initially survives—is essential to the poem's plot. These allusions are brief and difficult. Nothing even explicitly reminds the audience that this is the Lesser Ajax, not the Telamonian. Nestor has mentioned (Telamonian) Ajax's death at Troy but did not clearly identify which Ajax he meant. The suicide of Telamonian Ajax, though, was probably an especially familiar story. His inclusion with Achilles, Patroclus, and Nestor's own son Antilochus places him (3.109–12) in a grouping that is probably objectively traditional, for the same heroes are together in Hades (11.467–69).

At least, Proteus's allusiveness is appropriate to the narrative situation, since Proteus knows that Menelaus knows the story up to this point and that Menelaus will not be confused about which Ajax is meant or why Athena hates him. Nestor's reticence is more complicated, since he addresses Telemachus, a young man from an island on the margins. People assume, rightly, that Telemachus has heard of Orestes, but how much would Telemachus know about Locrian Ajax? Perhaps Nestor and Menelaus avoid clarifying the story because they are speaking to a young man, before whom specificity about sexual crime would be socially inappropriate. (Compare the disguised Athena's suggestion that "wild men" are preventing Odysseus's return at 1.198–99 and Telemachus's violent sexual disgust with the maidservants at 22.462–64.)[8]

---

8. If this is right, the second song of Demodocus, sung to the people at large with dancing by young men, requires explanation: either the difference marks the free and easy Phaeacians, it is acceptable to narrate sexual misbehavior of

Their vagueness is not unusual, however. In this case, whether or not Telemachus knows exactly what Locrian Ajax did to cause Athena's anger, the internal narrators structure their stories so that this information is irrelevant.

The external audience is in the same situation as Telemachus. Anyone who does not know why Athena hated Ajax and what that hatred had to do with her anger against the Greeks may be somewhat puzzled by these vague references. However, although this prior knowledge makes the story clearer, it is not important for the significance of the tale. Proteus's story makes Ajax's insane boastfulness the cause of his death; the moral is there. Similarly, in Nestor's and Menelaus's stories, the emphasis lies not on the original cause of the gods' anger but on the different ways these characters and Odysseus attempt to mollify the gods and relate to each other. Although there are advantages to knowing more, the knowledge is not essential. In exposition of the main narrative of the epics, the poet often requires the listener who is not well informed to wait for an explanation; in paradigmatic, secondary material, the explanation may not be provided at all, because it is not really needed.

Paradigms can be difficult as stories because they contain gaps that are never filled, as long as they succeed as paradigms. There are other examples. In the *Iliad*, for example, Glaucus opens his genealogy with the assertion that "many men" know it (6.151). Certainly his account is not always easy to follow. He moves from explaining his father's origins in Corinth to telling how Proetus drove him "out of the community of Argives" without specifying whether these events happened in Corinth (where Proetus does not belong) or, if elsewhere, why Bellerophon was there (6.157–59). After Proteus's wife falsely accuses Bellerophon of sexual assault, he agrees, without Glaucus's explaining why, to travel to Lycia, carrying "malevolent signs" on tablets on which Proetus has written "many life-destroying things" (6.168–69). Bellerophon, ordered to kill the Chimaera, succeeds by "obeying the portents of the gods" (6.153; Pegasus goes unmentioned). He then fights the Solymi and the Amazons and survives an ambush. Suddenly, after narrating Bellerophon's splendid heroic career and fruitful marriage, Glaucus says that "when he [Bellerophon] also came to be hated by all the gods, he wandered

gods more openly than that of mortals, or bards can sing of matters people normally avoid talking about.

alone over the Aleian plain, consuming his own heart, avoiding human paths" (6.200–202). Artemis kills Bellerophon's daughter, Laodamia, in anger of unspecified origin. The entire story is crammed with obscurity, in part because Glaucus becomes extremely vague whenever the story does not reflect well on his family. He chooses not to explain why his ancestor became hateful to the gods. Also, since he has claimed that "many men" know his genealogy, so long an explanation should not be necessary—and since Diomedes turns out to claim ancestral guest friendship with Glaucus, he probably knows the story of his grandfather's guest-friend and his children.

Some of the difficulty depends on the poet's own aesthetic. The vagueness of the allusion to the writing tablet surely belongs to the poet, who does not want to mention writing explicitly. This naturalistically minded poet also avoids mentioning Pegasus, although he must convey the monstrousness of the Chimaera, since Bellerophon's heroic achievement depends on it. Extreme compression plays a role, too. Whatever caused these gaps and imprecisions, the resulting narrative is extremely clear in the outlines of the story of Potiphar's wife, in its emphasis on Bellerophon's great achievements, and in naming his children. The narrative is vague about the role of the gods (even though it emphasizes divine power) and about the misfortunes of Bellerophon and his children.

I have already discussed the introduction of Theoclymenus in the *Odyssey* (see the preceding chapter). Although the narrator provides this information in his own voice, he uses the abbreviated style typical of characters and privileges the message over the details. This technique is not unparalleled: at *Odyssey* 21.13–38, the poet tells the story of Odysseus's bow in an abbreviated but understandable way.[9] Compare the genealogy of Theoclymenus to the version of Melampus's story that appears, without the hero's name, in the Catalogue of Heroines (*Od.* 11.287–97).

> . . . and besides these she also bore strong Pero, a wonder for mortals, whom everybody around came courting. But Neleus would not give her to anyone who would not drive off the twisty cows with broad foreheads from Phylace, from strong Iphiclus, a hard task. Only a blameless prophet promised it, to drive them. But a cruel fate from a god fettered him with harsh chains and rustic

---

9. See Friedrich 1975, 53.

cowherds. But when the months and the days were finished as the years came around and the seasons returned, then fierce Iphiclus released him, since he told many prophecies. And the plan of Zeus was accomplished.

The stories complement each other; points ignored in one appear in the other (the heroine's name appears in one, the hero's name in the other; the name of the father Phylacus in one, the name of Iphiclus in the other; Melampus's grievance against Neleus and vengeance in one, the reason he finally escaped Iphiclus in the other).[10] The concluding allusion to Zeus's plan shows that the poet imagines the story as a summarized epic. He probably knew it as an epic performance.

Both versions of the Melampus story are contextually determined. In the Catalogue of Heroines, where the summary narratives may be imagined as Odysseus's renditions of what each ghost told him, Pero is the center of interest. Melampus does not even need to be named, since the point is that Pero's marriage generated an adventure so significant that the events can be attributed to a plan of Zeus. The later genealogy primarily stresses the family's prophetic ability. It secondarily emphasizes the tendency of the family to wander and to get itself into trouble and its closeness to the gods. Even combined, the entry in the catalogue and the introduction of Theoclymenus are not entirely comprehensible without prior knowledge (that Neleus had a claim to the cattle, that Iphiclus was the son of Phylacus, that Melampus sought Pero not for himself but for his brother), and the narrative work of combining them would be extremely difficult for a listening audience without prior knowledge.[11] Even to remember the catalogue entry in such detail when Theoclymenus appears would be an impressive achievement. However, in neither case is the confusing part of the story essential. It is possible to grasp the message without prior knowledge. The poet probably expected that many listeners in his audience knew the story, but he does not demand prior knowledge if the hearer does not demand full transparency.

Compare the stories about Tydeus. At *Iliad* 4.372–400, Agamemnon compares Diomedes unfavorably to his father. He tells how Tydeus came

---

10. See Heubeck 1954, 20.

11. Fenik (1974, 236 n. 12) charts the complementarities of the stories with the note "Information in brackets is not supplied in the *Odyssey* and is assumed on the part of the audience."

with Polynices to Mycenae to seek help for the war against Thebes and would have received it had not Zeus "shown ill-omened signs" [παραίσια σήματα φαίνων] (4.381). The army sent Tydeus as an ambassador to Thebes. Despite being a hostile stranger, he challenged the Thebans to athletic contests at a feast and won everything easily, because Athena helped (4.390; this is a case where the hero's patron divinity is widely known, like Odysseus's). The angry Thebans sent an ambush after him, led by Maeon and Polyphontes; he killed them all except Maeon, "following the portents of the gods" [θεῶν τεράεσσι πιθήσας] (4.398).

The first part of the tale establishes that Diomedes should not feel that his help to Agamemnon is one-sided. The Mycenaeans would have helped his father had Zeus not shown his opposition. The second section stresses Tydeus's aggressiveness; Agamemnon's suggestion that Tydeus followed the signs of the gods surely anticipates Sthenelus's reply, in which the "recklessness" of the fathers—as displayed in Tydeus's failure to follow signs and perhaps in his challenging his enemies at a banquet—is contrasted with the sons' sense.

The challenge to the Thebans appears once more, at 5.800–808, when Athena again rebukes Diomedes for not living up to his father's standard. The same elements reappear: Tydeus is without supporters at a feast but issues a general challenge and wins easily with the help of the goddess; but the goddess, unlike Agamemnon, contrasts Tydeus's small size with his valor. Because it concentrates on this episode, this version makes Athena's help the climactic moment. Just as Tydeus could be confident to the point of recklessness because the goddess supported him, so his son should be.

Finally, Diomedes himself recites his genealogy in a claim on his hearers' respect at 14.113–25. Here he stresses his father's wealth and his general reputation for excellence with the spear, mentioning no particular heroic deed. He is, as usual, vague about the one episode where he suggests divine causality: Oeneus remained at home, but Tydeus wandered and came to live in Argos, "for thus, it seemed, was the will of Zeus and the other gods" (14.120).

The story of Tydeus's challenge seems objectively traditional. It appears twice with little variation (though the two instances are not widely separated). The challenge is a standard theme, but this particular form— the ambassador from a hostile power who challenges his enemies at a feast—is special; Tydeus's action is recklessly brave and probably socially indecorous. Killing a crowd of ambushers is surely a standard heroic achievement (Bellerophon does it, too), and leaving one survivor looks like a folktale motif. The Thebans later said that Maeon had buried Tydeus; this could be either an independent tradition or a gloss on this passage. The other leader, Polyphontes ("Much-slaying") son of Autophonus ("One who slays with his own hands"), has an obviously significant name and patronymic. We may suspect that he was introduced into the story at some point to provide a leader for Tydeus to kill. Significantly, the narrator says at 23.677–80, as he introduces Mecisteus's son, Euryalus, that Mecisteus (or perhaps his father) went to Thebes for the funeral of Oedipus and defeated all the Cadmaeans. Euryalus is the third Argive leader with Diomedes and Sthenelus, and Diomedes fusses over him in this episode. The association with Diomedes makes the poet remember (or assume) that other heroes' fathers performed exploits like Tydeus's.

Divine causality is strikingly obscure in many of these stories. Sthenelus boasts to Agamemnon that despite the relative weakness of their forces, he and his companions took Thebes, "trusting in the portents of the gods and the help of Zeus" (*Il.* 4.406–8). Their fathers, in contrast, perished "through their own recklessness" [σφετέρησιν ἀτασθαλίησιν] (4.409). These portents are as vague as those in the Bellerophon story and as the "cruel fate" in the tale of Melampus. The Melampus story is similarly vague about the nature of the prophecies the prophet told to win his freedom (of course, prophecies may reveal divine purposes). The poet alludes to Athena's anger against the Greeks during their return from Troy but is vague about its cause. We might assume that character narratives are simply exaggerating the usual rule that only the poet really knows what the gods do and think. However, the allusiveness extends not just to divine matters strictly speaking but to the human causes of misfortune, especially when divine forces are involved—to why Melampus suffered from *atê*, what Bellerophon did to antagonize the gods, why his children died, what offense exactly made Athena angry after the capture of Troy, and why Tydeus had to leave home.

Antinous is similarly vague when he warns the disguised Odysseus, who he assumes is drunk, not to demand the bow.

οἶνοσ καὶ Κένταυρον, ἀγακλυτὸν Εὐρυτίωνα,
ἄασ᾽ ἐνὶ μεγάρῳ μεγαθύμου Πειριθόοιο,
ἐς Λαπίθας ἐλθόνθ᾽· ὁ δ᾽ ἐπεὶ φρένας ἄασεν οἴνῳ,
μαινόμενος κάκ᾽ ἔρεξε δόμον κάτα Πειριθόοιο.

ἥρωας δ᾽ ἄχος εἷλε, διὲκ προθύρου δὲ θύραζε
ἕλκον ἀναΐξαντες, ἀπ᾽ οὔατα νηλέϊ χαλκῷ
ῥῖνάσ τ᾽ ἀμήσαντες· ὁ δὲ φρεσὶν ᾗσιν ἀασθεὶς
ἤϊεν ἣν ἄτην ὀχέων ἀεσίφρονι θυμῷ.
ἐξ οὗ Κενταύροισι καὶ ἀνδράσι νεῖκος ἐτύχθη,
οἳ δ᾽ αὐτῷ πρώτῳ κακὸν εὕρετο οἰνοβαρείων.

(Od. 21.295–304)

[Wine also caused *atê* to the Centaur, famous Eurytion, in the house
of great-hearted Perithous, when he visited the Lapiths. He entered
mental *atê* from wine, and in madness, he committed wrongs in the
house of Perithous. Grief seized the heroes, and they jumped up
and dragged him through the courtyard to the door and cut off his
ears and his nose with cruel bronze. And he, having entered *atê* in
his mind, went bearing his *atê* in his pained heart. That was the ori-
gin of the quarrel between centaurs and men, but he was the first
to suffer because of being drunk.]

Antinous relentlessly repeats a theme word, *atê*. Yet he is not at all pre-
cise about what Eurytion actually did, perhaps because trying to rape
the bride at a wedding is not especially close to Odysseus's behavior in
the scene. Filling in the gap in Antinous's story is not necessary and is
perhaps not even helpful. Filling in the gap increases the irony the nar-
rator directs against Antinous, since the suitors have abused women in
Odysseus's house. However, the vagueness of Antinous's language al-
lows the listener to imagine a parallel between Eurytion's actions and
all the misbehavior of the suitors, not just their sexual misdeeds. The
Melampus story shows that this is not just a realistic representation of
how speakers avoid unpleasant subjects, for the poet does it himself.
Vagueness is useful.

Similarly, Penelope delivers two quasi-paradigmatic narratives
about daughters of Pandareus. Speaking to the disguised Odysseus, she
compares her mental wavering to the nightingale's song: "through folly"
(19.518–23), the daughter of Pandareus killed with bronze her own child,
the son of Zethus, and sings in lamentation. The variety of the nightin-
gale's song and perhaps its sadness parallel Penelope's agonizing inde-
cision; but evidently, she chooses the comparison because she fears that
if she decides wrongly, her own son will die. Soon after, while praying to
Artemis, she tells another story of Pandareus's daughters: left orphaned

because the gods had destroyed their parents, they were cared for by Aphrodite; Hera, Artemis, and Athena all bestowed favors on them. But when Aphrodite asked Zeus to give them marriage, he, "for he well knows everything, fate and ill-fate of mortal humans, caused the storm winds/Harpies to carry them off to be servants to the Erinyes" (20.66–78). Here, the main comparison is Penelope's wish for escape from her present situation. But there are other connections. She feels isolated and friendless, as orphaned girls would; she is superior to other women, like girls blessed by the goddesses.[12] The story also has an unintended point. Instead of marrying, the girls become servants to the dark goddesses of vengeance. Penelope wishes that the gods would make her, like them, disappear (20.79); although she will not disappear, she will bring horrific vengeance on the suitors instead of entering a new marriage.

Neither story is attested elsewhere. The scholia offer supplements, but these look like not independent traditions but midrash-like expansions on the passages themselves. The two tales do not exactly contradict each other but they do not cohere either. It might be easier to imagine two fathers named Pandareus, and the appearance of Pandareus in two stories close to each other in performance time reflects the poet's associative processes. They are both very obscure as told, and as in other examples, the obscurity centers on the cause of human wrongdoing and on the gods' motives. The very emphasis on Zeus's knowledge of fate as a motive underscores the absence of real motive. Yet if everybody could and did fill in these gaps, the stories would lose some of their effect. In the scholiast's version of the nightingale story, Aedon kills her child while meaning to kill a nephew, because she is jealous of Niobe's children; in the version familiar from Ovid, Procne kills her child deliberately, as vengeance on her husband. Neither specific story is really paradigmatically useful for Penelope's situation, but the possibility of causing the death of one's child is.

Hence, paradigmatic stories are not at all obscure so far as their purposes require that they be explicit. When Phoenix tells how he came to be a surrogate father for Achilles, the poet has him explain exactly why he quarreled with his father, because the quarrel, a dispute over a concubine, parallels the *Iliad* and can serve as a negative exemplum for Achilles.[13] Phoenix's tale of the anger of Meleager in the embassy of the

---

12. See Lowenstam (1993, 240–41) discusses this aspect of the paradigm.
13. See Scodel 1982.

Iliad is obscure in a number of places, but it explains the background of the fight with the boar very clearly, as long as the hearer is comfortable with the regressive technique.[14] The Couretes were besieging Calydon; it all began when Oeneus failed to sacrifice to Artemis. As a character-narrator, Phoenix indicates his own ignorance of exactly why Oeneus did this; otherwise, motives are straightforward. Artemis sends the Calydonian boar; Meleager (identified as the son of Oeneus) gathers hunters from many cities. Phoenix wants his audience to sympathize with the Calydonians, so he narrates Oeneus's failure to sacrifice to Artemis; this standard folkloric cause of divine anger does not prejudice the audience against Oeneus. Similarly, he briefly but clearly tells the story of the boar hunt, because the Panhellenic hunt provides a setting not unlike the Trojan War.

The narrative jumps, though, from strife over the boar's head and hide (9.548–49) to war between Couretes and Aetolians. The initial stage of the war goes badly for the Couretes, who "could not remain outside the wall though they were many" (9.550–52). Where is this wall? It can hardly be the wall of Calydon. Then Meleager becomes angry and stays beside his wife. Since she is critical to the tale, she receives an elaborate but confusing introduction.

> He lay by his wife, lovely Cleopatra, daughter of Marpessa, the fair-ankled daughter of Evenus and of Idas, the mightiest of men on the earth in those days. For he even took up his bow face-to-face against the lord Phoebus Apollo for the sake of the girl with beautiful ankles. In their halls, then, her father and lady mother gave her the significant name *Alcyone,* because her mother had the fate of a grieving Halcyon and wept because the far-worker Phoebus Apollo had snatched her away. (9.556–64)

This digression is extraordinarily hard. Apparently, Apollo snatched Marpessa, and Idas somehow recovered her using his bow. The cause of Meleager's anger appears only at 9.566–72; he was angry because his mother had cursed him, and she did this because of the killing of her brother. Meleager's killing of his uncle, which is critical to the plot, is mentioned only here. When a series of embassies comes to try to convince Meleager to fight again, one includes his sisters and mother, with

14. See Schadewaldt 1966, 83–84; Krischer 1971, 136–40.

no explanation of her presence (9.584–85).[15] Thereafter, the tale is simple enough. Meleager's wife finally persuades him to fight, and he saves his city. The fulfillment of his mother's curse, however, is elided.

Most of these difficulties are the result of the paradigmatic function of the tale. In later tradition, the killing of the brother or brothers of Althaea takes place during the initial dispute over the honors of killing the boar. That would create a real problem for the Homeric narrative. The poet needs an initial period of successful warfare for the Aetolians, to establish that they needed Meleager as the Achaeans need Achilles. The curse must therefore be delayed. Furthermore, the killing of the mother's brother does not correspond easily to anything in the *Iliad*. It is not paradigmatically useful, whereas the quarrel over the honors of killing the boar is. The curse itself needs full emphasis, because Meleager must have a good reason to be angry—Phoenix does not want to seem to take Achilles's cause of anger lightly. The cause of the curse, however, is reduced, becoming as close to a mere function as it can.

Despite its areas of muddle, the story functions perfectly as long as the hearer does not worry about the obscurities. The tale is quite clear about the issues that matter: Meleager's refusal to fight, the peril of his city, the embassies, his final decision. So far as the listener concentrates on considering Meleager purely as a parallel for Achilles and ignores the problems the story has in itself, no information the narrator does not provide is required. The hearer should recognize the elaborate digression about Cleopatra as a signal that she will play a critical role. The reference to her father as one who was willing to fight with a god for his beloved fits the ethos of this story, in which Meleager yields to his wife rather than his friends. In one version, Meleager himself died at Apollo's hands (Hesiod frag. 280.2 M.-W.). Still, it does not much matter whether everyone understands exactly who bore the name *Alcyone* or why.

Because the allusiveness of subordinate narratives is so dependent on their functionality, it does not require a rule of transparency for a listener who follows the narratives with a view to their function. The authorial audience does exactly that. Often, this obscurity is indeed a particular form of traditional referentiality. In subordinate narratives, where the audience is prepared for a didactic message, the narrator employs a moral shorthand. He reduces entire sequences within stories— whether told before or potential, familiar or unfamiliar to audiences—

---

15. Kakridis (1949, 18–23) discusses the folk motif of the "ascending scale of affection" that occurs here.

to summaries of their functions: mistake, quarrel, divine helper. To evaluate and understand the story as a whole, the audience needs to understand only the markers of these functions: good/bad state of mind, good/bad attitude toward divine authority. Under the assumption of transparency, we must believe that the story of Maeon and Tydeus was not only objectively traditional but familiar to everyone. Everyone in the authorial audience should know that the phrase θεῶν τεράεσσι πιθήσας [trusting in the portents of the gods] does not require that the narrative be filled in. It adequately replaces such a narrative by announcing that the hero, despite his boldness toward mortals, respected divinely set limits and therefore prospered—we do not need to know how. Sthenelus claims the reverse of his fathers' colleagues: while the Epigoni were successful because they respected divine limits, the Seven against Thebes were foolish. We do not need to know what the portents were that the Epigoni followed. Penelope's vague story of a woman who killed her own child and her dream of being carried away like the maidens who serve the Furies are sufficiently parallel because they are obscure. The morals of the story of Locrian Ajax do not depend on what he originally did to anger Athena. However, it is very important that the other Greeks suffered as a result of his wrongdoing and that he might have escaped had he not foolishly boasted. These allusions are adequate expressions of thematic content—indeed, they can be more efficient than a fuller narrative.

The difficulty of compressed subordinate narratives interacts with another of their outstanding features. Their versions are often peculiar, incorporating details not found in other versions. Often, these details clearly serve the paradigmatic purposes of the speaker. Obscure allusion and apparently invented detail are functionally closely related; they are both characteristic of contextually determined narrative. Yet they are normally taken as evidence for opposite arguments, and scholars examine them separately rather than together. Under the assumption of transparency, gaps lead the interpreter to assume that the original audience knew the story already, while unusual details are often evidence for Homer's originality.

Consider the story of Niobe, a famous example of "invention" cited by Willcock.[16] Niobe and the outlines of her story are very familiar in Greek poetry and art: she is likely to have been traditional in the strongest

---

16. Willcock 1964, 141–42. The following passage, *Iliad* 1.399–406, is discussed on 143–44.

sense, known to everyone. She is appropriate as an exemplum for Priam precisely because she is the emblem of grief. Similarly, when Achilles says that even Heracles died (*Il.* 18.117–19), the example is powerful because everyone knows Heracles as the greatest of heroes. Achilles' version of Niobe's story is odd not only because Niobe eats in it but because petrifaction of the populace has no meaning at all in it. The gods must bury Niobe's children because the gods have intervened to help the as yet unburied Hector; this is the logic of paradigm. If the children are to lie unburied, however, Homeric narrative style demands a motive; the Niobe tale suggests petrifaction, since Niobe turns to stone. Once the children are to be buried by the gods, the petrifaction of the people is a fill-in, almost an inference.

Consider another of Willcock's examples, the story of how Thetis rescued Zeus.

> . . . other Olympian gods wished to bind him, Hera, Poseidon, and Pallas Athena. But you went and released him from his bonds, goddess, quickly calling to great Olympus the Hundred-Hander whom the gods call Briareus but all men call Aegaeon—for he is greater in might than his father—and he then sat beside the son of Cronus, glorying in his superiority. The blessed gods were afraid of him and no longer tried to bind Zeus. (*Il.* 1.399–406)

As Willcock points out, such a conspiracy of gods appears nowhere else in the tradition, and the gods involved are suspiciously identical to those who oppose Zeus in the *Iliad*. Why the Hundred-Hander should be mightier than his father is a mystery. The anecdote is composed of a mélange of traditional materials: both the motif of rebellion against Zeus, and the motif of a female goddess who rescues him appear elsewhere; the choice of gods is determined by the present context, while the detail of being "mightier than his father" belongs to Achilles himself. The story thus seems a perfect example of the creative adaptation of inherited themes.

Laura Slatkin has argued in detail that the theme of the succession myth lies behind the *Iliad* and how this passage depends on it.[17] Thetis, an apparently minor divinity, is more important than she seems, because her son was fated to be mightier than his father. If Thetis had had

---

17. Slatkin 1991.

sexual relations with Zeus or another major Olympian, her son would have had the potential to overthrow Zeus. Achilles' mortality is therefore not the mortality of all the other heroes: it is the cost of the survival of the world order. Yet the story could still signify all this even if it is an ad hoc recombination. Slatkin's interpretation does not depend on a prior existence of the story Achilles tells in the form in which he tells it. Indeed, if it were well known to everyone, it could hardly serve as a substitute for the "real" story, a way of explaining Thetis's ability to move Zeus that does not allow Achilles to know exactly his place in the order of the world.

However, the interpretation demands not just that the phrase "son mightier than his father" be objectively traditional in its application to Achilles but that its association with Achilles be strong and familiar enough that it evokes him through traditional referentiality. If the phrase seems to the authorial audience as fully appropriate and traditional for Briareos/Aegaeon as for Achilles, nothing directs a listener to the "repressed" story. It thus requires that the poet know the story that Thetis was fated to bear a son stronger than his father and that Zeus married her to a mortal for that reason. If the poet intended his audience to recognize this theme, he must assume that his audience also has heard this story before.

Homer never mentions the story that Thetis would have a son mightier than his father, and it was not the only story about her marriage to Peleus: according to the *Cypria*, Zeus married her to a mortal in anger after she refused him in deference to Hera (2 Davies). At *Iliad* 24.59–60, Hera says that she reared Thetis "and gave her in marriage to a man." Whether the *Cypria*'s story lies behind this passage or is an expansion of it, the *Iliad* does not, at the level of plot, presuppose the version in which marriage to Thetis threatens Zeus's power. Yet the phrase "mightier than his father" is meaningful in this context and pointless in association with the Hundred-Handers. It is probable, therefore, that the story has influenced Homer's view of Achilles and that the phrase "mightier than his father" reflects this influence. However, this is not necessarily an allusion the audience needs to pursue very far. As a member of the narrative audience, the hearer should not remember it at all. As a member of the authorial audience, the hearer will profit from having heard the story before, but by sharing in the poet's chain of associations, rather than by consciously reconstructing the full story. A recollection that Achilles, too, was fated to be mightier than his father gives

Thetis's plea and later references to Achilles' fate special pathos. Too sharp a concentration on this alternative tale would be distracting. The hearer does not need to know in advance either the tale Achilles tells or the one the poet omits, but the story the poet does not tell enrichs the *Iliad*, as long as it stays in the background. As often, a vague memory is here more helpful than a precise one.

Innovations, like allusions, generate gaps. If the details are truly innovations, however, the audience could not fill in these gaps correctly, because there is nothing behind them. The phrase "mightier than his father" does not refer to any story about Briareos. Similarly, there is no reason why the gods turned Niobe's people into stone. Achilles compares himself to Heracles.

> I will accept my fate, whenever Zeus and the other immortal gods wish to accomplish it. For not even mighty Heracles escaped death, although he was extremely dear to the lord Zeus, son of Cronus. Nonetheless, fate and the harsh anger of Hera overcame him. (*Il.* 18.115–19)

Although Hera's resentment of Heracles is central to his adventures both in the *Iliad*'s allusions and in later versions, her anger is not part of the story of his death as the poets or mythographers tell it. Achilles himself will die at the hands of Paris and Apollo. Although Achilles may not know this yet (Hector predicts it at 22.359–60, and Achilles replies by echoing this passage), the poet probably emphasizes Hera's anger because the parallel is controlling his narrative here. Such a passage can hardly be called an "invention," because no specific narrative is generated. Like many other character narratives, this one reduces divine causality to a function.

There is a similar question of what constitutes "invention" in one of the few allusive passages in the narrator's voice. The *Iliad* notoriously avoids mentioning the Judgment of Paris, except once, as the gods urge Hermes to steal the body of Hector from Achilles.

> ἔνθ᾿ ἄλλοις μὲν πᾶσιν ἑήνδανεν, οὐδέ ποθ᾿ Ἥρῃ
> οὐδὲ Ποσειδάων᾿ οὐδὲ γλαυκώπιδι κούρῃ,
> ἀλλ᾿ ἔχον ὥς σφιν πρῶτον ἀπήχθετο Ἴλιος ἱρὴ
> καὶ Πρίαμος καὶ λαὸς Ἀλεξάνδρου ἕνεκ᾿ ἄτης,

ὃς νείκεσσε θεὰσ, ὅτε οἱ μέσσαυλον ἵκοντο,
τὴν δ᾿ ᾔνησ᾿ ἥ οἱ πόρε μαχλοσύνην ἀλεγεινήν.

(Il. 24.24–30)

[Then it pleased all the others, but not Hera or Poseidon or the owl-
eyed maiden; they felt just as when they first came to hate holy Il-
ium and Priam and his people because of the *atê* of Alexander, who
spoke abusively to the goddesses when they came to his cattle pen
but who praised the one who provided him with misery-causing
lust.]

These lines are peculiar in a number of ways (and, as a result, have been
suspect since antiquity). First, Poseidon's enmity seems to have the
same cause as that of Hera and Athena, although he elsewhere speaks
at some length of Laomedon's treatment of him as the cause of his anger.
(This story, too, is confusing, since Apollo receives the same treatment
but is not angry.) Perhaps this is not a serious issue, precisely because
the poem has explicated Poseidon's hatred for Troy. But this passage im-
plies a different version of the Judgment of Paris from any extant one—
so different that Wilamowitz hypothesized that the lines allude to a
completely different earlier story, a version of the "god in disguise."[18]
For while ᾔνησ᾿ (praised) has weak meanings, νείκεσσε never means
anything milder than "reproached" or "addressed abusively." Some
have suggested that the goddesses would have been offended by losing,
so that abuse was implicit in the Judgment of Paris itself.[19] A poet,
though, who imagined Paris as having pronounced such a priamel as
"Hera is most powerful, Athena is wisest, but Aphrodite is the most
beautiful" would not have used the verb νείκεσσε.

The passage is very close to familiar versions of the Judgment of
Paris—too close, with Aphrodite's gift of satyriasis, to refer to any other
story—yet it is not exactly the same. This Paris not only rules against the
two goddesses but is gratuitously rude to them. The relative clause that
says so may be an embedded focalization, giving the goddesses' own

---

18. Wilamowitz-Moellendorff 1930, 142; see Stinton 1965, 1–3.
19. See Adkins 1969, 20; Davies 1981. Richardson (*Il. Comm.*, 6:279) com-
ments that "from this [sc. 'reproach'] to 'find fault with' and hence to 'insult' is
not a difficult transition."

version of events.[20] This version puts Hera and Athena in a better light, as character focalizations do, since gods may be expected to resent insults. However, we cannot completely separate the narrator from the judgments embedded in such focalizations. In choosing to give the characters' point of view through his own voice, he inevitably gives it some legitimacy. And Paris's rudeness, vague as it is, is not exactly a piece of narrative "invention." This passage lies in a gray area—it is not just a partisan account, but it is not quite a distinct version.

If this version justifies the goddesses' hatred for Troy, it makes Paris seem even worse than he already is. This prepares for Priam's abuse of his surviving sons, which assimilates them all to Paris.

> . . . all these worthless ones are left, cheaters and dancers, best at pounding the floor, snatchers of lambs and kids from their own community. (24.260–62)

The whole divine scene is extraordinary. It begins very much like the Achaean assembly of book 1: the plan to have Hermes steal Hector's corpse pleases all the gods but the three enemies of Troy, just as Chryses' plea meets with approval from all the Achaeans except Agamemnon. In this case, however, the resistance of Hera and the others prompts Zeus to craft another plan, one obviously superior in every way to the scheme to steal the body. By having Priam successfully ransom Hector, the gods show compassion for one hero without diminishing the honor of the other. Metapoetically, by presenting an alternative, blocked resolution, the narrator emphasizes the actual solution of the impasse, which is morally satisfying and aesthetically pleasing in achieving closure through a final use of the supplication theme. The poet needs the abandoned plan so that the audience will appreciate what actually happens, and he needs to motivate why the plan cannot be carried out. He must therefore explain Hera's hatred for Troy.

When Zeus earlier asks Hera why she hates Troy so much, the narrator wants her hatred to seem excessive, so she does not answer the question except to reiterate her hate, as if she were motivelessly malignant (4.30–67). Here, she is partly in the right, so the traditional motive is modified to make her relentless hatred more understandable. The poet invites the audience to see events Hera's way. Her way is probably

---

20. See de Jong 1987a, 120.

slightly different from any version familiar to the audience, but only slightly. Like Hera's anger in Achilles' account of Heracles' death, it is not sharp enough to be called an innovation, but it is surely generated by its immediate context.

Compare the moment at which Zeus sees Hera and is struck with desire, "as when first they two went to bed and joined in love, avoiding detection by their dear parents" (14.295–96). Here, once again, the narrator's voice conceals an embedded focalization: this is surely Zeus's memory. It is, however, certainly reliable. Yet it is hard to imagine a theogony in which Zeus and Hera slipped away for illicit sex—and their father was not "dear" to them in the story as we know it. This narrative implies a "normal" domestic life.[21] Yet within the deception episode, with its humor about the loves of Zeus, Zeus's relationship with Hera should appropriately begin with deceit of his parents, just as the loves he enumerates in his catalogue all mean that he deceived her.

Catalogues of exempla are a special subgenre within the surviving epics, used by only gods addressing other gods—Dione consoling Aphrodite (*Il.* 5.381–404), Zeus explaining to Hera how much he desires her (*Il.* 14.315–28), Calypso complaining to Hermes of the gods' jealousy (*Od.* 5.118–29). Most of this material must be objectively traditional and must have been familiar to audiences. Zeus's amours generate major heroes and the gods Apollo, Artemis, and Dionysus. Calypso cites the familiar Orion and Demeter's love for Iasion. However, nowhere else in extant Greek literature does Artemis kill Orion because the gods resent his sexual relations with the Dawn, as she does in Calypso's version. Dawn has many mortal lovers in Greek mythology, and the gods do not kill them. Similarly, Iasion is the father of Plutus at *Theogony* 969–74, and the ritual associations of the "triple-furrowed field" make it hard to imagine that storytellers often emphasized his premature death, rather than the fertility of the union. The Greeks had certainly become familiar with the Near Eastern idea that sexual union with a goddess was dangerous; but Calypso could not use such stories, since she is blaming the (male) gods.[22] In the corpus of Greek stories in general, it is simply

---

21. We may also suspect that Hera's claim that Oceanus and Tethys took care of her while Zeus overthrew Cronus (14.201–4) is contextually bound. Hera's lie needs a basis for her interest in Tethys and Oceanus.

22. See Giacomelli 1980 for the threat to the *menos* of men who have sexual relations with goddesses.

not the case that the gods resent goddess-mortal unions. These examples are slightly "off," since the mortals in them die because the gods want to separate them from their goddess-lovers, while Odysseus is "dead" on Calypso's island and returns to life by leaving her.[23] Calypso does not want to acknowledge her chthonic affinites. Of course, within the mimetic world, Calypso cannot be inventing these stories—why lie to another god? Instead, the narrator selects mortal unions with goddesses in which the man's ultimate fate was either varied enough or obscure enough that Calypso's versions are not blatantly innovative.

Dione's references are even trickier. She narrates first how the Aloadae imprisoned Ares.

> Ares endured, when Otus and mighty Ephialtes, sons of Aloeus, bound him in a strong bond. They imprisoned him in a bronze jar for thirteen months. There Ares, insatiable for war, would have perished had not their stepmother, lovely Eeriboea, reported it to Hermes. He stole Ares away. He was worn out, and the harsh imprisonment had subdued him. (*Il.* 5.385–91)

This story is unattested elsewhere; but Otus and Ephialtes, well known for their attempt to scale heaven, piling Mount Pelion on Mount Ossa to reach Olympos, are traditional enemies of the gods. The tale is both weird and circumstantial. That Hermes should steal the victim fits his traditional role (as the gods consider having him steal Hector's corpse), but how are we to imagine the communication between Eeriboea and Hermes?

Dione also says that Heracles wounded Hera in the right breast with an arrow and hit Hades in the shoulder with an arrow "in Pylos among the corpses" [ἐν Πύλῳ ἐν νεκύεσσι] (5.397). Hades was healed by Paeon, as Ares soon will be (5.899–901). Neither story is attested elsewhere, and the ancient exegetical commentary offers two explanations for Hera's wounding: either it was the same occasion as Hades', or the infant Heracles shot Hera in anger at her withdrawal of the breast. The attack on Hades presumably belongs either to the wars of Heracles with Pylos, of which we hear from Nestor (11.690–93) and in the Hesiodic *Ehoeae* (frags. 33–35 M.-W.), or to Heracles' descent to the underworld

---

23. See Crane 1988, 16–20.

to fetch Cerberus. It is hard to understand, though, what Hades (and perhaps Hera) were doing at Pylos.

However, the point of the exempla themselves is not hard to elucidate. Gods may have to endure much from mortals, but the consequences are not really serious. Otus and Ephialtes were huge and immensely powerful, but Apollo killed them before they reached full maturity (*Od.* 11.305–20). As Niobe is the traditional example of grief, they are the examples of theomachy punished. Dione cannot use their more famous attack on the gods, however, because no god was injured. Heracles, by contrast, is the hero who tests mortal limits most extravagantly but who does not perish as a result. Dione ends her speech by threatening Diomedes. Yet Diomedes—who later speaks piously about how he will not fight gods, since the consequences are bad (6.128–41)—will not suffer at all for wounding Aphrodite. In other words, the examples go beyond the speaker's intention to create an ambiguity—in this case, about whether mortals who fight with gods suffer or not. The examples, like Calypso's, are effective whether the stories are objectively traditional or not and, more importantly, whether they are familiar or not, because the characters in them are familiar and the stories depend on their traditional personalities.

Mabel Lang has argued that since a large group of apparently unconnected paradigms (and one brief mythic digression in the narrator's own voice) forms a single story about Heracles, the narrator clearly has an extended and complex tale in mind.[24] Presumably, the audience, too, can place each segment within this implicit narrative. The existence of the implicit story argues against the claim that the poet invented individual paradigms as he needed them; Lang sees a gradual process whereby paradigms and main narrative adapted to each other. She analyzes the following passages (the order of presentation is that of the *Iliad*, while the numbers indicate her reconstructed chronological sequence).

1. Hera, Poseidon, and Athena (or, in a variant, Apollo) attempted to bind Zeus, but Thetis saved him (1.396–406).
4. Hephaestus was thrown to earth when he tried to help Hera (1.590–94).
7. Heracles sacked Troy "for the sake of Laomedon's horses" (5.638–42).

---

24. Lang 1983.

6. Hypnus helped Hera put Zeus to sleep so that she could drive Heracles off course. Heracles was on his way home from Troy and landed in Cos. Hypnus would have been hurled had he not fled to Night (14.250–61).

3. Zeus punished Hera by hanging her (15.18–24) and hurling to Earth any god who tried to help her.

5. Hera was punished for driving Heracles off course so that he landed on Cos (15.24–28).

8. The Trojans and Athena built Heracles a wall as protection against the sea monster (20.145–48).

2. Poseidon and Apollo served Laomedon at the order of Zeus (21.441–57), Poseidon building the walls of Troy, Apollo tending cattle. (According to 7.452–53, Apollo and Poseidon both built the walls of Troy.)

By combining the various items and filling in gaps, Lang produces the following coherent story (parts supplied from later tradition appear in square brackets).

Apollo, Poseidon, and Hera conspire against Zeus. Zeus sends Apollo and Poseidon to serve Laomedon. Laomedon refuses payment and threatens the gods, [so Poseidon sends the sea monster]. [Laomedon hires Heracles to fight the monster, promising him horses as a reward, and Heracles succeeds, but] Laomedon again refuses payment. Heracles then sacks Troy. When Heracles is on his way home, however, Hera sends Zeus to sleep and drives Heracles off course to Cos, whereupon Zeus hangs Hera and throws Hephaestus to earth.

This is, indeed, a reasonably coherent story. It is less coherent than it appears at first glance, though. Why does Zeus not punish Hera for the initial conspiracy? Lang cites his remark at *Iliad* 8.407–8 that he is not as angry at Hera as he is at Athena, since Hera always opposes him. Yet within this same notional sequence, he punishes Hera after she drives Heracles off course, so he evidently does not regard such punishment as useless. In *Iliad* 8, he threatens to strike both goddesses with his thunderbolt (lines 404–5), even though he says he is less angry with Hera. Surely he would have to respond to a direct attack on his power. The connection between the gods' conspiracy and the service of Apollo and Poseidon to

Laomedon is pure speculation and is not especially well founded. Poseidon never even says that it was a punishment, and if Athena is the other conspirator, she is not punished at all. Gods who serve mortals are a frequent motif in Greek mythology. An alternate tradition has the gods deliberately test Laomedon. Why, when Laomedon cheated Apollo as well as Poseidon, is Apollo a pro-Trojan god (Poseidon asks this very question)? What was the cause of the initial conspiracy?

Later tradition allows us to fill in the links that make sense of the story once the gods serve Laomedon, but it is vague up to that point. What exactly did Apollo do for Laomedon, since one passage says that he helped build Troy's walls, while the other says that he herded? Zeus says that he hurled from Olympus any god who tried to help Hera; was Hephaestus the only one? Can we be certain that this was the occasion on which Hephaestus tried to help Hera, since quarrels between Zeus and Hera seem to be frequent? What was the occasion when Hera threw Hephaestus into the sea, where Thetis and Eurynome rescued him (18.395–405)? Are we to assume that Homer's audience knew the answers to all these questions?

If a real song lies behind these episodes, it was a song about Heracles. These are fragments of his story (the gods' quarrels are there because they explain Heracles' misfortunes). The poet has at least one section of Heracles' whole story—the first sack of Troy and its aftermath —clearly defined in his mind. His ability to use pieces of it so freely surely implies that he knew it well and that it was part of his narrative inheritance. His audience probably also knew it. The tale of Poseidon's and Apollo's service to Laomedon is an explanatory detail within this tale; being so subordinate, it does not need further antecedents. Pindar tells it as an incident in the story of the Aeacids (*Ol.* 8.31–51).

However, the existence of a traditional story about Heracles' sack of Troy does not mean that the audience would fit into its framework every story that could belong there. The conspiracy of the gods is not really part of this story: if we omit the conspiracy, the gods' service to Laomedon is unmotivated, but if we keep it, the absence of motivation has simply moved back one stage. Hephaestus's attempt to help Hera could belong to this story or to another; nothing makes the connection necessary. Further, not every detail in Homer's allusions to this story must be either objectively traditional or familiar to the audience. Instead, the familiar frame is useful precisely because it allows the poet to maintain traditionality while adapting allusions to their context.

The story of Heracles' birth that Agamemnon tells at *Iliad* 19.95–133 is closely related to this sequence. Zeus, tricked by Hera, swears an oath that the child descended from himself and born that day will rule among his neighbors; Hera causes Eurystheus to be born before Heracles. In his rage over this, Zeus throws Atê from heaven, so that she now afflicts mortals. Hera apparently goes unpunished. This is a doublet/variant on the same themes surrounding Zeus, Hera, and Heracles elsewhere— Zeus deceived by Hera, Heracles victimized, and a divinity thrown from Olympus. But Atê is thrown instead of Hephaestus. Many have wondered whether the role of Atê here is an innovation. Indeed, some scholars have thought that Agamemnon, rather than Homer, is the inventor. On this reading, the poet expected his audience to recognize the innovation and understand that Agamemnon, in his search for self-justification, is inventing mythology. The narrative is certainly peculiar, since mortal characters do not ordinarily repeat the direct speech of the gods, as Agamemnon does here.[25] However, the basic frame of the story, Hera's tricking of Zeus at Heracles' birth, is very likely to be traditional. In other words, the consistency of the basic structure of Heracles' adventures does not prove anything about the details. Instead, it seems that the poet has a repertory of traditional cycles of stories that he can vary to meet his characters' and his own needs.

Similarly, the narrator is clearly fully in systematic control of a substantial body of information about the antecedents of the plot of the *Iliad* itself. The Great Foray, as scholars sometimes call it, is clear in his mind—or its most important parts are.[26] The Catalogue of Ships informs us that Briseis comes from Lyrnessus (2.689–94), the city of King Mynes (who receives a genealogy going back to his grandfather). That the catalogue names the king and his brother and that Achilles and Briseis mention the facts of the sack suggest that the poet has inherited these details. Achilles later says that he wishes Briseis had died when he took Lyrnessus (19.59–60). Achilles claims to have sacked twelve cities by sea and eleven by land (9.328–29). The poem only names six of these. Thebe and Lyrnessus are mentioned several times each. Aeneas associates Pedasus with Lyrnessus (20.92), while it is the native town of Lycaon's mother (21.87) and of Elatus, killed by Agamemnon at 6.33–35. *Pedasus* is also the name of one of a pair of twins, sons of an illegitimate

---

25. See de Jong 1987a, 172–73; Rabel 1991, especially 112.
26. On the Great Foray see Jones 1995.

son of Laomedon, killed at 6.20–28, and of the horse Achilles took from
Thebe (16.152, 467). Diomede, with whom Achilles sleeps at 9.664–65,
comes from Lesbos, and her father is Phorbas, whose name is the same
as the father of a Trojan at 14.490; the attack on Lesbos is important in
book 9, where Lesbian women are offered to Achilles, but it is not men-
tioned elsewhere. Patroclus sleeps with Iphis, who comes from Scyrus
(9.666–68). If the Scyrus that Achilles sacks is the same island where
Neoptolemus is growing up (19.326), this raid is hard to understand,
while a Scyrus in the Troad mentioned by the scholia is otherwise unat-
tested. Also, it seems odd that while the father of the king of Lyrnessus
is Evenus (whose name is also that of the father of Marpessa), the father
of Iphis is Enueus (9.666–68), an anagram of Evenus.

It appears that some allusions to Achilles' earlier sacks of towns are
fixed, while others may not be (even) "objectively" traditional. The poet
seems to wish to avoid having more than one captive woman from the
same place. Each one represents a separate heroic achievement. Fur-
thermore, each needs to be dignified with a genealogy. The poet uses his
traditional skills to amplify the information he has inherited. The sacks
of Thebe and Lyrnessus, though, display a consistency that most con-
sider a sign of traditional status; earlier poets had surely mentioned how
the Achaeans took these places.

The *Cypria* narrated at least part of the Great Foray: "[Achilles]
drives off the cattle of Aeneas and sacks Lyrnessus and Pedasus and all
the surrounding cities" (Proclus 80–82 Davies). However, according to
the exegetical commentary (schol. bT) on 2.690, that poem had Briseis
come from Pedasus, not Lyrnessus. Evidently, the *Cypria* disagrees with
the *Iliad* on this point. The disagreement can hardly be ideologically or
politically motivated. It has no apparent significance at all. Evidently,
then, the *Cypria* poet learned the story slightly differently. However, one
could interpret this difference in very divergent ways, since it does not
necessarily imply that the captures of the women were part of the ear-
lier tradition. The *Cypria* poet may have heard songs featuring Briseis
and a capture at Pedasus instead of Lyrnessus. However, the opposite
is also possible: the *Cypria* poet may have had heard a song about the
capture of Lyrnessus in which Briseis did not figure. That would not
mean that Briseis's capture at Lyrnessus was not objectively traditional.
The capture of Briseis is only important as a preface to the events of the
Iliad, and a performer who did not intend to allude to the *Iliad* story
might not have mentioned her. The *Cypria* poet, however, had heard the

Iliad so she mattered to him.[27] If the story as he had learned it did not put her at Lyrnessus, he therefore decided that she must have come from elsewhere. Since he knew of no other women from Pedasus, he deduced that she must have come from there. In any case, however traditional the material may be, Achilles' speech does not assume vast knowledge on the part of the audience.

Areithous the "club man" appears at *Iliad* 7.8–11, where his son is killed. At 7.132–57, Nestor tells a paradigmatic story of his youth: he killed Eurythalion, who had been the attendant of Lycurgus, who killed Areithous "by cunning, not might." Nestor has already mentioned the killing of Eurythalion at 4.319. The two stories contradict each other chronologically. A hero whose son is at Troy can hardly have been killed by a man whose heir fought the young Nestor. Further, the topology of the second tale is extremely difficult. Nonetheless, they clearly complement each other; the second glosses the epithet "club man," left obscure by the first. Areithous is surely objectively traditional, as his unique epithet suggests, and that Nestor refers twice to his killing of Eurythalion as an exploit of his youth suggests that it, too, was inherited. The connection between the two, though, could be a new recombination in response to the need to expand a battle about which the poet did not know very much.

Sometimes, it would be genuinely helpful to know whether specific details are objectively traditional, because further interpretive consequences can depend on the question. For example, Garvie uses the argument from transparency to claim that the content of the first song of Demodocus in the *Odyssey* is traditional.[28]

> He sang from a song whose fame then reached wide heaven, the quarrel of Odysseus and Achilles, son of Peleus—how they came to strife, with harsh words, at an abundant feast honoring the gods, and the lord of men, Agamemnon, rejoiced in his mind, because the best of the Achaeans were fighting. For thus Phoebus Apollo had declared to him in oracular speech at holy Pytho, when he crossed the stone threshold to consult the oracle. For the beginning of trou-

---

27. Burgess (1996) argues for a *Cypria* entirely independent of the *Iliad* and perhaps indeed telling the entire story of Troy.

28. Garvie 1994, 249: "The allusive treatment supports the view that the story was in fact familiar to [Homer's] audience." Cf. Danek 1998, 142–50.

ble was rolling forward for the Trojans and Danaans through the plans of great Zeus. (*Od.* 8.74–82)

Garvie argues that because the reference to the oracle is "almost unintelligible," Homer must be alluding to a familiar story. Others have argued the opposite: that when Homer says that the song's fame reached heaven then, he implies that it is not well known now.[29] Scholars who believe this passage is "invented" have argued that it alludes to the *Iliad:* In one interpretation, Agamemnon rejoices because he wrongly thinks that this quarrel between the "best of the Achaeans" means that the war will soon be won, not realizing that the quarrel meant by the oracle is the quarrel of the *Iliad*.[30]

From the perspective of the audience of the *Odyssey*, it is not very important whether the story is strongly traditional, objectively traditional, or a contextually determined recombination. The *Odyssey* clearly defines its hero as Achilles' rival as well as his friend, as their encounter in the underworld shows. Odysseus tries to praise Achilles, but Achilles insists that Odysseus is the more fortunate man (11.477–91). Quarrels between heroes are clearly a standard heroic theme, and a quarrel between these two would be relevant to the *Odyssey* whether the quarrel was strongly traditional or not. The oracle is a particularly elaborate example of the divine causality that is so frequent in compressed narratives; it is a marker of divine interest, so we do not need to know exactly what it said.

For Nagy, this tradition of a quarrel between Achilles and Odysseus—a quarrel the scholiast suggests concerned the relative importance of cleverness and strength in the capture of Troy—is symptomatic of a deep antagonism between the two characters.[31] Nagy bases his interpretation of the embassy scene of *Iliad* 9 and its famous, difficult duals on the enmity inferred from this quarrel. This reconstruction is important, because if a story in which Achilles and Odysseus quarreled was not part of the repertory, there is no other reason to think that Achilles and Odysseus were traditionally enemies. It is worth noting, though, that there was an epic story about the tension between might and cunning—but the opposition is between Ajax and Odysseus, not

---

29. See Marg 1956; Clay 1983, 96–103; Taplin 1990.
30. See Pucci 1987, 218–19.
31. Nagy 1979, 15–58.

Achilles and Odysseus. Yet this tension is inherent in the very different characters of Achilles and Odysseus; it is a possibility that the epics do not exploit. If we avoid reifying the tradition, the story in the song of Demodocus becomes an expression of this tension, whether it had ever been sung independently or not.

The compressed narratives of Homeric epic do not demand that the audience be familiar with large amounts of mythological detail. They ask the audience not to fill in the gaps but to concentrate on the point. Transparency is not required. The poet can recombine details in new ways or refer in passing to material the audience may not fully understand. The abbreviated narratives certainly demand a general familiarity with important traditional characters, such as Niobe, Otus and Ephialtes, and Heracles. They have a reductive tendency, however, that is unique to the subgenre, compressing what could be whole epic episodes, especially those of divine involvement or human folly, into functions. At the same time, they positively require just as expository passages sometimes do, that the listener not bring to bear everything someone might know. Indeed, as I have already suggested, knowing where to stop the play of memory is an important competence in traditional referentiality.

Narrative Teases

The Homeric poems make themselves accessible to listeners who have only a general familiarity with the traditional stories; those who know more will enjoy them more. However, their rhetorical strategy constructs an extremely knowledgeable narrative audience. Homeric narrative is thus not always transparent, and there is a significant gap between the well-informed narrative audience and the far less fully informed authorial audience. This rhetoric of inclusion partially explains why Homer so often delays exposition to a moment at which it can easily be naturalized. The delay can be very brief. For example, the disguised Odysseus suddenly worries that Eurycleia will recognize his (previously unmentioned) scar when she washes his feet (*Od.* 19.390–91). She recognizes it "immediately" in both story time and performance time (19.392–93), and the narrator explains her memory with a full explanation of the scar. For just a moment, the listener is baffled: what scar?

Sometimes this practice takes an exaggerated form. The narrator speaks of less familiar characters as if they were well known to everyone, delaying his exposition and generating tension. Eumaeus's name does not appear in the first half of the *Odyssey*. Only at 4.640 is he fleetingly mentioned. The suitors are surprised to learn that Telemachus has gone to Pylos, because they had assumed that he was "there in Ithaca, on his estates, with either the sheep or the swineherd."[1] This allusion does not imply that Telemachus has an especially close relationship with the swineherd, although it does not exclude that possibility, since it is only one of a pair of alternatives. Telemachus could be expected to visit his rural holdings occasionally. If the hearer knows versions of the story

---

1. S. West (*Od. Comm.*, 1:233, ad loc) comments, "The casual reference to the swineherd is interesting; Eumaeus, who is to play a major role in the second half of the poem, has not yet been introduced, and it sounds as if he was a well-established character in the saga of Odysseus' homecoming." Here, again, is the assumption of transparency.

in which the swineherd plays a significant part, this passing mention is a reminder of the character, but it is not a flag for anyone who is not prepared for it.

When Odysseus has reached Ithaca, Athena tells Odysseus to go to the swineherd's hut.

> αὐτὸς δὲ πρώτιστα συβώτην εἰσαφικέσθαι,
> ὅς τοι ὑῶν ἐπίουρος, ὁμῶς δέ τοι ἤπια οἶδε,
> παῖδά τε σὸν φιλέει καὶ ἐχέφρονα Πηνελόπειαν.
>
> (13.404–6)

[You yourself go first to the swineherd, who takes care of your pigs and is well disposed toward you as before, and he loves your child and wise Penelope.]

Odysseus follows her command.

> Αὐτὰρ ὁ ἐκ λιμένος προσέβη τρηχεῖαν ἀταρπὸν
> χῶρον ἀν' ὑλήεντα δι' ἄκριας, ᾗ οἱ Ἀθήνη
> πέφραδε δῖον ὑφορβόν, ὅ οἱ βιότοιο μάλιστα
> κήδετο οἰκήων, οὖσ κτήσατο δῖος Ὀδυσσεύς.
>
> (14.1–4)

[But Odysseus went along the rough path from the harbor, through a wooded area along the ridges, where Athena had directed him to the godlike swineherd, who cared most for his property out of all the servants whom godlike Odysseus had acquired.]

This is clearly an adequate introduction in the Homeric style. The most important fact about Eumaeus in this situation is his loyalty, and Odysseus goes to his hut because the goddess has told him that it is a safe place. The narrative will strongly emphasize both the swineherd's devotion to Odysseus and his excellent care of Odysseus's property.

The still-unnamed swineherd receives the heroic epithet δῖος (etymologically connected to the name *Zeus*) at 14.3. The epithet is striking. Δῖος/ν is a very common epithet of heroes. Except where it modifies ὕφορβος/ν, it appears without a proper name only once in the Homeric epics, in the phrase δῖον γένος (*Il.* 9.538, of Artemis). In the *Odyssey*, the nominative is used most often for Odysseus but also for Orestes. More-

over, the epithet is rare in this metrical position. The irregularities invite
the audience to wonder why a swineherd is close to Zeus, especially
since the author's and Athena's praise of Eumaeus has been praise ap-
propriate to a subordinate of very low status.[2]

Eumaeus has a strange place in the formulaic system. The poet re-
peatedly apostrophizes him (as Εὔμαιε σύβωτα [[you] Eumaeus the
swineherd]), as he does Patroclus and Menelaus in the *Iliad*. Like them,
Eumaeus serves as a sympathetic double of a more important character,
Odysseus.[3] The apostrophes replace the usual nominative epithet pre-
ceding speeches and show special sympathy.[4] In Eumaeus's other "stag-
ing" formula for speeches, his name does not appear: he is συβώτης,
ὄρχαμος ἀνδρῶν [the swineherd, leader of men]. The cowherd Philoetius
also receives this epithet (20.185, 254). Eumaeus is literally a leader of
men, since he directs other swineherds; Philoetius is likewise probably
the head of a group. Nonetheless, earlier in the poem, this phrase is a
line-end epithet for Pisistratus, Nestor's son, who is not yet a leader but
will be a king, and for Polites at 10.224, at the moment of a significant
intervention; when Odysseus calls him "the dearest and favorite to me
of all my companions." In the *Iliad* (2.837, 12.110), is used for Asius. Ὄρ-
χαμος ἀνδρῶν, like δῖος, is a heroic epithet.

As I have already mentioned, Eumaeus is also called the "godlike
swineherd." This formula appears repeatedly where epic usually has
epithet plus name. Otherwise, the only occupational term that replaces
a hero's name in this way is μάντις in the formula μάντις ἀμύμων—and
the prophets so identified are all acting as prophets. Eumaeus, however,
is still the swineherd—at least to the poet—even when he has helped kill
the suitors (22.194), although Odysseus has promised that he and
Philoetius will be comrades and brothers of Telemachus (21.215–16).
There is a remarkable passage at 17.505–8. Penelope has been speaking
of the wickedness of the suitors and their mistreatment of the beggar.

ἡ μὲν ἄρ' ὣς ἀγόρευε μετὰ δμῳῆσι γυναιξὶν
ἡμένη ἐν θαλάμῳ· ὁ δ' ἐδείπνει δῖος Ὀδυσσεύς.
ἡ δ' ἐπὶ οἷ καλέσασα προσηύδα δῖον ὑφορβόν·

2. Foley (1999, 213–26), suggests that the definition of the epithet is unim-
portant; it marks the importance of the character.

3. See Block 1982.

4. See Kahane 1994, 111–12.

"ἔρχεο, δῖ᾽ Εὔμαιε, κιὼν τὸν ξεῖνον ἄνωχθι
ἐλθέμεν . . ."

[She then spoke thus, sitting in her room among her servant women. Meanwhile, godlike Odysseus was having his meal. But she, calling for him, addressed the godlike swineherd, "Come, godlike Eumaeus, go and bid this stranger come . . ."]

In a passage like this, one suspects that the poet has applied "godlike" to Eumaeus because its proper referent, Odysseus, is absent.

Throughout the *Odyssey*, the epithets of Eumaeus stress simultaneously his humble status and his nobility. Some of the peculiarities of the formulae are doubtless based in meter—the name is a difficult one. But other solutions to the technical problems of the name were possible. The formulae were clearly created for Eumaeus as we see him in the poem, not for some other story. Since he is not only of noble birth but will participate in heroic battle, the honorifics are appropriate; at the same time, the poet emphasizes that Eumaeus is (only) a swineherd, because the thematic center of the Ithacan books is a beggar who is really the hero. The epithet system for Eumaeus does not prove that the poet inherited him as a developed character—its oddities perhaps suggest the opposite. Certainly these epithets could not have been created for a version of the return significantly different from this one or very much shorter. The role of Eumaeus clearly belongs to the elaboration of a single-performance song of the hero's return (like Serbo-Croatian return songs) into a monumental epic. It was thus less likely to be universally familiar than was the basic tale of return.

When Odysseus arrives at Eumaeus's steading, the place receives an extended description according to arrival conventions (14.5–28). Eumaeus built it during the absence of both Odysseus and Laertes; this fact both defines him as an exceptionally loyal servant and informs the audience that the scene is unfamiliar to Odysseus. Eumaeus's name does not occur until 14.55, in a narrator's apostrophe. The narrator never formally introduces him, nor does Eumaeus formally introduce himself. Odysseus addresses Eumaeus by name when he blesses him at 14.440, having earlier called him "stranger" and "friend."[5] At 15.363–70, as Eumaeus explains why he grieves for Odysseus's mother,

---

5. This is often taken to be a slip, but surely we are to assume that the other

he describes how she reared him and cared for him only slightly less than her own daughter (this is the only mention of Odysseus's sister). At the request of the disguised Odysseus, Eumaeus describes at length how he came to be enslaved (15.390–429). These passages combined provide a full history.

Significantly, Eumaeus was the son of a king whose name means "wealthy," living on a faraway and happy island. His nurse, a Phoenician woman sold into slavery by Taphian pirates, was seduced by a Phoenician sailor. When she told him her origin, he offered to take her home, and she agreed to steal some gold and the child in her care. After a year, the Phoenicians were ready to leave; the sailor came to the king's house and signaled to the nurse while displaying a precious necklace. The nurse successfully abducted the child but died on the voyage, and Laertes bought Eumaeus. The tale helps explain Eumaeus's loyalty to his master, for the nurse exemplifies the bad consequences of disloyalty. It also explains his generosity to the stranger, who, like Eumaeus, is far from his homeland and a victim of a terrible fall from good fortune.[6] The story also provides a formal basis for Eumaeus's heroic epithets, since he is of royal origin. Eumaeus's patronymic is an obviously significant name; neither the father nor Eumaeus's homeland has any legendary existence outside this tale. Even more than the epithets, they belong to this particular narrative situation, this very *Odyssey*.

The character of Eumaeus belongs to the elaborate mechanism whereby the poet avoids revealing too much about Odysseus's plans. Throughout the Ithacan intrigue, the narrator is reticent about exactly what Odysseus will do.[7] He does not hint at the contest of the bow until Penelope announces it to the disguised Odysseus; instead, he prepares elaborately for Telemachus and Odysseus to attack the suitors suddenly. He likewise gives no hint that Eumaeus will actually fight on behalf of Odysseus, although he establishes Eumaeus's loyalty so that it is not shocking when he does.

The use of heroic epithets for a swineherd fits neatly with the narrator's refusal to introduce the character. The inclusive rhetoric implies that everyone knows all about this swineherd. At the same time, the jux-

---

swineherds have used the name in the course of the various actions narrated at 14.410–39.

6. See Minchin 1992.

7. See Olson 1995, 145–48; Scodel 1998.

taposition of the heroic and the mundane is a puzzle for the audience: what kind of swineherd is "godlike"? The puzzle then receives two solutions. First, the revelation that Eumaeus is really a king's son justifies his epithets. Then, when he fights beside Odysseus against the suitors, the epithet gains a richer reference. Eumaeus's problematic epithets are thus part of the narrator's general refusal to inform the audience too fully of the course of the action in this latter part of the poem. One of the themes of the Ithacan books is precisely the unpredictability of human affairs (the moral of Odysseus's story to Antinous at 17.415–44), and the narrator encourages the audience to appreciate this unpredictability by making his tale surprising.

The presumption of such narrative teasing also offers a new explanation of one of the most familiar problems in Homer, that of Phoenix and the duals of *Iliad* 9. There are two interconnected difficulties. First, when Nestor proposes that he "lead" the embassy to propitiate Achilles, Phoenix has not been mentioned before.

ἀλλ᾽ ἄγετε κλητοὺς ὀτρύνομεν, οἵ κε τάχιστα
ἔλθωσ᾽ ἐς κλισίην Πηληϊάδεω Ἀχιλῆος.
εἰ δ᾽ ἄγε τοὺς ἂν ἐγὼ ἐπιόψομαι οἳ δὲ πιθέσθων.
Φοῖνιξ μὲν πρώτιστα Διΐ φίλος ἡγησάσθω,
αὐτὰρ ἔπειτ᾽ Αἴας τε μέγας καὶ δῖος Ὀδυσσεύς·
κηρύκων δ᾽ Ὀδίος τε καὶ Εὐρυβάτης ἅμ᾽ ἑπέσθων.

(9.165–70)

[But come, let us rouse ambassadors, who will go as quickly as they can to the hut of Achilles, son of Peleus. Or rather, I will see to them, and let them obey. First, let Phoenix, dear to Zeus, be leader, but then great Ajax and godlike Odysseus. Among heralds, let Odius and Eurybates follow.]

Without any explanation, this previously unmentioned character is present at the council of the Greek chiefs. The most recent commentator remarks, "His introduction here as if he were as well-known a figure as Hector . . . is awkward."[8] The moment of selection is especially noteworthy because Nestor at first suggests calling for volunteers, then

---

8. Hainsworth, *Il. Comm.*, 3:85–86 (on 9.182).

changes his mind and selects the ambassadors himself. The change of mind emphasizes his confidence that he knows who is best.

Once the three ambassadors and two heralds set off, the poet uses the dual form of the verb as he describes their progress (9.182, 183, 185).

> τοῖσι δὲ πόλλ᾽ ἐπέτελλε Γερήνιος ἱππότα Νέστωρ
> δενδίλλων ἐς ἕκαστον, Ὀδυσσῆϊ δὲ μάλιστα,
> πειρᾶν ὡς πεπίθοιεν ἀμύμονα Πηλεΐωνα.
>   Τὼ δὲ βάτην παρὰ θῖνα πολυφλοίσβοιο θαλάσσης
> πολλὰ μάλ᾽ εὐχομένω γαιηόχῳ ἐννοσιγαίῳ
> ῥηϊδίως πεπιθεῖν μεγάλας φρένας Αἰακίδαο.
> Μυρμιδόνων δ᾽ ἐπί τε κλισίας καὶ νῆας ἱκέσθην . . .

> (9.179–85)

[The Gerenian cavalryman Nestor, glancing at each one, but especially at Odysseus, gave them many instructions about trying to persuade the blameless son of Peleus.

So the two of them walked along the shore of the resounding sea, uttering many prayers to the earth holder, earth shaker, that they would easily persuade the great mind of the descendant of Aeacus. And they came to the huts and ships of the Myrmidons . . .]

When the ambassadors reach Achilles' camp, they find him singing and playing the lyre.

> τὸν δ᾽ εὗρον φρένα τερπόμενον φόρμιγγι λιγείῃ
> καλῇ δαιδαλέῃ, ἐπὶ δ᾽ ἀργύρεον ζυγὸν ἦεν,
> τὴν ἄρετ᾽ ἐξ ἐνάρων πόλιν Ἠετίωνος ὀλέσσας·

> (9.186–88)

[They found him delighting his mind with a high-toned lyre, a beautiful, elaborately crafted one with a silver crossbar, which he had gotten from the booty when he destroyed the town of Eetion.]

The ambassadors advance without further ado.

> τὼ δὲ βάτην προτέρω, ἡγεῖτο δὲ δῖος Ὀδυσσεύς,
> στὰν δὲ πρόσθ᾽ αὐτοῖο· ταφὼν δ᾽ ἀνόρουσεν Ἀχιλλεὺς
> αὐτῇ σὺν φόρμιγγι λιπὼν ἕδος ἔνθα θάασσεν.

> (9.192–94)

[The two of them went forward, and godlike Odysseus led, and they stood in front of him. In astonishment, Achilles jumped up, still holding the lyre, leaving the seat where he had been sitting.]

In this passage, the hut seems to be a simple structure, without a porch on which visitors could wait to be noticed. Still, it is remarkable that the ambassadors do not wait by the door, as Patroclus does when he visits Nestor's hut (*Il.* 11.644). Achilles is apparently disconcerted by this suddenness. It is unclear whether the phrase "Odysseus led" means that Odysseus is excluded from the two going forward (i.e., a separate leader) or is leading as one of the two (Greek idiom allows both interpretations).

Achilles then uses the duals in his apparently polite address to the ambassadors at 9.197–98.

χαίρετον· ἦ φίλοι ἄνδρες ἱκάνετον ἦ τι μάλα χρεώ,
οἵ μοι σκυζομένῳ περ Ἀχαιῶν φίλτατοί ἐστον.

["Welcome. Truly you two are dear heroes who come. Surely there is great need,[9] you two who are the dearest to me of the Achaeans, angry though I am."]

The poet and Achilles then stop using the dual to refer to the members of the embassy. When the embassy leaves (without Phoenix, who stays with Achilles), only plurals are used.

Hainsworth's commentary provides a helpful summary of the different approaches scholars have taken to the problem of the duals (here listed not in his order and with some additions).[10]

1. Grammatical—the dual is simply used for the plural (the view of Zenodotus, no longer argued by anyone).
2. Analytic (Phoenix is a later intrusion and the heralds do not count) or Neoanalytic (the poet slips into the language of an ear-

---

9. The meaning here is difficult: is the "need" a social propriety (they should visit their friend) or the situation of the Achaean army? I think it is the former.

10. Hainsworth, *Il. Comm.*, 3:85–87. There is also a good introduction in Griffin 1995 (23–25) and a useful bibliography in Heubeck 1974 (71–74).

lier version, either one with two ambassadors or a general epic embassy-type scene with two heralds).[11]

3. The duals refer to two groups, the ambassadors and the heralds.[12]
4. Phoenix, being of lower social status than the others, is counted with the heralds and excluded.[13]
5. The duals refer to the heralds.[14]
6. The earlier duals refer to the heralds, in an echo of their earlier taking of Briseis; the later ones refer to Odysseus and Ajax.[15]
7. The earlier duals refer to Ajax and Odysseus, because Phoenix is ahead "leading," but then Odysseus goes ahead, and the later duals refer to Phoenix and Ajax, since Odysseus is not one of the dearest of the Achaeans to Achilles; or the earlier duals evoke a traditional two-ambassador embassy.[16]
8. Achilles focalizes the scene. Since Phoenix can be taken for granted by Achilles, he does not include him in his greeting, and since the narrator is taking Achilles' perspective, he adopts Achilles' duals.[17]
9. The dual as such echoes the earlier visit of the heralds, but the failure to identify the referent of the dual prepares for the uncertainties of the scene to come; "the very identity of the participating figures is posed as a question."[18]

All these approaches have difficulties. Although there are other difficult duals in Homer, there are none like these, and nowhere does a dual refer to two distinct groups, each including several people. The duals are really problematic, not just a rare grammatical form. Several explanations make them a slip of some kind, whether incompetence on the part of the rhapsode who added Phoenix to the embassy, or the poet's

---

11. See, e.g., Page 1959, 297–300. The fullest analytic discussion is Noé 1940.

12. See Thornton 1978; Gordesiani 1980.

13. See Köhnken 1975, 1978.

14. See Stanley 1993, 351–53 n. 9. However, for Achilles to call the heralds his dearest friends is not courtesy but nonsense.

15. See Segal 1968.

16. See Nagy 1979, 49–55. For the duals as a "reactivation" of an older version, see Nagy 1997, 179–80.

17. See Martin 1989, 236–39.

18. Lynn-George 1988, 54.

drifting into a familiar pattern with the dual.[19] The duals, though, are used repeatedly and by Achilles as well as the narrator, so a slip is hard to credit.

Any answer that requires that the narrator's duals and Achilles' duals refer to different people is inherently difficult, unless the poet is fumbling badly. A listener, having decided who the pair was, would surely attach the duals to the same characters throughout: would the poet have expected his audience to know to whom he referred? Would the poet represent Achilles as greeting the heralds and ignoring the others? "Allusive" interpretations demand too much of the audience. The duals are not a detail in an abbreviated narrative that a listener can overlook without missing the essential point.

There is no real evidence that Odysseus and Achilles were traditional enemies—indeed, the epics make them friends, though opposites and rivals. Achilles does answer Odysseus's speech in this scene by saying that he hates the man who says one thing and keeps another in his heart (9.312–13), and Odysseus is not an ingenuous speaker. But Achilles is here explaining why he himself will be forthright. If Achilles and Odysseus were enemies, it would be extraordinarily foolish for Nestor to propose Odysseus as ambassador. The poet would not make Nestor a fool, and the significance of the embassy vanishes if it is doomed to failure from the start because its members would rouse Achilles' hostility. Even if Achilles hated Odysseus, it would be very rude for him to greet the other two graciously and ignore Odysseus, who is clearly with them. If he did ignore Odysseus, could Odysseus ignore the snub and speak first, as if he had a chance to persuade him? Though Achilles could perhaps ignore Phoenix, if he is of lower status (as well as the heralds, who in this context are clearly subordinate), why would the narrator ignore him? Phoenix will soon deliver an exceptionally long and important speech. Achilles can hardly focalize a scene he does not even know is happening; and the narrator's view is usually quite distinct from Achilles', whose perceptions are limited and wrong. While I agree that Achilles uses the dual because he takes Phoenix for granted, it does not make sense to attribute this attitude to the narrator.

The most convincing suggestion has been that the duals are a mean-

---

19. Janko (1998, 8) uses the mistake as evidence for a dictated text, since the poet did not correct the mistake.

ingful allusion to the earlier visit of the heralds.[20] However, this explana-
tion requires a hearer who can make the association and realize that the poet
has distorted his grammar in the interest of allusion. That is not a realistic
expectation. Moreover, if the poet had wanted the audience to remember
the heralds, he could have repeated the language of the earlier scene more
closely than he does (τὼ δὲ βάτην παρὰ θῖνα πολυφλοίσβοιο θαλάσσης
echoes τὼ δ᾽ ἀέκοντε βάτην παρὰ θῖν᾽ ἁλὸς ἀτρυγέτοιο). (The heralds were
"unwilling" as the referents of the duals are not, and the difference in the
first half of the line means that the sea is "loud-resounding" rather than
"unharvested.") The discussion of Lynn-George (cited in note 18), which
requires a permanent suspension of determinacy, makes the *Iliad* a post-
modernist fiction hard to imagine in oral performance.

   Once we abandon the assumption that the poet seeks immediate
transparency and that any failure of transparency is therefore a slip, we
may link the duals with the sudden presence of Phoenix. Phoenix has no
legendary deeds to make him familiar outside the *Iliad*. Indeed, his role
as educator of Achilles conflicts with Chiron's.[21] Phoenix's father also
has no substance in legend. Both Phoenix's patronymic and his father's
are suspiciously appropriate for the situation at hand: A name meaning
"defender, son of one who rouses himself" denotes a striking pair of an-
cestors for a hero who tries to convince Achilles to return to battle.[22]

   Phoenix himself may be objectively traditional. The details that give
him his character, though, are all contextually bound. What epic per-
formance would include the description of little Achilles on Phoenix's
lap except in an appeal like this one? The Phoenix, Meleager, and *Iliad*
stories have all evidently influenced each other, so that this Phoenix—
the old, loyal, childless tutor of Achilles—belongs only to our *Iliad* or its
immediate predecessors. It is therefore possible and even likely that he
was not well known to everyone, even if his name was familiar.

----

   20. For discussions of the parallels, see Segal 1968; Lohmann 1970, 227–31;
Edwards 1980, 16–17. Edwards points out that in both cases, a messenger scene
becomes a hospitality scene.
   21. March (1987, 22–24) thinks Chiron's role is an innovation aimed at ex-
plaining Achilles' knowledge of medicine, since several passages imply that
Thetis lived with Peleus during Achilles' childhood and that the boy would
have had a "normal" home life—but Thetis also speaks of being at home at his
imagined return (18.440–41; cf. 18.330–32), although she lives with her father in
the sea.
   22. See Mühlestein 1987, 147.

Both the failure to introduce Phoenix and the use of the duals, could be unusually bold extensions of the rhetoric of inclusion. The narrator speaks as if everyone knew exactly who Phoenix was and exactly whom the duals referred to and why the narrator was using them. This creates considerable suspense and perplexity for anyone who does not know these things. The initial passage in which the duals appear is not paradigmatic, so the audience will not disregard the problem and concentrate on the message: instead, the listener will be (mildly) confused.

The embassy includes two major heroes; one hero unknown or little known, who is "leading"; and two heralds.[23] As they leave, Nestor exhorts "each member of the embassy," but especially Odysseus, to try to persuade Achilles. There is already a slight perplexity. Nestor himself has said that Phoenix should "lead." This can hardly mean that the others do not know the way to Achilles' encampment, so it seems to indicate a more general, political leadership. A moment later, though, Nestor seems to be placing his trust primarily in Odysseus.

When the duals start, the hearer must consider who is performing these actions. The listener is unlikely to imagine that the heralds are worrying how to persuade Achilles. The heralds are attendants, guarantors of the truth and solemnity of the actions. Since Odysseus is present, he will surely speak—he has already displayed his persuasive gifts in the poem, and Nestor has given him special instructions. At 9.183, two characters are apparently praying to Poseidon that they will easily persuade Achilles; these should be those who are actually going to speak to him, so Odysseus must be one of them. Odysseus and Ajax are major heroes, so the audience will surely guess that they are meant, but there must be some uncertainty about the function of Phoenix.[24] Perhaps Phoenix was to "lead" literally, by going ahead, but nothing helps the audience decide. It simply has to wait for clarification. At 9.192, two of the ambassadors come forward, with Odysseus in the lead. The listener can infer that Phoenix has not led by going ahead, since Achilles is interrupted while singing to himself.

---

23. Some have speculated that Phoenix was borrowed from lost epic sources; see Kullmann 1960, 133. I find this hard to imagine.

24. Tsagarakis (1979) argues against Köhnken (1975, 1978) that Phoenix is not of lower status than the other ambassadors. He is, however, unquestionably a lesser figure from the audience's point of view.

Achilles' "astonishment" at seeing the ambassadors is not mere mild surprise. The half-line formula ταφὼν δ᾽ ἀνόρουσε [in astonishment he jumped up] appears elsewhere in arrival scenes. The young Achilles leaps up in surprise when he first sees Nestor and Odysseus at the porch of Peleus's home in Phthia (*Il.* 11.777). Eumaeus is mixing wine when Odysseus remarks that someone whom the dogs know must be coming, but when Telemachus then appears, Eumaeus jumps up in astonishment and drops the bowls (*Od.* 16.12–13)—similarly, Achilles forgets to put down his lyre when the embassy arrives. The arrival of the heroes in Phthia is unexpected and welcome; Eumaeus has worried that Telemachus would never return. The formula also describes Achilles' shock after his dream vision of dead Patroclus (*Il.* 23.101). Other usages of the participle ταφών confirm that it indicates not just mere surprise but a response to the supernatural: it is used of Ajax when he perceives Zeus's hostility (*Il.* 11.545), of Patroclus when he is attacked by Apollo (*Il.* 16.806), and of Priam when, on his catabasis-like journey to Achilles' tent, he sees the young man who is actually Hermes (*Il.* 24.360). Achilles' response, then, seems excessive, especially since he might well be expecting an overture from Agamemnon. In any case, his visitors are not travelers from afar or supernatural beings.

The embassy evokes not only the earlier visit of the heralds but the original embassy of Nestor and Odysseus to recruit Achilles, a visit that will be an important topic of Odysseus's speech to Achilles (9.252–59) and of Nestor's later plea to Patroclus (11.765–90). Each of these speeches develops its own moral by using the theme "a father's parting advice, . . ." but each also implicitly contrasts Achilles' enthusiasm for war and his willingness to follow his elders with his withdrawal now. The enthusiasm of the young Achilles was surely an inherited subject. Even a listener who had never heard a full version of the embassy to Achilles could easily infer it, for a great hero is usually eager to fight at the first opportunity (according to *Il.* 11.717–19, Nestor, typically, fought although his father had forbidden him as too young). In relation to this type-scene, Phoenix stands in for Peleus, while Odysseus represents himself. The echo helps explain why Odysseus steps forward and causes Achilles' astonishment: Odysseus is contaminating the theme of the embassy to an angry hero with the recruiting theme. However, the poet has not yet activated (or created) audience memory of Odysseus's role in recruiting Achilles or of Phoenix's ability to represent Peleus.

After his initial surprise, Achilles greets two of his visitors with con-

siderable courtesy and has a meal prepared. This greeting deepens the
mystery and gives it special point. Achilles sounds polite, and he was
extremely gracious to Agamemnon's heralds, who did not expect it
(1.327–44), so the audience will not assume that he is insulting anyone.
After the meal, Ajax nods to Phoenix, and Odysseus notices and begins
to speak (1.223–24). This surely piques the auditor's curiosity further.
Ajax apparently thinks that Phoenix should now speak, but Odysseus
begins instead; the sequence replicates the events that created confusion
about "leading" a minute earlier. But once Odysseus's great speech
starts, the auditor cannot worry about Phoenix or his role; all attention
must be on Odysseus and Achilles.

After Achilles' angry response to Odysseus, Phoenix begins to
speak (9.434), and if this episode is really following the narrative pat-
tern I have suggested, it is no surprise that he explains at length who he
is. His speech conceals the expository function it serves for the external
audience within its function as a pathetic reminder to Achilles of what
he owes Phoenix. Phoenix tells Achilles the story of his life before he
came to Phthia: how he seduced the concubine of his father, Amyntor,
at his mother's behest; how his father cursed him with childlessness;
and how he fled from home in anger and was received by Peleus. Of
course, Achilles knows this already. Phoenix tells it as a *captatio benevo-
lentiae*, a way of asserting his rhetorical authority relative to Achilles,
and also because his flight from home is a negative example for Achilles,
who avowedly intends to leave Troy.[25] The narrative is perfectly "natu-
ral," but once it is over, everyone knows that Phoenix stands in a very
special relationship to Achilles.

Phoenix begins his speech by implying that if Achilles goes home,
Phoenix will not wish to stay behind without him; this gives us a delicate
relationship, in which Phoenix can apparently choose whether to go with
Achilles or remain at Troy. Yet he came to Troy because Peleus sent him.

> How could I be left here alone without you, dear child? It was for
> you that the old horse-driver Peleus sent me, on the day that he sent
> you from Phthia to Agamemnon, still an infant, with no knowledge
> yet of shifting war or of assemblies, where men become distin-
> guished. That's why he sent me, to teach all these things, to make
> you an orator in speech and an achiever in action. (*Il.* 9.437–43)

---

25. See Scodel 1982.

This possibility is confirmed by Achilles' answer.

> You should not love him [sc. Agamemnon], lest you become hateful to me, even though I love you. It is noble for you to join me in caring about the one who cares for me. Be king equally with me and share half my honor. These men will carry their report, but you stay here and sleep in a soft bed. When dawn appears, we will consider whether to go home or stay. (9.613–19)

These passages imply that Phoenix could leave Achilles but that this is not a realistic choice for him. In doing so, he would fail Peleus, his benefactor, and leave himself with no social role. Having no son of his own, Phoenix is dependent on Achilles for his own protection (9.495) and ultimately for that of his land and people. Apparently, he does not regularly sleep in Achilles' own hut as Patroclus does (cf. 9.659–61), but the narrator does not say where he usually stays—presumably nearby in the Myrmidon camp.

The first part of the autobiography of Phoenix seems closely related both to the Meleager story Phoenix is about to tell and to the *Iliad* itself: it involves a quarrel over a woman, a parental curse, and an angry young hero. The second part is closely linked to themes of the poem and to the rhetorical needs of the passage. Peleus is a receiver of exiles elsewhere in the *Iliad*—like his wife, Thetis, he is characteristically a rescuer. Phoenix describes Peleus's generosity toward him.

> He loved me as a father loves a son, an only one, late-born, heir to many possessions, and he made me rich and bestowed on me a large following, and I lived at the border of Phthia and ruled over the Dolopes. (9.481–84)

Phoenix's sense of obligation to Peleus makes his fear of failing him as a substitute father even more poignant. It should perhaps rouse Achilles' sense of duty to his father, since Odysseus has already reminded him and the audience that Peleus explicitly warned his son against anger (9.254–58).

Phoenix then narrates the care he gave the young Achilles:

> But I made you as great as you are, Achilles like the gods, loving you from my heart, since you would not go with another to the feast

or eat in the halls before I sat you on my knees and gave you your fill of food, cutting it up for you and holding out the cup of wine. Often you wet the front of my clothes over my chest, spitting up wine in childish indigestion. (9.485–91)

This passage contradicts what has just preceded it, for if Phoenix lived at the borders of Phthia, he could hardly have been the constant attendant of little Achilles: but this is paradigmatic material, so the audience listens for the point.

As exposition, this speech completely clarifies Phoenix's role in the embassy. Obviously, Nestor chose him for the embassy because of his close association with Achilles. His "leadership" was presumably intended to get the embassy through the door and win them a fair hearing.[26] His presence explains the otherwise abrupt entry; accompanying an intimate of the house, the visitors do not need to wait at the door. The duals Achilles used were addressed to Odysseus and Ajax, the surprise visitors. Phoenix's own arrival would not be a surprise. He does not require such special greeting. By using the duals, Achilles temporarily avoids facing the obviously official nature of the visit and addresses himself to his friends as friends. The earlier duals, then, also referred to Odysseus and Ajax, and the narrator used them *in order* to cause perplexity: Phoenix's role in the embassy is ambiguous, and the narrator wants this to be noticed without explaining it.

If Phoenix was to "lead" the embassy by putting Achilles in a mood to listen and by ensuring that Achilles would not simply refuse to listen to the ambassadors, there might be some tension between Phoenix and Odysseus or, perhaps, between Nestor and Odysseus. From the start, Nestor expects Odysseus to give the important speech and directs his instructions mainly to him, but he is nervous about how Achilles will receive the group and makes Phoenix "leader." He presumably expects that Phoenix will introduce the others if necessary. Phoenix perhaps does not pray on the way to Achilles' tent because he does not expect to have to persuade Achilles to end the quarrel; he only expects to persuade Achilles to listen. Odysseus takes the lead as soon as they enter, however, perhaps overconfident in his persuasive gifts. Thus, Achilles is taken unawares.

Achilles initially justifies Odysseus's confidence by welcoming the ambassadors courteously. Odysseus reasonably misinterprets Achilles'

---

26. Wyatt (1985, 402–3) discusses why the group needs a guide.

behavior as a sign that he is open to persuasion, so he does not wait for Phoenix to speak. Phoenix therefore does not serve the function for which Nestor chose him. But Nestor turns out to have been right that Phoenix would be useful. He is not needed to win the embassy a hearing, but he dissuades Achilles from his initial angry decision to sail home.

On this hypothesis, there is good reason for readers to find the duals confusing—because they are confusing. They increase the mystification around Phoenix. They could be perplexing even to someone who already knows quite well who Phoenix is. Such an auditor would guess that Phoenix is the excluded ambassador, especially when Achilles fails to include one of his visitors in his greeting, but the point of this distinction between Phoenix and the others can only become clear after the speeches. Only someone who is familiar with exactly this version will be immune to surprise. This surprise does not serve merely as a narrative effect. It is revelatory of Achilles' character and state of mind. He is both easier to approach than Nestor feared and more difficult to persuade. Odysseus's recital of Agamemnon's offered gifts only makes Achilles angrier. Phoenix reaches Achilles with the example of Meleager, but Achilles finds in the tale a positive point instead of a dissuasive one and declares that he will fight only at the last minute. Ajax touches him with his appeal to friendship but cannot overcome his anger. Achilles defies expectation.

The narrative never explains why Phoenix was at the meeting of the Achaean leaders, either because the poet had no good mimetic reason to place him there (Phoenix was there so that he could go on the embassy) or because any explicit reason would be distracting and unnecessary. Because it is never explained, however, the audience must take his presence on faith. They may of course speculate about why he was there. Since the Meleager tale indicates that embassies are a feature of the stories about angry heroes that often appear in the tradition (*Il.* 9.574–87; cf. *Od.* 8.75–82), the audience can expect the characters to know the protocol.[27] The audience may assume that Phoenix was present because Nestor or Phoenix himself knew he would be needed. Such guesses do not interfere with the poet's authority to place Phoenix where he wishes.

---

27. Schadewaldt (1966, 142–43) and Kakridis (1949, 47–49) discuss the hero's anger as a traditional theme.

Eumaeus and Phoenix are outstanding instances of the rhetorics of traditionality and inclusion. In the case of Phoenix, the poet delays his explanation to emphasize the unpredictability of Achilles. In the case of Eumaeus, the peculiar effect has ideological implications. The poet constantly, through his language, accents the disjunction between the heroic stature of Eumaeus (who plays a heroic role against the suitors) and his actual social position. The *Odyssey* clearly teaches that nobles may be worthless and impious evildoers, while swineherds may be godlike. The poet, however, places Eumaeus firmly within the tradition. By implying that everyone knows this story already, the poet avoids responsibility for it and declines to draw any moral for the real world. By distancing the implications of the character from himself, he makes the potential message even more powerful, for its authority is not his but the tradition's. He also reduces the danger of offending elite members of the audience. The bard's work is a continual exercise in discretion.

The Social Audience

The Homeric epics practice considerable mystification in the interest of capturing the widest possible audience. They create a narrative audience of connoisseurs. Inviting everyone into the audience, they expend considerable narrative effort to make themselves accessible and to bridge the distance between the narrative and authorial audiences. At the same time, they exploit this distance: others have told the story before, and the narrative audience has heard it before. Thus, they leave no room for questions or disagreements. Likewise, they distance themselves from self-interested, contextually determined storytelling. By providing himself with a source of authority remote from both the oral tradition and the occasion of performance, the poet protects himself from poetic and narrative difficulties. Reliance on the Muses, together with the poet's expository techniques and handling of subordinate narratives, makes it very difficult for anyone in the audience to distinguish familiar, unfamiliar, and invented. Homer tries to control his reception so that the audience will accept everything as equally traditional, equally new.

However, Homeric inclusiveness is not just an approach to narrative technique. The discussion of Eumaeus in the preceding chapter has shown that political and social issues are also involved. Audience members differ not just in how many performances and stories they have heard before and how carefully they have listened to them but in their social identities. They come from specific communities, belong to age-groups, are defined by gender roles, possess or lack wealth, and have varying status in their communities' hierarchies, so the relationship between performer and authorial audience entails more than the audience's familiarity with epic stories. If the bard aims at inclusiveness, he must bridge these distances among the members of his audience. I call this aspect of the authorial audience the *social audience*. Social audiences differ particularly in their reception of the thematic aspects of a story, those that are, at least implicitly, generalizable: audiences who have different experiences and interests may also allot sympathy and criticism differently.

While the *Odyssey* denies that epic performances depend on their immediate contexts, it certainly does not deprive them of relevance. On the contrary, the songs of Phemius and Demodocus have significances that neither their performers nor their internal audiences appreciate. Despite their lack of obvious morals, their subjects— Athena's revenge on the Greeks for their impiety, a quarrel between two great heroes, a god and goddess taken in adultery, the destruction of a city—invite both intense emotional response and moral evaluation. The epics are obviously morally serious in import and have political implications: the *Iliad* treats the consequences of a quarrel between leaders of the Greek army, the *Odyssey* the return of a long-absent king. The poems take place largely in significant public spaces: council meetings, assemblies, palaces where chieftains gather, athletic competitions, the battlefield. With audiences whose political interests were not identical, such political poetry is a likely field of conflict.

Like the other contexts of its composition, the social context of Homeric epic is not easy to reconstruct. The poems themselves, along with the Hesiodic corpus, provide the most important evidence for their social world, the only way to supplement the material record.[1] Scholars disagree about the extent to which the social world represented in the poems is realistic or contemporary with their composition. Since the dates of composition are also in dispute, both the use of Homer as a historical source and the attempt to understand the epics within their historical context are constantly in danger of becoming an endless loop of circular argument. Even if the political and social structures of the epics reflect a real society, scholars disagree about how to describe that society. Is it tribal or already a protostate? Is the *basileus* a king, a chief, or a "big man," and do the poems reflect struggles between kings and the rest of the elite?[2] This is the period of the rise of the polis, the city-state, in which all

---

1. Olson (1995, 199–202) makes some good comments on this problem. The most familiar argument for an (incoherent) amalgam is Snodgrass 1974.

2. I translate βασιλεύς as "king" because I see the *basileus* as having an institutionalized status and making a claim to divine authority. His power, however, is far from absolute. On the *basileus* as king/"big man," see Donlan 1981–82; Qviller 1981. Sale (1994, 40–54) rejects the translation "king" but argues that the Achaean leaders are absolute monarchs in their communities. For the

citizens were in some sense participants, while in the archaic period, aristocrats shared power through rotating offices. The full form of the polis does not yet appear in Homer, but where does Homeric society stand in its evolution?[3] To what extent is Homeric society socially stratified?[4] Is there a class struggle? The poems touch on a variety of issues: the rise of the polis opened to dispute the independence of the individual household, the particular balance of power both among members of the dominant group and others, the composition of the ruling group, and the forms by which ruling elites claimed legitimacy.[5]

Recently, many scholars have placed less emphasis than before on the Homeric epics as historical "sources" and have instead examined them as ideological productions—not as innocent images of a real world, but as interventions in it.[6] This chapter is concerned with a slightly different but related question: how do the epics successfully appeal to a differentiated social audience? To be successful, the epics need not have presented their audiences with a perfect reflection of their own situation or interests. To be appreciated, oral poems need not be set in a contemporary social order; they need to bear relevant, contemporary meaning—a completely different matter.[7] As Koljević says of Serbian epic, "the oral epic singing at its best was both a way of coming to terms with history and a means of getting out of it."[8] Audiences need not share the

---

basileus within the history of Greek kingship, see Carlier 1984, 185–230. There is a rich survey of views of Homeric society in Gschnitzer 1991; I am impressed by Gschnitzer's argument that we need to separate the fluctuating political relations that the epics show from the underlying institutions that they assume.

3. Recent consensus sees the polis as central in Homer: see Raaflaub 1997; Olson 1995, 184–204; van Wees 1992. Scully (1990) sees Homer's polis as largely contemporary yet including the Myceanean citadel in a composite "city."

4. There is a survey of opinion in Thalmann 1998, 243–71.

5. See Donlan 1979. Rose (1992, 43–91) argues that Homer's treatment of aristocracy, particularly of claims of birth, is ambiguous and indeed critical (see also Rose 1997). Stanley (1993, 248–96) connects the *Iliad*'s distance from and irony toward its heroes with written composition.

6. Notable are Morris 1986; Rose 1992, 43–140; Tandy 1997, 166–93; Thalmann 1998.

7. Morris (1986) trivializes "epic distance" as if it were merely decorative. Bani Hilali, for example, clearly takes place in a world quite different from that of its audiences (rural or urban).

8. Koljevic 1980, 320.

specific opinions implied in a performance to enjoy and applaud it; Athenian audiences praised Aristophanes but did not often follow the policies he urged. However, audiences reject narratives whose basic values they do not share.[9] The Homeric epics cannot have been meaningful and relevant to the members of their audience if the broader political questions the stories raise had no parallels in their lives. It is thus possible to consider the social rhetoric of the epics without closely addressing the question of how precisely they depict the contemporary world and reflect its allotments of power.

Understanding the social rhetoric does demand some attention to the reality of the social audience. Other scholars have studied the gendered audience,[10] so I shall not discuss it here. The most important remaining difference among audience members is, crudely put, that between elite and nonelite. Some people were called ἄριστοι (best) in their communities and had both competitive and cooperative relations with their peers in other settlements. Some scholars locate the Homeric epics exclusively within an aristocratic milieu—though the extent to which a true "aristocracy" existed in this period, with high status inherited and clear boundaries between the aristocracy and those outside it, is fiercely disputed.[11] If a well-defined aristocracy existed and its members were the only audience, the epics' ideological function was simple: the aristocrats identified with the heroes of the past and felt justified in their privilege. Even if we believe that the evidence points to less distinction between local chiefs and the most prosperous peasants and to a dominant group whose power was less secure, it clearly makes a difference whether the poets performed only for the chiefs or addressed only them.[12]

The evidence tells strongly against such a restriction of the audience, although the presence of bards at elite feasts certainly implies that some people had more opportunity than others to enjoy epic performances. Demodocus's name, meaning "welcome among the people," sug-

---

9. In New Criticism, the attempt to read sympathetically becomes an important pedagogic goal; see, for example, Brooks and Warren 1959, 276. Cf. Rabinowitz 1987, 34–36; Booth 1988.

10. See Doherty 1995.

11. For arguments for aristocracy, see Murray 1980, 38–57; Latacz 1996, 48–66. For arguments against inherited status, see Ulf 1990, 1–50; Raaflaub 1991, 230–38.

12. Strasburger (1953, 106–10) stresses the peasant-like qualities of the Homeric "kings."

gests that the bard's importance is not confined to the elite.[13] The poet calls him "honored by the people" [λαοῖσι τετιμένον] (*Od.* 8.472), and a few lines later, Odysseus says that bards receive honor and respect among "all human beings on the earth" [πᾶσι . . . ἀνθρώποισιν ἐπιχθονίοισι] (8.479). Demodocus performs at the games, before a "great crowd, thousands" (8.09–10), though his song is not about heroes. Outside strictly bardic performance, Eumaeus is an important internal audience.[14] The self-presentation of song needs to be treated with suspicion; this is socially inclusive rhetoric. If aristocrats were the only patrons and audiences of epic, however, it is hard to understand why such an inclusive rhetoric would prevail. There is certainly no reason in the comparative evidence to associate heroic poetry with exclusively aristocratic audiences: the audiences of many epic traditions have consisted largely of peasants, whether in Bosnia, Egypt, or Rajasthan.[15]

Hesiod offers a different picture. In the *Works and Days*, the speaker is not a professional bard but a farmer. Not only is he independent of the local elite, but he is intensely critical of the "chiefs." The internal audience of the *Works and Days* is the speaker's brother, Perses, and the "chiefs"; the implied audience is willing to share Hesiod's highly critical attitude toward the "chiefs" and evidently consists of people not unlike the speaker, who are in a position to take his advice. These are not members of the most powerful local social group, but Hesiod expects them to have aspirations to attain wealth. He warns them against the temptation to spend winter days in the smithy or the *lesche*, the public gathering place (492–95). They are evidently free to spend time as they choose; they are far from being at the bottom of the social hierarchy, but they are not at the top. Ithaca also has such a public gathering hall (*Od.* 18.329), and it is a plausible location for informal performances.

Hesiod offers further evidence for the actual social inclusiveness of epic performance. Hesiod's *Theogony* praises Hecate's power to help speakers in the assembly, warriors, kings in judgment, athletic com-

---

13. See Kirk 1962, 278–81.

14. Louden (1999, 62–66) argues that the treatment of Eumaeus shows that lower-class people are in the *Odyssey*'s intended audience.

15. By contrast, Alhā excludes women completely (see Blackburn et al. 1989, 197); a standard performance venue in Egypt and Bosnia was the coffeehouse, which excludes women; in Dhola, women are in the audience only when their own households or neighbors are the patrons (see Blackburn et al. 1989, 220).

petitors, horsemen, fishermen, and herds. The lines describing Hecate's help in increasing flocks suggest that her attention belongs to the herds themselves and that their actual caretakers (not their absentee owners) should remember her.

> ἐσθλὴ δ᾽ ἐν σταθμοῖσι σύν Ἑρμῇ ληΐδ᾽ ἀέξειν·
> βουκολίας δὲ βοῶν τε καὶ αἰπόλια πλατέ᾽ αἰγῶν
> ποίμνας τ᾽ εἰροπόκων ὀΐων, θυμῷ γ᾽ ἐθέλουσα,
> ἐξ ὀλίγων βριάει κἀκ πολλῶν μείονα θῆκεν.[16]

(445–48)

[She is good for increasing the flock in the steadings, with Hermes' help. If she wishes, she makes herds of cattle and broad herds of goats and herds of woolly sheep great instead of small or smaller instead of many.]

The notional audience, from which the poet could have excluded real audience members who did not "count," extends through the social scale. As I have already suggested, this particular kind of inclusive rhetoric does not have any point unless these listeners were really part of a possible audience.

M. L. West has argued that the *Theogony* was the poem with which Hesiod won a tripod at the funeral games of Amphidamas. There were no fishermen in Hesiod's inland hometown, and the catalogue of those Hecate helps fits funeral games exceptionally well—if we assume that ordinary people, such as fishermen, were in the audience.[17] These games are the one historical occasion from this period on which we know a poetic competition took place (*Works and Days* 656–57). Like the event Alcinous sponsors on Scheria, the funeral surely included both athletic and musical contests. Such an event included the local population in the audience, while it also attracted competitors and elite guests from farther afield. Not only were nonelite listeners present, but the poet judged it more appropriate to acknowledge than to ignore them, although he places great emphasis on those of high status. While Hesiod

---

16. The text cited is that of West 1966; the textual difficulties are not relevant to my argument.

17. West 1966, 45. I have listed the catalogue entries according to their order in the manuscripts, not according to West's edition.

himself sang a hymn, it is probable that other competitors on this occa-
sion performed heroic poetry, especially since Hesiod includes it among
theperformances that allay grief (*Theog.* 98–100) and expects his audi-
ence to be familiar with epic heroes. A king's funeral is precisely the kind
of occasion on which we expect a display of social cohesion. Even if the
Theogony was not Hesiod's prizewinning hymn, the catalogue of those
Hecate helps implies that the potential audience of this poem, at least,
was not socially restricted. The *Theogony,* as extant, ends with a list of
unions between goddesses and mortals and their heroic progeny
(969–1018) and with the proem to Hesiod's *Catalogue of Women.* There is
no sharp distinction here between a theogony and genealogical poetry
about heroes.

Some scholars see the poems as aristocratic propaganda; Ian Mor-
ris compares epic to a political pamphlet. He suggests that a patron had
it put in writing to save its aristocratic ethos from the change inevitable
in oral tradition, because aristocratic rule was under challenge from the
excluded.[18] The epics, though, can hardly have been such deliberate
self-promotion by patrons acting on behalf of their class. Such a strat-
egy presupposes an exceptional awareness of the fluidity of oral tradi-
tion and a surprising faith in the influence a written text could have.
Even more difficult, it requires full class consciousness and historical
awareness and class solidarity. Certainly the elites of different Greek
communities in the eighth century both cooperated and competed with
each other. But would they have had the kind of class consciousness that
would prompt a Panhellenic effort to influence a long-term historical
process? The patron would have had to make an immense investment
on behalf of his class as a whole. It is easy to believe that the epic ap-
pealed to members (or would-be members) of the elite and that they
used it in various ways to legitimate their power, but this is a very dif-
ferent thing from producing a text with propagandistic intent.

The modern historian, whose perspective is inevitably teleological,
sees that the city-state, all of whose citizens are members of a commu-
nity, inevitably constrained the independent hero of Homeric epic. That
does not mean that the members of the contemporary elite naturally rec-
ognized the rise of the polis as a threat. To many, it may very well have
appeared as an opportunity to formalize and ensure continuing power.
For example, the building of permanent temples—a conspicuous de-

---

18. Morris 1986, 124.

velopment of the period—is an eminently civic activity surely requiring elite patronage and leadership.[19] There could be no single, uniform, Panhellenic aristocratic ideology to promote.

Richard Janko suggests that the poems were written down by a local king to support monarchy and that Pisistratus revived them for that reason;[20] here, too, such historical self-consciousness seems out of place. Contestations were surely more often local and particular, not theoretical, and individual political motives for particular acts of patronage are far more plausible than generalized ones. A patron who sponsored the writing of an epic surely wanted to magnify his own prestige, in competition with his peers. More significantly, such speculations depend on a reductive reading of the texts. Just as the epics pursue various strategies to make themselves accessible at the level of plot, they open themselves to a variety of receptions and appropriations.

If the Homeric epics address nonelite as well as elite audiences and attempt to create an experience of social unity, how do they provide a past that is usable for everyone? Whatever society the poems reflect, they claim to describe the past, and within Greek culture, they provided a durable and shared past that made later Greek identity possible. Greek society and political organization changed enormously not only during the period when the Homeric epics arose and achieved textualization but as they diffused and became canonical. Adequate political and ideological readings should account for their successful reception under widely differing political and social conditions. That rhapsodic competitions continued to be an important part of the Panathenaea in democratic Athens is surely significant.

The epics are textualized, stable enough to be recognizable in repeated performances before different audiences. The avoidance of local reference allowed the same song to be performed in different places on different occasions. The cohesion the epics seek is first and foremost that of an immediate audience, united through shared emotion. This audience may be a crowd temporarily gathered for a festival or a funeral, not

19. On temple building, see Murray 1980, 65. I am not saying that the temples were "class monuments" (cf. Starr 1962, 320). The role of the elite in tomb cult is similarly uncertain (see the bibliography in Raaflaub 1991, 232 n. 94).

20. Janko (1998, 12) writes, "Only a cultural or ideological motivation can account for the desire to record these epics."

a group that could easily define itself by repeated interactions. The imagined audience extends through time, invited by the rhetoric of traditionality to join earlier audiences and later ones. Each performance unites its present audience, but members of each audience may know that the same song is also performed elsewhere. The artificial dialect not only marks the performance as special but invites the audience to enlarge its imaginary temporal and spatial boundaries. Whoever listens and is moved joins an imagined community, one that by the classical period, included all Greeks.

This invented community shares some basic values. Homeric narrative seeks to guide the audience's judgment about central moral concerns: no competent listener commends the suitors or fails to approve the ransom of Hector. Such moral concerns have political implications. The epics create their community in part by representing public opinion as shared and communal. On the surface, the *Iliad* especially represents internal audiences whose reactions—once allowance is made for their different allegiances as Greeks or Trojans—are all the same. Just as ritual allows for individual meaning within a communal, consensual action, Homeric epic creates a mystified unanimity without imposing the hearer's acquiescence in specifics. Both epics evoke basic values that could transcend class boundaries. The *Odyssey*, for example, exploits everyone's attachments to home and community to create sympathy for its hero. Everyone can be expected to admire hospitality and to be horrified at mistreatment of strangers and guests in a story (however different real life might be). The low-status Eumaeus most embodies this virtue. The poem does not allow disagreement about Eumaeus's merits, though it does not dictate particular real-life conclusions.

Just as the poet's complete independence from the circumstances of performance is a fiction, so too is the harmony of audience response— yet not completely. It is surely reductive to assume that any individual in the late Geometric period had a single, unambiguous set of ethical values and political allegiances. Rather, the epics arose within a range of genres and individual performances that supplemented and corrected each other, with audiences that sometimes differed and sometimes overlapped. Hesiod's didacticism and Archilochus's antiheroic attitudes are other sides of the world that created Homeric epic, not a later response to it or voices of a completely different class. There are clear traces of "peasant" attitudes beside the generally "aristocratic" ethos in Homeric epic itself.[21]

Within this loose system, Homeric epic is the genre of social cohesion. This cohesion requires the people to accept elite dominance but simultaneously allows them to view individual aristocrats with a critical gaze. It celebrates a shared moral perspective that gives the common people a decisive voice, even as it defines their opinions as based on the same principles as those of the elite. In praising generosity, epic often simultaneously demonstrated it: a performance sponsored by one aristocrat or a group for the people is itself an action of appropriate generosity and so invites the audience to believe that the patron or patrons share some of the excellence of the heroes.

This surface unity that the shared performance creates does not mean that the epic is interpretively closed. Just as it is condescending and reductive to imagine that everyone in an oral audience has the same knowledge of epic technique and epic stories, there is surely no culture in which stories and their meanings are immune to disagreement and negotiation. Certainly, this period's obvious manifestation of the desire to use the past, cult at old tombs, seems to have had different meanings at different sites and was an area of contest.[22] Indeed, the epics themselves are not univocal. The *Iliad* and *Odyssey* have different political and theological emphases; but there is no reason to believe they had significantly different audiences.[23] Other poems in the epic repertory seem to have diverged even more from the monumental epics than from each other. Patently, the epics were available for different understandings; otherwise, they could not have achieved the canonical status they did during a period of immense change. In Homeric paradigms, the story is always "true," but the application is open to dispute; the epics distinguish themselves from paradigmatic speech by leaving applications open. In practice, the individual hearer can apply the poetic message as he or she chooses; the epics, however, stress a unified public understanding of the past.

That does not mean that the poems are ideologically empty. In the era in which the Homeric epics were created, elites had developed a va-

---

21. See Donlan 1973, 150–54.

22. On early tomb cult and early hero cult, see Whitley 1988; Morris 1988; Antonaccio 1995.

23. For the theological differences, see Kullmann 1985.

riety of new ways to claim legitimacy both within their city-states and beyond them. Epic patronage was surely one of these ways. By concentrating on the deeds of kings, the poems imply that their lives and actions are more worthy of memory than those of common people. Epic as a genre marginalizes most of everyday life.[24] Furthermore, epic views itself as a tradition of praise: heroes eagerly seek to be remembered in it, and the formulaic system constantly reminds the audience of the heroes' excellences. By representing the exemplary past as a society in which great heroes ruled over anonymous crowds, epic legitimates such a social order.

At the same time, epic distance defines the heroes of the past as unmistakably greater than those of the present, and the material world of the epics is more splendid than any reality its audiences could have known. The *Iliad* repeatedly contrasts the strength of its heroes with that of men of its present (οἷοι νῦν βροτοί εἰσ᾽ [as mortals are now], 5.304; 12.383, 449; 20.287). The comparison is to the disadvantage of all mortals of the poet's own time; it implicitly discourages anyone from claiming too close an identification with the heroes, and it makes all present-day mortals equally inferior. So far as epic expresses nostalgia for vanished greatness and grief for the deaths of heroes, it unites the audience in sorrow. Similarly, epic's ability freely to portray the gods means that it constantly reminds the audience of the barrier between mortal and immortal, a barrier that establishes a form of equality among all members of the audience. When the gods serve as internal audience, even the most humble member of the external audience is, in a sense, godlike. When the heroes meet in the presence of a vast assembly, everyone, even the most powerful member of the external audience, is, in a sense, among the crowd. Yet at the same time, everyone can identify with the heroes.

Athletic competition is in some ways parallel to epic performance. Both activities enact conflict while seeking to create cohesion, and both display elite merit for popular approval. Conflicts arise both at the Phaeacian games of the *Odyssey*, when Euryalus offends Odysseus, and at the funeral games of Patroclus in the *Iliad*, where Antilochus and Menelaus argue over second place in the chariot race and where the lesser Ajax insults Idomeneus. In both poems, however, social order is restored without violence, because authoritative arbiters (Achilles, Al-

---

24. See Rose 1997, 165.

cinous) intervene and because the characters have peaceful procedures (the challenge to an oath) for resolving disputes. Conflict is essential to both athletics and narrative; without it, there is nothing to watch or hear. Yet the athletic event usually manages to contain conflict. The bow contest of the *Odyssey* is an attempt to use athletic competition to settle a particular local dispute. In Homeric narrative, athletic competition becomes dangerous when a foreigner defeats local elite, who are thus diminished before their people: Alcinous cleverly deflects the tension caused by Odysseus's evident superiority to Alcinous's own people (*Od.* 8.234–53), while the Thebans attempted to murder Tydeus after such an incident (*Il.* 4.387–98).[25] Ideally, however, participation in athletic competition marks all athletes as excellent, and each competitive event celebrates all its elite participants, even while individuals contend for position within each competing group.[26]

Epic narrative has related social functions. Instead of presenting real, present elite members in competition, however, it tells about violence and conflict in the past, distancing these from a harmonious, though inferior, present. While different members of an audience may have particular preferences among the heroes or somewhat different responses to any given action, these differences are at least partially subsumed in shared enjoyment and emotion.

When Demodocus performs at the Phaeacian games, the young men of the aristocracy also dance and compete athletically with each other for the entertainment of the whole community. The day begins with Alcinous's formal introduction of the stranger to the marveling people in the assembly, and toward evening, Alcinous displays gifts for the stranger from himself and the other twelve "leaders" (*Od.* 8.100–417). Epic performance is thus part of a whole complex of forms of aristocratic display before the people. Alcinous has the singer fetched, and everyone enjoys the same song: the performance is part of a political ritual, an enactment at once of social hierarchy and of cohesion. Everyone present—at least every male—participates as audience, while the elite provides both patronage and competitors.

It is perhaps significant that Demodocus performs at the games a song exclusively about gods. At one level, because the participants are

---

25. Van Wees (1992, 200–206) has an excellent discussion of community involvement in such competitions.

26. Cf. Kurke 1991, 98–99.

divine and so safe from real consequences, the story of adultery can be performed for amusement. The song eases the tension caused by Euryalus's insult to Odysseus and by Odysseus's display of athletic superiority to his hosts. The gods, though, are everyone's social superiors. The human audience can share the laughter of the gods at the embarrassment of Ares and Aphrodite; at the same time, they may be aware that similar events in their own lives would not be funny at all. They are united as inferiors who can judge their superiors and laugh at them.

In the *Theogony*, Hesiod's treatment of the Muses as inspirers of "kings" points in the same direction. Although Hesiod's idealized king helps the injured and so must actually take action for one side or the other in a case, Hesiod emphasizes the ease and authority with which such a king settles a dispute.

> ὃ δ᾿ ἀσφαλέως ἀγορεύων
> αἶψά τε καὶ μέγα νεῖκος ἐπισταμένως κατέπαυσεν.
> τοὔνεκα γὰρ βασιλῆες ἐχέφρονες, οὕνεκα λαοῖς
> βλαπτομένοισ ἀγορῆφι μετάτροπα ἔργα τελεῦσι
> ῥηϊδίως, μαλακοῖσι παραιφάμενοι ἐπέεσσιν.
>
> (85–90)

[And he, speaking unerringly, immediately settles even a great quarrel competently. That is why kings are "intelligent," because they accomplish acts of restitution in the public assembly for the injured, easily, persuading with gentle words.]

In this description, there is some tension between μετάτροπα ἔργα (actions that reverse an earlier injustice) and the passage's emphasis on how easily and quickly the king ends a dispute. Although the king's judgment must favor one of the contending parties, his persuasion causes them to agree, so that restitution apparently ends the quarrel without bitterness. The king's speech is different from that of the bard in being fitted to an immediate situation, but the Muses are appropriate inspirers for kings because such idealized kings, like poets, are neither self-serving nor servants of any faction. Similarly, Odysseus and Nestor are the great orators of the *Iliad* because they consistently seek a communal good. Hesiod's passage illustrates one kind of socially inclusive rhetoric. It might well flatter chiefs who heard it, but it would be relatively easy for even a peasant who deeply resented the local elite to sympathize with the speaker of this passage. He need only judge his own local "kings" not "intelligent" or blessed like those praised here. By praising an idealized king, the passage confers a general legitimacy on kingship but not necessarily on individual kings. Hesiod does not contradict himself in praising the king here and criticizing the chiefs of the *Works and Days*. Instead, both Homer and Hesiod endorse elite rule but criticize elite members who do not deserve its privileges. Left open, however, are the actual politics of how the people could control the powerful when public opinion failed.

When epic characters imagine themselves as subjects of future song and story, they assume these songs will evaluate them. Audiences thus control the long-term glory that is the heroes' greatest goal. According to the dead Agamemnon, Clytemnestra will be the subject of "hateful song" (στυγερὴ . . . ἀοιδή, *Od.* 24.200), whereas the gods will create a lovely song for Penelope (24.197–98). Agamemnon and Hector both assume that a fantasized future judgment should influence one's present actions: it will be shameful for later men to hear that the Achaeans failed to take Troy, while Hector hopes to achieve before dying a deed worthy of remembrance (*Il.* 2.119, 22.305). Penelope, who will be a subject of song, tells the disguised Odysseus that how she treats him will affect her reputation in oral tradition (*Od.* 19.325–34). Agamemnon, Nestor reports, left his wife in the care of a bard, probably because he hoped that being reminded that song remembers human actions, good and bad, would deter her from wrongdoing (*Od.* 3.267–68). Aegisthus disposed of the bard on an uninhabited island, perhaps not only because abandoning the corpse is especially wicked but because a tomb of the bard would itself be a reminder of the power of memory.[27] Social memory is a force of social control. When characters imagine themselves in song, the future audience is undifferentiated and indeed universalized. The verdict of social memory in song is uncontested: good or bad actions lead to appropriate, popular, shared memory.

---

27. Kraus (1955, 69) suggests that the bard would protect the queen through his power to relieve anxiety; Marg (1971, 38) thinks that his intimacy as a frequent entertainer makes him a suitable guardian. Svenbro (1976, 31) suggests that the bard sings about Agamemnon himself. S. West (*Od. Comm.*, 1:176–77) discusses the possibility that the ἀοιδός is a eunuch. Scully (1981) sees the bard as the voice of social norms, while Anderson (1992) argues that Homeric bards do not enforce moral standards and that the poet gives this role to the bard to mark Agamemnon's loss of fame.

Helen apologizes to Hector for the burdens she has caused.

δᾶερ, ἐπεί σε μάλιστα πόνος φρένας ἀμφιβέβηκεν
εἵνεκ᾽ ἐμεῖο κυνὸς καὶ Ἀλεξάνδρου ἕνεκ᾽ ἄτης,
οἷσιν ἐπὶ Ζεύσ θῆκε κακὸν μόρον, ὡς καὶ ὀπίσσω
ἀνθρώποισι πελώμεθ᾽ ἀοίδιμοι ἐσσομένοισι.

$$(Il. 6.355–58)$$

[Brother-in-law, since the burden is especially on your mind be-
cause of me, bitch that I am, and because of the *atê* of Alexander.
Zeus laid a cruel fate on us, so that in the future, we could be top-
ics of song for people who are to come.]

The double causation is significant. In this passage, moral responsibility
clearly belongs to Helen and Alexander; Zeus has caused their wrong-
doing to have spectacular consequences worthy of epic memory. Helen
uses the most neutral and inclusive language for the audiences who will
hear these songs and judge their characters: they are not Greek or Tro-
jan, male or female. The most frequent formula characters use in imag-
ining their future reputations is καὶ ἐσσομένοισι πυθέσθαι [even for
people of the future to hear about]. While only Helen refers directly to
song instead of future reputation more generally, characters within the
poems do not need to make this distinction: whether as audiences of epic
or participants in oral tradition, everyone is a potential judge of the he-
roes of the past. Nobody ever hints that these listeners and narrators of
the future might disagree about how to judge the past. The social con-
trol exerted by concern for memory belongs to the widest possible hu-
man community. This unanimity is of course a mystification. Greek po-
etry reveals intense disagreements about how to assess the heroes: Helen
herself, Odysseus, and Heracles were topics of intense disagreement.
The epics carefully select their stories to control audience sympathies.

The audience is nearly always wiser than the characters, since the
omniscient Muse tells the hearer so much. This knowledge gives addi-
tional force to the significant form of power that the epics offer to every
potential member of the audience: the opportunity to praise or blame
the heroes. Within the epic, the poets enact the power of even the low-
est-status members of the audience by showing their kingly heroes as
constantly observed and judged by their own followers. Furthermore,
either praise or criticism directed at characters within the story could

reflect well or badly on the contemporary world. For Hesiod in the *Works and Days* (156–173e), the excellence of the "demigods" who fought at Thebes and Troy does not justify the present-day "kings"; it shows their injustice all the more sharply by contrast. There are thus, crudely, four possible "political" responses to any moment in the action, as the listener evaluates it favorably or critically and then judges that some corresponding person or situation in the contemporary world is similar or different.[28]

As audiences instinctively realize and Helen reminds us (*Il.* 6.356–58), a serene social order does not generate epic narrative, which must always therefore tend to represent the weaknesses of a social system rather than its strengths. A few passages show what ideal communities look like, and although they are hardly egalitarian, the people share in prosperity and festivity. On Achilles' shield, in the City at Peace, women enjoy the music, dancing, and processions from their doors, while the men attend the assembly as supporters of each side (*Il.* 18.491–508). The plowmen receive cups of wine at the end of each furrow, while a feast awaits the harvesters (18.544–46, 558–60). The *Odyssey* offers the peaceful and prosperous communities of Pylos and Sparta and remote Phaeacia. When Telemachus arrives at Pylos, a sacrifice is in progress at which nine groups of five hundred men each offer nine bulls each (3.5–8). The event clearly includes all the adult males of the community, and the meat supply from the bulls is abundant. When Odysseus begins his story by praising the pleasure of listening to the bard, he says that happiness prevails among the whole people (ἐϋφροσύνη μὲν ἔχῃ κατὰ δῆμον ἅπαντα, 9.6). He can be reasonably sure that this is so, having seen the vast crowd enjoying the games. The praise of the good king includes his justice and the prosperity and well-being of his people (*Od.* 19.109–14). When Achilles abuses Agamemnon by saying that he is a δημοβόρος βασιλεύς "a king who eats his people" (*Il.* 1.231), he appeals to a stereotype of bad kingship. Kings are open to judgment on the basis of their treatment of the people and the extent to which the people fare well under their rule. The poems never show merit, either in war or in council, in the absence of noble birth; even the virtuous slave Eumaeus is a king's son. The poems thus support an aristocratic order. Yet they also show

---

28. I thus agree with Thalmann (1998) that there is a dominant aristocratic point of view, but while he thinks the traces of other views indicate a failure of repression, I see them as a deliberately inclusive strategy.

nobly born leaders who fail to exhibit the excellence their positions require, and they show the conflict between the status conferred by ability and that conferred by birth, wealth, and followers.[29]

Although the *Iliad* and *Odyssey* construct their social audiences somewhat differently, both poems show communities that suffer terribly because of the self-indulgence of spoiled leaders. Whatever the merits of individual heroes, communities fare badly. Indeed, this is a traditional theme: the phrase "destroyed the people" is formulaic for a king's folly.[30] The *Iliad* is defensive about the Trojan War itself. When the Trojan elders see Helen, they say:

οὐ νέμεσις Τρῶας καὶ ἐϋκνήμιδας Ἀχαιούς
τοιῇδ᾽ ἀμφὶ γυναικὶ πολὺν χρόνον ἄλγεα πάσχειν·
αἰνῶς ἀθανάτῃσι θεῇς εἰς ὦπα ἔοικεν·
ἀλλὰ καὶ ὣς τοίη περ ἐοῦσ᾽ ἐν νηυσὶ νεέσθω,
μηδ᾽ ἡμῖν τεκέεσσί τ᾽ ὀπίσσω πῆμα λίποιτο.

(3.156–60)

[It is not a proper cause for righteous indignation that the Trojans and Achaeans with fine leg-armor suffer grief for a long time for such a woman. She is terribly like the immortal goddesses to look at. Still, even so and even as she is, let her go home in the ships, and may she not remain as a source of grief for us and our children in the future.]

Nobody denies that an action is nemesis unless he or she expects someone else to think that it is, and there is indeed a later tradition that condemns the Trojan War. Herodotus has the Persian wise men say that only fools would fight over a woman (1.3). Following the version according to which Helen was in Egypt, he argues that the Trojans would never have let their city be destroyed rather than give her up (2.18.2). The chorus of Aeschylus's *Agamemnon* makes the pursuit of Helen through war an aristocratic excess for which the common people suffer, parallel to Alexander's crime. Here, class implications are overt: spoiled princes frivolously sacrifice their people. In the *Cypria*, Nemesis was Helen's mother (F. 7 Davies). The war itself was Zeus's contrivance for relieving

---

29. See Donlan 1979 on "position" versus "standing."
30. Haubold 2000 is a study of this theme.

the overburdened earth of its excessive population—a borrowing from the Near Eastern flood stories.[31] The adaptation of this motif to the war could be "defensive" of the heroes—making the apparent folly of the war the inevitable result of Zeus's plan—or hostile to them. In one version, the god who suggests the war as a solution to overpopulation is Momus, personified Blame. He is probably based on the Babylonian god Mummu, but his appearance in this context implies that the war, unlike natural catastrophes, makes the deaths the fault of mortals themselves.[32]

Although the Trojan elders defend those who fight for Helen, the elders themselves want to restore her to Menelaus. The *Iliad* does not accept the hostile interpretation of the conflict, but neither does it suppress the critique of the war. Instead, Homer demonstrates the failure of leadership on the Trojan side: Priam is among the elders who among themselves urge the return of Helen. When Antenor urges the return of Helen and Paris angrily refuses, however, Priam effectively sides with his son. Apparently, he would rather continue the war than quarrel with his son before the assembly. Neither the elders nor the people, who want peace, prevail. The *Iliad* also reminds us that Alexander successfully bribed the elder Antimachus (11.123–25). Remarkably, the heralds who report the Trojan assembly to the Achaeans insert a wish that Alexander had died before he brought Menelaus's treasure to Troy (7.390) and say that the Trojans want him to return Helen (7.393). Although they speak before a full assembly, the Trojans address the leaders only—"Son of Atreus and other leading men of the Achaean alliance" (7.385).[33] At Troy, the will of the people does not prevail, so perhaps the heralds assume that they have no reason to address the Achaean people. Hector then compounds this general failure by rejecting the wise advice of Polydamas (18.284–309) and so dooming himself and his city.

Although the poet avoids suggesting that the war is not a worthy cause for the Greeks, the Achaean leaders are open to criticism.[34] The *Il-*

---

31. See Burkert 1992, 100–102; West 1997, 480–82.

32. Momus and Mummu, see Burkert 1992, 103.

33. Sale (1994) argues that Troy is an oligarchy, like the contemporary polis, and that the Achaean kings are monarchs in an unsteady alliance; I think, however, that Priam's weakness is personal, not institutional.

34. Nicolai (1983) argues that the pattern in which individual irrationality leads to collective disaster implies politically that aristocratic councils should control leaders more.

iad does not explicitly refer to the story that Helen's suitors took an oath to defend her husband, so it emphasizes Agamemnon's personal stake in the war. This emphasis makes it even worse that when he quarrels with Achilles, Agamemnon worries more about his own wealth and prestige than about the long-term welfare of his people. Monarchy does not fare well, then; but Achilles also prefers his anger to helping his friends. Similarly, in the *Odyssey,* the Ithacan elite allows its sons to plunder Odysseus's wealth. The suitors assume all the privileges of power with none of the responsibilities—they do not defend the community, oversee their land, conduct festivals to the gods, or settle disputes. Odysseus kills them rather than accept compensation, and only direct divine intervention prevents him from killing their families as well.

The authorial audience that judges the action is modeled inside the poems, not so much by the audiences of the *Odyssey*'s poetic performances, who do not evaluate their action or characters, but by the audiences of the action, who do. In the *Iliad,* both the noncombatant Trojans and the gods constitute audiences for the action.[35] Both the old men who sit on the walls and Andromache, who pleads with Hector, would like the action to take a completely different direction: to save the city, the elders, as a body, would send Helen back (3.154–60); Andromache begs Hector to adopt a more defensive strategy (6.431–39). These hopes are in vain. In speaking them, however, these characters share in the audience's helplessness to change the traditional story. They become model spectators. The gods often have the same function. Because they theoretically have the power to change the course of the action, the *Iliad* poet portrays them not as helpless to convince the human actors but as committed to the events as fated. Thus, when Zeus asks Hera whether to allow the Achaeans and Trojans to settle their dispute peacefully, she not only indignantly insists on the destruction of Troy but tells Zeus that she will not begrudge him the sacking of her own favorite cities of Argos, Sparta, and Mycenae (4.51–54)—a remark that points to the collapse of Mycenaean power.[36] By pointing to the reality of historical change, the poet insists on

---

35. For the gods as audience, see Redfield 1975, 158–59, 213–14, 220–21; Griffin 1980, 179–204; Bremer 1987, 41–43.

36. Kirk (*Il. Comm.,* 1:336) comments that Argos was not destroyed, and he considers this fact evidence against the interpretation of these lines as pointing to the fall of Mycenae. But the Dorian dialect of Argos would surely have been enough to convince Homer's contemporaries that the site had suffered disruption.

both the traditionality of the events he tells and their historical distance. Although, from one point of view, the plan of Zeus defines epic action, the occasions when even Zeus decides not to intervene to save Sarpedon and Hector make him, too, a spectator (16.431–58, 22.167–85). The poet constantly reminds the audience that the events cannot be changed, but that the audience can understand and judge them.

Membership in audiences thus extends from the gods, through the Trojan women and elders, to the ordinary soldiers at Troy and the Ithacans. An audience seems to be present whenever the space of action is not distinctly private, and where reputation is at issue, oral tradition can acquire an astonishing efficiency. At *Iliad* 9.34–36, Diomedes complains before the assembly of how Agamemnon called him "unwarlike and without valor," and he asserts that all the Argives, "young and old," know all about it.[37] He refers to Agamemnon's rebuke of him during the Epipolesis at 4.365–400, which he exaggerates: Agamemnon did not go quite this far, though he did say that Diomedes was inferior to his father in battle. Yet Agamemnon did not deliver this rebuke in an assembly; the only participants in the scene are Agamemnon, Diomedes, and Sthenelus, and the only likely witnesses are Diomedes' own troops. Diomedes assumes, though, that Agamemnon's negative evaluation is public knowledge, and he refers to it in the presence of the entire army, who thus know it now if they did not before. Diomedes apparently takes it for granted that such a rebuke will be a topic of universal gossip, and he speaks before the assembly to vindicate his valor publicly, to the army at large. Suggesting that Agamemnon claims that all the Achaeans are unwarlike and without valor (9.41), he invites the entire audience to share his indignation. The common soldiers do not speak in the assembly, but they are an important constituent of the audience before whom the heroes perform.

Homeric characters constantly watch each other, and they are constantly aware of how others will or might see them. Consider, for example, Sarpedon's famous statement of the "heroic code."

Γλαῦκε, τίη δὴ νῶϊ τετιμήμεσθα μάλιστα
ἕδρῃ τε κρέασίν τε ἰδὲ πλείοις δεπάεσσιν
ἐν Λυκίῃ, πάντες δὲ θεοὺς ὣς εἰσορόωσι,

---

37. The text of Zenodotus reads ἡγήτορες ἠδὲ μέδοντες [leaders and counsellors] instead of "young and old," which is surely inferior.

καὶ τέμενος νεμόμεσθα μέγα Ξάνθοιο παρ᾽ ὄχθας
καλὸν φυταλιῆς καὶ ἀρούρης πυροφόροιο;
τῷ νῦν χρὴ Λυκίοισι μέτα πρώτοισιν ἐόντας
ἑστάμεν ἠδὲ μάχης καυστείρης ἀντιβολῆσαι,
ὄφρά τις ὧδ᾽ εἴπῃ Λυκίων πύκα θωρηκτάων·
οὐ μὰν ἀκλεέες Λυκίην κάτα κοιρανέουσιν
ἡμέτεροι βασιλῆες, ἔδουσί τε πίονα μῆλα
οἶνόν τ᾽ ἔξαιτον μελιηδέα· ἀλλ᾽ ἄρα καὶ ἲς
ἐσθλή, ἐπεὶ Λυκίοισι μέτα πρώτοισι μάχονται.᾽
ὦ πέπον, εἰ μὲν γὰρ πόλεμον περὶ τόνδε φυγόντε
αἰεὶ δὴ μέλλοιμεν ἀγήρω τ᾽ ἀθανάτω τε
ἔσσεσθ᾽, οὔτέ κεν αὐτὸς ἐνὶ πρώτοισι μαχοίμην
οὔτέ κε σὲ στέλλοιμι μάχην ἐς κυδιάνειραν·
νῦν δ᾽ ἔμπης γὰρ κῆρες ἐφεστᾶσιν θανάτοιο
μυρίαι, ἃς οὐκ ἔστι φυγεῖν βροτὸν οὐδ᾽ ὑπαλύξαι,
ἴομεν, ἠέ τῳ εὖχος ὀρέξομεν ἠέ τις ἡμῖν.

(Il. 12.310–28)

[Glaucus, why are we outstandingly honored in Lycia, in seating, with meat, with extra cups of wine, and everyone looks toward us like gods, and we cultivate a great *temenos* [land allotment] by the shores of Xanthus, fine both in orchards and in grain-bearing plowland? Therefore we should go and stand among the front line of Lycians and meet parching battle, so that one of the heavy-armed Lycians may say, "Our kings do not without glory rule in Lycia and consume rich wine and choice sweet wine. No, there is noble strength in them, too, since they fight in the forefront among the Lycians." Dear friend, if it were the case that if we escaped this war, we would thereafter be permanently ageless and deathless, neither would I myself fight at the front, nor would I send you into battle where men win glory. But since, in fact, there are over us anyway ten thousand death demons, which no mortal can flee or evade, let us go, and we will give someone reason to boast, or someone will give it to us.]

Sarpedon's exhortation falls into two distinct parts. One argument for risking one's life is that death is inevitable in any case; the other, however, depends on the hero's status. Sarpedon receives various privileges as a king. He does not imply that if he does not fight bravely, he will lose these advantages. Instead, he imagines what his own community will say. If he fights well, his honor and his material advantages will not be resented.

This concern is distinct from the common heroic anxiety about general reputation after death: Sarpedon is thinking specifically of his own people and what they think of him. The formula μάχης καυστείρης ἀντιβολῆσαι appears only one other time in the *Iliad*, when Agamemnon rebukes Odysseus and Menestheus, and there, too, the theme is the contrast between fighting and feasting (4.342). Battle is hot and consuming, while an elite that does not fight (or otherwise govern) merely consumes. The suitors of the *Odyssey* represent such a group.[38] Still, the anonymous speaker evidently feels that the community shares in the prestige of its leader's fame. Sarpedon is fighting for his Trojan allies, not to defend Lycia or benefit his own community directly. The exchange between leaders and people is thus not straightforwardly material, with one side surrendering its material surplus and providing deference in return for protection or the maintenance of justice—an important function of kings that Sarpedon ignores here. Instead, the community participates vicariously in the kings' competition for glory. This view projects onto the common people what the elite would like them to think; but it also gives them a basis on which to blame the elite.

Such anonymous representative comments are an important device of the epic. Their judgments are not performances by their speakers and are not attempts at persuasion. The comments are brief, and it is easy to allow for any ironies or hyberbole in them, whereas other ideologically marked passages, such as the speeches of the Thersites episode, are persuasive performances that do not pretend to represent accurately their speakers' "real" judgments. The *Iliad* and *Odyssey* use representative comments very differently, however.[39] In the *Iliad*, both the "real" representative comments reported by the narrator (nine in the *Iliad*, fourteen in the *Odyssey*) and the representative comments imagined by the characters (eight in the *Iliad*, three in the *Odyssey*) locate the heroic actors in a world of critical inferiors. Judging is largely what these speeches do, directly or indirectly. At *Iliad* 2.271–78, the (Achaean)

38. See Rose 1992, 100–101. However, I do not agree with Rose that the suitors are "oligarchs." Except in their hopes of becoming *basileus*, they are apolitical. On the suitors more generally see Said 1979.

39. See de Jong 1987b.

speaker praises Odysseus for his handling of Thersites; at 3.297–302, the (Achaean or Trojan) speaker prays for the complete destruction of whoever violates the peace oath; at 3.319–23, he prays for peace and for the death of whoever is responsible for the war. At 4.80–84, the speaker responds to Athena's descent by recognizing that whether there will be war or peace depends on Zeus; the speaker at 7.178–80 (again an Achaean) prays that Ajax, Diomedes, or Agamemnon may win the lot to fight Hector, and at 7.201–6, he prays that Ajax may win or that there be a tie. At 17.420–22, an anonymous Trojan urges his comrades to fight even if they all perish, while at 22.372–74, an Achaean comments on how it is much easier to touch the dead Hector than it was while Hector was attacking the ships. The passage at 7.178–81 is particularly revealing, because the narrator comments a moment later that Ajax was "whom they themselves wanted" (7.182), identifying the general judgment even more clearly than does the prayer itself. This evaluation concurs with the authorial statement in the Catalogue of Ships that Ajax was the best man after Achilles (2.768–69). Six of the nine representative comments reported by the narrator in the *Iliad* either openly or implicitly evaluate the main actors. All but the Trojan's words of encouragement in battle are the comments of spectators, men who cannot themselves act effectively and who must instead watch and pray.

The tone of the anonymous speech over Hector is hard to judge, for the speaker both vaunts over Hector's death and admits that he himself could not resist him. Other narrative information confirms these evaluations. Before the duel between Menelaus and Paris, both sides pray for an end to the war and for the death of the man responsible. After Paris disappears, the narrator explains that the Trojans and allies would not have concealed him from Menelaus, "for he was as hateful as black death to all of them" (3.454). The device of allowing one speaker to pronounce a sentiment for everyone makes these opinions communal. Furthermore, the two armies have a right to judge. The authorial audience need not concur, perhaps, but the narrator certainly invites his hearers to sympathize with their situation, and their assessments are reasonable. Where the actions of the leaders and the judgments of the people are sharply at odds, as when the Trojans do not return Helen, the leadership has failed.

The *Iliad*'s heroes frequently consider what such representative others will say about them. Hector especially fantasizes: he imagines the Greek who will see Andromache in slavery and remember Hector's valor (6.460–61); he imagines a future Trojan who will say that Astyanax is much better than his father (6.469); he imagines seafarers who will see the tomb of a warrior Hector has slain in single combat (7.87–91); he urges that the duel end with an exchange of gifts, so that a Trojan or Achaean may comment that Hector and Ajax separated in friendship after fighting (7.299–302); he imagines an inferior who will say, "Hector destroyed his people through overconfidence in his own might" (22.106–7). Agamemnon, fearing that the wounded Menelaus will die, imagines a Trojan who jumps on his tomb and boasts (4.176–81). Menelaus asks the "leaders and advisors of the Argives" to judge fairly between Antilochus and himself, lest anyone sometime say that Menelaus, though his horses were inferior, defeated Antilochus through falsehood and higher status (23.573–78).

The last example is especially interesting, for it is not completely clear whether the issue is Menelaus's reputation alone or that of the other Achaeans also. Again, is Menelaus concerned only that his second-place victory receive the praise it deserves, untainted by any suspicion of unfairness, or is he worried about acquiring a broader reputation for using social pressure to get his way? At the very least, the value of winning is diminished if the audience believes the victory unfair. If the concerns are taken broadly, the reputations of all the Achaean leaders are in danger: Menelaus turns to them precisely so that the judgment may compel public assent as the verdict of the entire elite. Then, however, he changes his mind and demands an oath instead. So it is Antilochus whose public standing is endangered, since to be truly successful, he must not only take the oath but persuade the crowd that his oath is true. Once he yields, Menelaus gives him the prize, "in order that these men, too, may know that my mind is never proud and harsh" (23.610–11). He thereby echoes Antilochus's earlier insistence that if Achilles wishes to console Eumelus, he should not distort the order of victory but should give Eumelus an additional prize, "either in the future or right now, so that the Achaeans will praise [Achilles]" (23.551–52). Anonymous speech, real or imagined, is the voice of communal control. Even though Zeus regularly bullies the other gods and insists that he is more powerful than all of them combined, he, too, yields to the modest threat phrased "we other gods will not praise you" (16.443, 22.181), without questioning whether Hera and Athena speak only for themselves.

Praise and blame are the weapons of the weak. The *Iliad* heroes' concern for what the people will say does not always lead to wise action. Hector fears the immediate criticism of the people and ignores the possibility of even more severe criticism in later tradition. Nonetheless, the heroes' frequent worry about public opinion prompts the audience to participate in evaluating them. At the same time, the poet implies that this evaluation will be stable and shared. Members of the elite disagree furiously with each other in the assembly, with the people as audience; but the people's responses are unanimous.

In the *Odyssey*, by contrast, anonymous speech does not primarily mark the force of positive social control. Reputation is as powerful a force as it is in the *Iliad*—Athena sends Telemachus on his travels to win him a good reputation and reminds him of the good fame Orestes has won. But the poet seldom uses anonymous speech to represent social control. Nausicaa imagines a social inferior who will criticize her if he sees her with Odysseus (6.275–84), and she herself would criticize a young woman who violated the norms of sexual behavior (6.285–88). Eurymachus does not want to allow the beggar to try the bow.

> We are ashamed at the talk of men and of women, lest someone else, inferior among the Achaeans, may say, "Truly, lesser men by far are courting the wife of a blameless man, and they cannot bend his polished bow. But someone else, a beggar, came wandering and easily bent the bow, and shot it through the iron." So they will say, and it will be a reproach to us. (21.323–29)

Eurymachus has already called it a reproach "even for those in the future to hear about" that the suitors are so much weaker than Odysseus and cannot bend the bow (21.253–55). Penelope tartly points out the paradox of this worry about reputation: those who dishonor a king's house by devouring his substance have no good reputation among the people (κατὰ δῆμον) anyway (21.331–33).[40] The suitors, however, are not afraid of public disapproval in itself; they—or, at any rate, Eurymachus and Antinous—are afraid of contempt, which would reduce their power. That Eurymachus feels shame at what the Ithacans will say about the bow contest is itself a comment on his lack of shame about public opinion more generally.

---

40. I do not agree with Adkins (1960, 38–39) that Penelope is here engaging in persuasive definition. Consider Menelaus's comment that when Odysseus comes, the suitors will be like fawns left in a lion's den (4.333–40): the suitors' behavior prompts unfavorable comparisons.

The *Odyssey* does not report a negative public opinion about the suitors. In the Ithaean assembly, Halitherses warns the suitors and the people (2.161–76); Mentor rebukes the people for not restraining the suitors (2.239–41). The people are thus implicated in the suitors' deeds, but the poet does not use anonymous speech to report public opinion. Although Antinous says that Telemachus is trying to attach blame to the suitors (μῶμον ἀνάψαι, 2.86), there is no sign that the Ithacans apart from the two speakers in the assembly criticize the suitors. The narrator does not report their thoughts. Instead, he most often reports anonymous speeches by the suitors. Only when a passerby hears music and dancing inside Odysseus's house and criticizes Penelope for remarrying (23.148–51) does the anonymous voice serve social control.

The *Odyssey* probably differs so much from the *Iliad* in its use of anonymous speech partly because it is so concerned with deception and partly because it demands a less complex distribution of sympathy. The *Iliad* tries to generate pity for the Trojans while making it clear that they are in the wrong. It demands identification with Achilles along with recognition of the terrible consequences of his actions. Anonymous comments place the actions of the leadership within their social context. The *Odyssey* has a much sharper distinction between good and bad, and its chief effort in directing audience response goes toward maintaining complete sympathy for its hero despite his loss of his crew and the ruthless killing of the suitors. While the *Iliad* blames the sufferings of the Trojans mostly on Paris and secondarily on the rest of the Trojan elite, who failed to control him, the *Odyssey* blames the deaths of Odysseus's men and, even more, the deaths of the suitors on themselves.

The people, too, are portrayed as being in the wrong for not stopping the suitors.[41] But the demos is incapable of action without strong leadership from above. When Telemachus summons the assembly, it has not met since Odysseus left (2.26–27), which suggests that the people have lost the habit of collective action or even judgment. Antinous urges the suitors to murder Telemachus "in the country far from town or on the road" (*Od.* 16.383–84), before he can address the people. He fears that Telemachus will be able to rouse the populace to drive the suitors into exile when he divulges their unsuccessful attempt to murder him; "they will not praise evil deeds when they hear about them" (16.375–86). He assumes, however, that once Telemachus is dead, the people will ac-

---

41. See Olson 1995, 202–3.

quiesce, both because nobody will lead them and because there will be no alternative. Alive, Telemachus can use the attempt to kill him against the suitors. Popular action requires both leadership and a focus for anger.

In a meeting after the slaughter of the suitors, Eupeithes, Antinous's father, rouses the suitors' families against Odysseus, claiming that it will be "an outrage for those in the future to hear about" if they do not avenge themselves on the killers of their sons and brothers (24.433–35). Medon comes from Odysseus's house to warn the group that Odysseus had divine help, while Halitherses reminds the people that they themselves are to blame, because they did not restrain the suitors (24.451–62). These speeches blur the distinction between the people attending this meeting, initially a gathering of relatives collecting the suitors' corpses (24.417–19), and a full assembly of Ithacans. They begin with the formula Κέκλυτε δὴ νῦν μευ, Ἰθακήσιοι, ὅττι κεν εἴπω, which introduces assembly speeches (24.454 = 2.25, 2.161, and 2.229, and 24.443 is identical in the first two-thirds of the line). One group then follows Eupeithes, while others are convinced by Halitherses.[42] The poet thereby gives the audience a group with whom to identify.

Characters also regularly blame the people for ingratitude toward Odysseus, idealizing his rule and praising him as a king who deserves gratitude for his exceptional benignity toward his people. Penelope says to the herald Medon:

οἳ θάμ' ἀγειρόμενοι βίοτον κατακείρετε πολλόν,
κτῆσιν Τηλεμάχοιο δαΐφρονος. οὐδέ τι πατρῶν
ὑμετέρων τὸ πρόσθεν ἀκούετε, παῖδες ἐόντες,
οἷος Ὀδυσσεύς ἔσκε μεθ' ὑμετέροισι τοκεῦσιν,
οὔτε τινὰ ῥέξας ἐξαίσιον οὔτε τι εἰπὼν
ἐν δήμῳ: ἥ τ' ἐστὶ δίκη θείων βασιλήων·
ἄλλον κ' ἐχθαίρῃσι βροτῶν, ἄλλον κε φιλοίη.
κεῖνος δ' οὔ ποτε πάμπαν ἀτάσθαλον ἄνδρα ἐώργει·
ἀλλ' ὁ μὲν ὑμέτερος θυμὸς καὶ ἀεικέα ἔργα
φαίνεται, οὐδέ τίς ἐστι χάρις μετόπισθ' εὐεργέων.

(4.687–95)

---

42. The Greek of the relevant passage is difficult, so that it is uncertain whether the majority, who jump up yelling, belong to Eupeithes' or Halitherses' party; I agree with Heubeck (*Od. Comm.*, 3:410) that the majority is probably with Eupeithes.

[You gather often and lay waste much substance, the property of
wise Telemachus. Did you not hear from your fathers, when you
were children, what kind of man Odysseus was to your parents? He
never did anything unfitting to anyone or said anything unfitting
among the people. That is the norm among godlike kings: he will
hate one person and may love another. Yet that one did nothing out-
rageous at all to any man. But your minds and your ugly actions are
clear enough, and there is no gratitude for prior benefactions.]

Penelope is of course an interested speaker trying to convince. The poet
does not expect his audience to assume that most kings are habitually
unfair; criticism of kings is not the point of the speech.[43] Rather, the poet
expects his audience to take human imperfection for granted. Kings, be-
ing only human and having power, sometimes act arrogantly, unfairly,
or whimsically. According to Penelope, Odysseus, however, never in-
jured anyone at all: his fairness exceeded the usual mortal standards.
Such extraordinary virtue demands gratitude, shown by protecting his
heir and property. It is difficult to be certain at whom exactly Penelope
directs this reproach; she seems to slip from the suitors to the Ithacans
or not to distinguish between them. If Penelope is including Medon
himself in her accusation, she is being unfair, since he has come to re-
port the suitors' plot against Telemachus, which he has overheard. But
she is not speaking publicly, and rebukes tend to be exaggerated and un-
fair. They are a performance genre, to be evaluated for rhetorical effect,
not literal truth.[44]

    The poet has already developed the theme of the Ithacans' ingrati-
tude: various speakers (Telemachus at 2.47; Mentor at 2.230, 234; Athena
at 5.8, 12) have claimed that Odysseus as king was "as kind as a father"
or "kind and gentle." Penelope's complaint thus reiterates and specifies
this "kindness" of Odysseus. Mentor and Athena have both couched

---

    43. Van Wees (1992, 78–79) ignores the rhetorical exaggeration of blame
speeches, whether the are aimed at princes or people.
    44. Stanford (1967, 287) says that at 4.686, Penelope identifies Medon with
the suitors' destructiveness, while at 4.688, she addresses Medon and the Itha-
cans; West (*Od. Comm.*, on 4:686) also takes the verb κατα κείρετε as referring to
Medon and the suitors. But Penelope's second-person plurals may not really in-
clude Medon; because he is a herald, she speaks as if she were giving him a mes-
sage to deliver.

their praise of Odysseus's kingship as an ironic imperative for other kings:

μή τις ἔτι πρόφρων ἀγανὸς καὶ ἤπιος ἔστω
σκηπτοῦχος βασιλεύς, μηδὲ φρεσὶν αἴσιμα εἰδώς,
ἀλλ' αἰεὶ χαλεπός τ' εἴη καὶ αἴσυλα ῥέζοι,
ὡς οὔ τις μέμνηται Ὀδυσσῆος θείοιο
λαῶν, οἷσιν ἄνασσε, πατὴρ δ' ὣς ἤπιος ἦεν.

$$(2.230–34 = 5.8–12)$$

[Let not any scepter-bearing king be wholeheartedly kind and gentle anymore, and let not any be right-minded; instead, may he be harsh and act wickedly, since nobody among the people he ruled remembers godlike Odysseus, though he was gentle as a father.]

Here, there are two extremes for the king: the complete benignity of an Odysseus and the harshness of a ruler who has realized that virtue is unrewarded.

These passages in praise of Odysseus appear early in the poem because the narrator needs to establish Odysseus's cause as worthy from the start. Because this particular praise of Odysseus implies that nobody could have a legitimate complaint about him, it enables sympathy for the hero to escape politics altogether. Although the specific qualities of Odysseus's kingship are not those of Hesiod's Muse-inspired king, the effect that the praise of him has on the listener is similar—this praise demands respect even from the potentially disaffected. The poet does not invite questions about the structure of the political order, such as whether the aristocracy in general deserves its privileges. Instead, he depicts one group, the suitors, who fulfill neither the functions for which Sarpedon deserves his people's praise nor those for which a Hesiod can praise kings: the suitors neither fight nor promote cohesion by resolving disputes. Indeed, the suitors encourage a fight between the disguised Odysseus and the beggar Irus for their own entertainment. On the other side is a king whose observance of norms has been exemplary. The poem encourages a common response that unites listeners across the social hierarchy. However, the fairy-tale division into good and bad—and the reminders that Odysseus's goodness was extraordinary—discourages the audience from drawing too simple a political moral.

The flight to the ships and Thersites' intervention in the *Iliad* seem to be glaring exceptions to the Homeric epics' usual attempts to unify audience responses. Here, the protagonist, Odysseus, appears so to invoke social order against the common soldiers as to antagonize nonelite members of the audience. Scholars thus tend to interpret the episode either as a straightforward affirmation of aristocratic dominance or as the expression of a counterideology.[45]

This is an immensely complex sequence from the perspective of audience response. With a false dream, Zeus impels Agamemnon to initiate a full-scale battle, so that Achilles' prayer may be fulfilled. Agamemnon then decides to feign discouragement to test his troops. The audience is better informed than the leaders, who in turn know more than the ordinary soldiers. The audience also knows the basic structure of the Trojan story, in which the *Iliad* is a mere interruption, and thus that the Achaeans will soon take Troy. In such a narrative situation, amid multiple ironies, no simple responses are likely. The modern reader is likely to sympathize with the current in Greek thought that sees the war itself as futile and foolish and that thus easily supports the move homeward. Within the episode, though, the only apparent reason the Achaeans wish to abandon the war is their despair about not winning it, and the listener knows that this despair is misplaced. The flight to the ships is an affront both to Greek pride and to "fate" (2.155)—to the story as the audience knows it. The combination encourages the audience to place its sympathy with Odysseus.

Odysseus's rhetoric is not socially inclusive, however. As he stops the army's rush to the ships, he rebukes the leaders and the ordinary soldiers in very different terms—although he uses the same vocative for both, δαιμόνιε (meaning, literally, "under the influence of a supernatural force)."[46] He speaks gently to kings but even uses the scepter to drive the common men back (2.199). The difference in treatment is especially striking because Athena has told him only to "restrain each man with gentle words" (2.180). Yet he speaks to the troops insultingly.

---

45. The fullest treatment is Thalmann 1988, with bibliography.

46. The word is frequent and is used to refer to anyone whose behavior seems unusual to a speaker, marking the speaker's emotional involvement; see Brunius-Nilsson 1955, 42 ("uttered spontaneously and impulsively at especially emotional moments").

δαιμόνι᾽, ἀτρέμας ἧσο καὶ ἄλλων μῦθον ἄκουε,
οἳ σέο φέρτεροί εἰσι, σὺ δ᾽ ἀπτόλεμος καὶ ἄναλκις,
οὔτέ ποτ᾽ ἐν πολέμῳ ἐναρίθμιος οὔτ᾽ ἐνὶ βουλῇ·
οὐ μέν πως πάντες βασιλεύσομεν ἐνθάδ᾽ Ἀχαιοί·
οὐκ ἀγαθὸν πολυκοιρανίη· εἷς κοίρανος ἔστω,
εἷς βασιλεύς, ᾧ δῶκε Κρόνου πάϊς ἀγκυλομήτεω
σκῆπτρόν τ᾽ ἠδὲ θέμιστας, ἵνα σφίσι βουλεύῃσι.

(2.200–206)

[You fool, sit down peacefully and listen to the speech of others who
are mightier than you, while you are unwarlike and without valor,
of no account either in war or in council. We Achaeans cannot all be
kings here. Rule by many is not a good thing. Let there be one ruler,
one king, to whom the son of wily Cronus has given the scepter and
the traditional laws, so that he shall be king over them.]

Odysseus's rebuke is harsh. It is not the case, however, as some inter-
preters have thought, that the troops are only doing what Agamemnon
has just urged.[47] While Agamemnon's speech suggested that they aban-
don the expedition, the protocols of the assembly clearly do not enjoin
that anyone respond to such a speech—even when made by the com-
mander—by rushing out to the ships and yelling without waiting to see
how the other leaders will respond. Agamemnon's speech, while urg-
ing the army to give up, has also stressed the shame that will result—
shame even people in the future will hear—because the Achaean army
fought so long without result (2.119–20). The wise listener would hesi-
tate in responding. The troops here show themselves to be not only
undisciplined but an incompetent audience.

Rebukes in the poems are often less than entirely fair, as I have al-
ready shown, and hearers schooled in the traditional style knew how to
adjust for this exaggeration. Only a little later in the poem, Agamemnon
rebukes Odysseus himself (4.338–48). He accuses Odysseus of being
slow to enter battle and calls him "excellent in evil deeds of cunning"
and "crafty-minded," to which Odysseus replies angrily. Even later,
when Agamemnon yet again suggests flight (14.65–81), Odysseus re-
bukes him abusively (14.83–102), saying that Agamemnon's remarks are

47. See Martin 1989, 67–77. Fenik (1968) discusses "the rebuke pattern" in Il-
iadic battle; rebukes are so frequent that they are clearly a part of the machinery.

both stupid and unworthy of a man in his position. Experienced listen-
ers know that mutual loyalty does not prevent epic characters from
speaking harshly to each other.[48]

In the case of Odysseus's rebuke of the fleeing trooops, the listener
may also be somewhat distanced from the crowd in the story, since the
audience knows that flight is mistaken. By itself, then, this passage might
not alienate from Odysseus's side even a nonelite listener who would re-
sent such treatment in real life. Further, interpreters have not sufficiently
acknowledged the strangeness of the last section of Odysseus's rebuke.
There is no "one ruler" or "one king" who directs this army, and each
of those to whom Odysseus spoke more gently is himself a "king"
(βασιλεύς, 2.188). The whole intention of the test was that when Aga-
memnon proposed flight, the other "kings" should speak against the pro-
posal. The "one ruler" must be Agamemnon, yet the narrator describes
Odysseus himself as "ruling" (κοιρανέων) the army as he brings it under
control. Odysseus here glides from insisting on the nonelite status of the
common soldiers to placing everyone except Agamemnon in the same
category. This rhetorical swerve prepares for the rest of the episode (in
which Agamemnon's position is an important theme), but it also softens
the contrast between kings and others. Odysseus demonstrates the be-
havior he encourages by acting on behalf of Agamemnon.

When the Achaeans return to the assembly, Thersites speaks. The
poet carefully marks Thersites' abnormality: Thersites is extraordinarily
ugly, receives no patronymic, and regularly violates the norms of epic
speech.[49]

> ... ὃς ἔπεα φρεσὶ ᾗσιν ἄκοσμά τε πολλά τε ᾔδη
> μάψ, ἀτὰρ οὐ κατὰ κόσμον, ἐριζέμεναι βασιλεῦσιν,
> ἀλλ᾽ ὅ τι οἱ εἴσαιτο γελοίϊον Ἀργείοισιν
> ἔμμεναι·

> (2.213–16)

---

48. See Holoka 1983, 6 (although he does not recognize that Diomedes, e.g.,
shows his resentment of Agamemnon's rebuke later, at 9.34–36, in another situ-
ation [i.e., assembly] where harsh speech is authorized.

49. The poet does not uncritically equate merit with good looks: the phrase
εἶδος ἄριστε, [best [only] in appearance], is an insult for Paris (3.39, 13.769), while
the handsome Nireus is otherwise completely undistinguished (2.673–75). How-
ever, these disjunctions are striking because they are supposed to be exceptions,
and Thersites' extreme ugliness is surely a sign of his social exclusion.

[. . . who had many words without any order in his mind, to no
point, inappropriate, for provoking the kings—whatever he thought
would be ridiculous for the Greeks.]

Unfortunately, the lines that describe the emotional state of the Achaean
audience are difficult.

ἔχθιστος δ᾽ Ἀχιλῆϊ μάλιστ᾽ ἦν ἠδ᾽ Ὀδυσῆϊ·
τὼ γὰρ νεικείεσκε· τότ᾽ αὖτ᾽ Ἀγαμέμνονι δίῳ
ὀξέα κεκλήγων λέγ᾽ ὀνείδεα· τῷ δ᾽ ἄρ᾽ Ἀχαιοὶ
ἐκπάγλως κοτέοντο νεμέσσηθέν τ᾽ ἐνὶ θυμῷ.
αὐτὰρ ὃ μακρὰ βοῶν Ἀγαμέμνονα νείκεε μύθῳ·

(2.220–23)

[He was extremely hateful above all to Achilles and Odysseus. For
he abused those two. But this time, he spoke reproaches against
godlike Agamemnon, shouting shrill. The Achaeans were furiously
angry at him, and their minds were full of indignation. But he, call-
ing loudly, abused Agamemnon in a formal speech.]

Is the "him" at whom the Achaeans are furious Agamemnon or Ther-
sites? If the former, Thersites is the otherwise suppressed voice of the
multitude, who sides with Achilles.[50] If the latter, then the people in the
crowd, although they may be eager to abandon the war, are not neces-
sarily resentful of Agamemnon.

It is far likelier that the army is angry at Thersites. As E. Lowry has
shown, Thersites is αἴσχιστος, both "ugliest" and "most shameful," and
there is a close association in Homeric language and thought between
shame and righteous indignation, the νέμεσις implicit in the verb νε-
μέσσηθεν.[51] The crowd's approval of Odysseus's repression of Thersites
is odd if Thersites really speaks the crowd's feelings. Furthermore, the
opening of Odysseus's speech after the Thersites episode assumes that
the host will feel ashamed at the thought of failing Agamemnon: "Son
of Atreus, now the Achaeans wish to make you, lord, the most disgraced
among all mortal kings . . ." (2.284–85). Ostensibly addressed to
Agamemnon, these words clearly appeal to the Achaeans' sense of ob-

---

50. See Leaf 1900–1902, 1:65 (on *Il.* 2.222); Thalmann 1988, 18.
51. Lowry 1991, 22–26.

ligation and loyalty to the king. If the troops generally were furiously angry at Agamemnon, the suppression of Thersites would hardly change their feelings, but they respond enthusiastically to Odysseus's speech (2.333–35). If the poet intended the antecedent of the dative-case pronoun to be Agamemnon, the outcome of Thersites' speech shows that the army is angry not because of the distribution of booty but only because they are tired of being at Troy. They perhaps resent how he has aroused their homesickness only to repress it.

Thersites' speech is not directly relevant to what has immediately preceded it.[52] While Agamemnon had spoken about the general frustration of the unsuccessful war, Thersites complains about the distribution of booty (echoing and perhaps parodying Achilles' complaints in his quarrel with Agamemnon).[53]

> Ἀτρεΐδη, τέο δηαῦτ' ἐπιμέμφεαι ἠδὲ χατίζεις;
> πλεῖαί τοι χαλκοῦ κλισίαι, πολλαὶ δὲ γυναῖκες
> εἰσὶν ἐνὶ κλισίῃς ἐξαίρετοι, ἅς τοι Ἀχαιοὶ
> πρωτίστῳ δίδομεν εὖτ' ἂν πτολίεθρον ἕλωμεν.
> ἦ ἔτι καὶ χρυσοῦ ἐπιδεύεαι, ὅν κέ τις οἴσει
> Τρώων ἱπποδάμων ἐξ Ἰλίου υἷος ἄποινα,
> ὅν κεν ἐγὼ δήσας ἀγάγω ἢ ἄλλος Ἀχαιῶν,
> ἠὲ γυναῖκα νέην, ἵνα μίσγεαι ἐν φιλότητι,
> ἥν τ' αὐτὸς ἀπονόσφι κατίσχεαι; οὐ μὲν ἔοικεν
> ἀρχὸν ἐόντα κακῶν ἐπιβασκέμεν υἷας Ἀχαιῶν.
> ὦ πέπονες, κάκ' ἐλέγχε', Ἀχαιΐδες, οὐκέτ' Ἀχαιοί,
> οἴκαδέ περ σὺν νηυσὶ νεώμεθα, τόνδε δ' ἐῶμεν
> αὐτοῦ ἐνὶ Τροίῃ γέρα πεσσέμεν, ὄφρα ἴδηται
> ἤ ῥά τί οἱ χἠμεῖς προσαμύνομεν, ἦε καὶ οὐκί·
> ὃς καὶ νῦν Ἀχιλῆα ἕο μέγ' ἀμείνονα φῶτα
> ἠτίμησεν· ἑλὼν γὰρ ἔχει γέρας αὐτὸς ἀπούρασ.
> ἀλλὰ μάλ' οὐκ Ἀχιλῆϊ χόλος φρεσίν, ἀλλὰ μεθήμων·
> ἦ γὰρ ἄν, Ἀτρεΐδη, νῦν ὕστατα λωβήσαιο·
>
>   (2.225–42)

[Son of Atreus, what are you criticizing about your situation, and what do you want? Your huts are full of bronze, and there are in

---

52. See Kullmann 1955, 170.
53. See Schadewaldt 1966, 152.

your hut many select women, whom we Achaeans give to you first, whenever we capture a town. Or are you short of gold (which some horse-taming Trojan may bring from Troy as the ransom of his son—someone I captured or some other of the Achaeans) or a young woman, so that you can join with her in love, one you keep apart for yourself? It is not proper that one who is leader bring the Achaeans into trouble. You weaklings, good-for-nothings, women, no longer men, let us go home with our ships and leave him here in Troy to digest his prizes, so that he can see whether we, too, protect him or not. Just now he has dishonored Achilles, a much better man than he. For he has appropriated and keeps his prize, having himself taken it away. But there is no anger in Achilles' mind; he is slack. Otherwise, son of Atreus, this would be your last outrage.]

The poet says that Thersites' favorite targets of abuse were Achilles and Odysseus (220–21), but in this speech, before Thersites criticizes Achilles, he praises him as a way of isolating Agamemnon. Thersites echoes Achilles' own words (2.242 = 1.232), but with a significant twist. Achilles, dissuaded by Athena from killing Agamemnon, publicly implies that it is lack of support from the people as a whole that restrains him: "People-eating king, since you rule over good-for-nothings! Otherwise, son of Atreus, this would be your last outrage" [δημοβόρος βασιλεύς, ἐπεὶ οὐ-
᾿τιδανοῖσιν ἀνάσσεις· / ἦ γὰρ ἂν ᾿Ατρεΐδη νῦν ὕστατα λωβήσαιο]. Later Achilles identifies the Greeks with Agamemnon (1.299); he implies that the entire community is taking away his prize, even as he threatens to kill Agamemnon in the presence of the Greeks if he tries to take anything else. Achilles apparently refers to both leaders and common soldiers with the word οὐτιδανοῖσιν (good-for-nothings); he uses the same word for what he would be if he always yielded to Agamemnon (1.293). Achilles evidently believes that sufficient social pressure would control Agamemnon, so he blames the community as a whole for failing to restrain him. Manhood and stature depend on resisting aggression, whether inside or outside the community.

Thersites agrees that to fail to resist Agamemnon is emasculating, but rather than urge the community to force Agamemnon to behave properly, he urges it to abandon the war, while he blames Achilles for not killing Agamemnon. Ordinarily, abandoning the war and thus permitting the Trojans to boast would be a failure of manhood (cf. Menelaus's rebuke to the Greeks at 7.96–100). Achilles still believes in the possibility of social order, while Thersites' speech of blame is completely destructive.

Thersites' speech does not really offer a counterideology; it appropriates one significant aspect of the dominant norms. The legitimacy of the political and social hierarchy depends in part on the implied impossibility of maintaining order in any other way. Odysseus's rebuke to the commoners leaves no choices between monarchy and anarchy. The elite, however, also wants to be seen as a meritocracy, as Sarpedon's speech shows. If commoners do not believe that kings are usually wiser and better in war than themselves, the system loses legitimacy. The issue in dispute between Agamemnon and Achilles is the relative standing given by inherited position and by merit in war. Neither side, however, questions that both inheritance and merit provide status and that those who have appropriate status may speak freely in the assembly.[54]

In speaking as if he himself or any other Achaean is likely to have performed heroic deeds, such as capturing enemies worthy of ransom, Thersites claims the status given by merit, so that his exact social position, which the poet does not clarify, is irrelevant. Hence, although, in this passage, Thersites appears to be a nonelite soldier, Kullmann has vigorously argued that Homer knew and suppressed the tradition that made Thersites Diomedes' cousin.[55] The context makes it clear that Thersites' claim to merit in war is completely without validity, so the question of whether a common soldier could claim status on these grounds is not really asked. The poet leaves the further implications open. The passage thereby avoids making the episode a clear representation of popular discontent with the dominant ideology.

In response, Odysseus insists that Thersites should not strive against the kings, since he is the worst of those who followed Agamemnon to Troy. In emphasizing that Thersites is alone (οἶος, 2.247) in voicing his criticism, Odysseus perhaps implies also that Thersites is alone in his opinion. In addition to this claim that Thersites lacks standing, Odysseus argues substantively that he should not seek to return, because it is not yet certain whether the Achaeans will be successful or not (2.251–53). The rest of Odysseus's speech consists of threats to strip and beat Thersites, and Odysseus concludes by striking Thersites with the scepter. Thersites cries and bends over; in thus submitting to Odysseus's

54. See Donlan 1979.
55. Kullmann 1960, 146–48.

abuse, he effectively acknowledges that he is no Achilles. The troops, though unhappy, laugh at Thersites and praise Odysseus with hyperbolic irony that nonetheless must indicate genuine praise ("this is the greatest deed he has done among the Greeks," 2.274). Thersites' complaints arouse no support among the soldiers and so are unlikely to be theirs. The army is unhappy not because of Agamemnon's treatment of Achilles or because of resentment of the leader's prerogatives but because the war has lasted so long without success. Hence, both Odysseus and Nestor remind the troops of the favorable omens at their departure for Troy.

Once Odysseus has silenced Thersites, both he and Nestor use strikingly inclusive language in addressing the assembly.[56] Both accuse the group of behaving like their inferiors. Odysseus says, "like young children and widows, they lament to each other about returning home" (2.289–90), while Nestor says that they conduct the assembly "like little children, who have no business with deeds of war" (2.337–38). These speeches implicitly unite both kings and men as male warriors who would lose, not vindicate, their virility by abandoning the expedition. Both speakers also cite promises that the Achaeans made before they came to Troy (2.286–88, 339–41), again without distinguishing the leaders from the mass. Odysseus calls the whole assembly "friends" in sympathizing with their frustration while urging them to be patient (2.296–298), in a striking change from his earlier rebukes. Nestor suggests that only "one or two" Achaeans are truly disaffected (2.346–47), and he urges no one to be eager to leave until he has slept beside a Trojan's wife—a reply to Thersites' complaint that Agamemnon had an unfair share of captive women (2.226–33), as well as an implicit promise that Troy will provide booty for all. As we have already seen, in the ideal Homeric world, goods are unevenly distributed, but the supply is so abundant that nobody is deprived. Perhaps the fact that Odysseus and Nestor attempt to win over the mass of the Achaeans is more important than what they say. In addressing the people, Odysseus retracts his earlier statement that they do not count.

This apparent tension between divisive and inclusive rhetorics within the poem is visible again at 12.165–76. There, the Aiantes are going along the rampart, urging the army on. The narrator says "they rebuked one man with gentle [μειλιχίοις] words, another with stern

---

56. On the relationship between the speeches, see Lohmann 1970, 51–58.

[στερέοις] words, whenever they saw someone completely hanging back from battle." The narrator then quotes a single speech.

ὦ φίλοι Ἀργείων ὅς τ᾽ ἔξοχος ὅς τε μεσήεις
ὅς τε χερειότερος, ἐπεὶ οὔ πω πάντες ὁμοῖοι
ἀνέρες ἐν πολέμῳ, νῦν ἔπλετο ἔργον ἅπασι·

(12.269–71)

[Friends, both the man among the Argives who is outstanding, and the one in the middle, and the inferior one—since men are not at all equal in war—now there has come to be work for all.]

The Aiantes explicitly stratify the army by fighting merit rather than social position, and even though the poet says that they used harsh reproaches toward some, the single speech is clearly "gentle" and inclusive.

The poet does not encourage nonelite members of the audience to identify with Thersites; but the authorial audience does feel pity for the Greek army, forced to remain so long away from home. Odysseus's harsh rebuke to the fleeing soldiers threatens the usual Homeric picture of solidarity between elite and commons and thereby threatens also the cohesion of the audience. But if this is a realistic depiction of a near collapse of social order, both the soldiers' flight and Odysseus's insults are equally symptoms of breakdown. The flight to the ships breaks the hierarchy, while Odysseus's rebuke exaggerates it, first giving the common soldiers no value at all, then making Agamemnon an absolute monarch over all the other Greeks. The following actions re-create social cohesion. Thersites' attempt to make Agamemnon the butt of laughter fails, allowing Odysseus to unite the group through laughter against Thersites. Then Odysseus and Nestor both speak inclusively and bring about cohesion by assuming and enacting it. They also, by reminding the crowd of the favorable omens that promise Troy's capture, emphatically remind the audience of the fact of Troy's fall. Agamemnon's dream led to an ironic distance between characters and audience; as long as the characters were hoping to capture Troy on this very day, the audience had to be aware that all their actions were deluded. Nestor and Odysseus instead refer to the true omens of Aulis and so bring audience and characters closer even as they bring army and leadership together. To refuse to join this group is to refuse the capture of Troy as a worthwhile goal. The cohesion that the *Iliad* invites here is a cohesion against an enemy. For the external audience, the basic structure of epic fails if Nestor and Odysseus cannot unite the army, so its members must support the speakers.

Perhaps the greatest achievement of the *Iliad* is that it can create such cohesion in its audience without demonizing the Trojans. The *Iliad* and the *Odyssey* constantly vary both focalization in the technical sense and point of view more generally.[57] The hearer is often in the position of a god watching the human characters or of the crowd judging the hero, and the narrator even more often invites the audience to feel and act along with the hero. To listen to the epic is to experiment with a variety of social roles. Both epics make the audience blame for problems those who violate conventional norms of behavior or ignore their social place. Thersites is not the only victim of the mocking laughter of the community; when Locrian Ajax, who is rude to his elder Idomeneus (23.473–81), slips in the manure of slaughtered cattle, the Achaeans laugh at him (23.774–84). Similarly, the *Odyssey* assigns blame to the upper-class suitors, to Odysseus's companions, and to disloyal slaves. The narrator allots sympathy with an even more generous hand.

In the final narrative movement of the *Iliad*, the temporary experience of bonding between Achilles and Priam implies both the possibility of transcending all social barriers, even those between friends and enemies, and the impossibility of sustaining such transcendence in ongoing social life. The poet produces one of his most powerful effects by suddenly shifting the point of view from Priam, whose story he has been telling since 24.160; to a focalization through Achilles and his companions at 24.477–84, when they are astonished as he stands before them; to a shifting focalization at 24.509–12, as both men remember and weep, but for different people. This is the ideal experience of the epic itself: both men participate in the same action, yet it is not precisely the same for both.

It is easy to criticize this broad sympathy as a mere disguise of support for the status quo. The *Iliad*'s strongest ideological effect is the resignation that so much of its action invites. In the *Iliad*, the human condition appears to be so poignantly unalterable that the poem discourages its audience from imagining that mere social change could be very significant. Near the end of the *Iliad*, Achilles tells Priam how

---

57. The most extreme case is perhaps *Od.* 6.90, where the focalizers are the mules.

Zeus gives men either a mixture of troubles and blessings or all troubles (24.529–33); Achilles completely ignores human responsibility. The *Odyssey* opens with a programmatic speech in which Zeus attributes human suffering partly to the gods, partly to human folly and wrongdoing (1.32–43); here, however, examples like Aegisthus and the suitors make the only issue individual moral behavior. In Homeric epic, political and social structures have no effect on human suffering. Yet in part because Homeric epic's political implications are easily forgotten in its humanistic and inclusive appeal, Athenian democrats could listen to it as enthusiastically as Ionian aristocrats had.

Works Cited

Commentaries of the *Iliad* and the *Odyssey* are cited by the following abbreviations.

Il. Comm.   G. S. Kirk, ed. *The* Iliad: *A Commentary*. Cambridge, 1985–93.
                G. S. Kirk. Vol. 1, books 1–4. 1985.
                G. S. Kirk. Vol. 2, books 5–8. 1990.
                J. B. Hainsworth. Vol. 3, books 9–12. 1993.
                R. Janko. Vol. 4, books 13–16. 1992.
                M. Edwards. Vol. 5, books 17–20. 1991.
                N. Richardson. Vol. 6, books 21–24. 1993.

Od. Comm.   *A Commentary on Homer's* Odyssey. Oxford, 1988–92. Rev. trans.
                of *Omero: Odissea*, 6 vols. (Milan, 1981–86).
                A. Heubeck, S. West, and J. B. Hainsworth. Vol. 1, introduction and books 1–7. 1988.
                A. Heubeck and A. Hoekstra. Vol. 2, books 9–16. 1989.
                J. Russo, M. Fernández-Galiano, and A. Heubeck. Vol. 3, books 17–24. 1992.

Adkins, A. W. H. 1960. *Merit and Responsibility*. Oxford.
———. 1969. "Threatening, Abusing, and Feeling Angry in the Homeric Poems." *JHS* 89:7–21.
Ahl, F., and H. Roisman. 1996. *The* Odyssey *Re-Formed*. Ithaca.
Andersen, Ø. 1977. "Odysseus and the Wooden Horse." *SO* 52:5–18.
———. 1987. "Myth, Paradigm, and 'Spatial Form' in the *Iliad*." In *Homer: Beyond Oral Poetry: Recent Trends in Homeric Interpretation*, ed. J. M. Bremer, I. J. F. de Jong, and J. Kalaff, 1–13. Amsterdam.
———. 1990. "The Making of the Past in the *Iliad*." *HSCP* 93:25–45.
———. 1992. "Agamemnon's Singer (*Od.* 3.262–272)." *SO* 67:5–26.
———. 1998. "Allusion and the Audience of Homer." In *Homerica: Proceedings of the 8th International Symposium on the* Odyssey, ed. M. Paisi-Apostolopoulou, 137–49. Ithaca.
Antonaccio, C. 1995. *An Archaeology of Ancestors: Tomb Cult and Hero Cult in Early Greece*. Lanham, Md.
Armstrong, C. B. 1969. "The Casualty Lists in the Trojan War." *G&R* 16:30–31.
Austin, N. 1966. "The Function of Digressions in the *Iliad*." *GRBS* 7:295–312.
Bakhtin, M. 1981. *The Dialogic Imagination*. Trans. C. Emerson and M. Holquist. Austin.

Bakker, E. 1997. *Poetry in Speech: Orality and Homeric Discourse.* Ithaca.

Bassett, S. 1938. *The Poetry of Homer.* Berkeley.

Basso, K. 1985. *A Musical View of the Universe.* Philadelphia.

Ben-Amos, D. 1984. "The Seven Strands of Tradition." *Journal of Folklore Research* 21:97–131.

Bethe, E. 1927. *Homer: Dichtung und Sage.* Vol. 3, *Die Sage vom troischen Kriege.* Leipzig.

Beye, C. R. 1964. "Homeric Battle Narrative and Catalogues." *HSCP* 68:345–73.

Biebuyck, D., and K. C. Mateene. 1969. *The Mwindo Epic from the Banyanga (Congo Republic).* Berkeley and Los Angeles.

Blackburn, S. 1988. *Singing of Birth and Death.* Philadelphia.

———. 1996. *Inside the Drama House: Rama Stories and Shadow Puppets in South India.* Berkeley and Los Angeles.

Blackburn, S., P. J. Claus, J. Fleuckiger, and S. Wadley, eds. 1989. *Oral Epics in India.* Berkeley and Los Angeles.

Bliss, F. R. 1968. "Homer and the Critics: The Structural Unity of *Odyssey* 8." *Bucknell Review* 16, no. 3:53–73.

Block, E. 1982. "The Narrator Speaks: Apostrophe in Homer and Virgil." *TAPA* 112:7–22.

Booth, W. C. 1988. *The Company We Keep: An Ethics of Fiction.* Berkeley and Los Angeles.

Bowra, C. M. 1930. *Tradition and Design in the* Iliad. Oxford.

Braswell, B. K. 1971. "Mythological Innovation in the *Iliad*." *CQ* 65:16–26.

———. 1982. "The Song of Ares and Aphrodite: Theme and Relevance to *Odyssey* 8." *Hermes* 110:129–37.

Bremer, J. M. 1987. "The So-called Götterapparat in Iliad XX–XXII." In *Homer: Beyond Oral Poetry: Recent trends in Homeric interpretation,* ed. J. M. Bremer, I. J. F. de Jong, and J. Kalaff, 31–46. Amsterdam.

Brooks, C., and R. P. Warren. 1959. *Understanding Fiction.* 2d ed. New York.

Brown, C. G. 1989. "Ares, Aphrodite, and the Laughter of the Gods." *Phoenix* 43:283–93.

Brunius-Nilsson, E. 1955. ΔAIMONIE. Uppsala.

Burgess, J. 1996. "The Non-Homeric *Cypria*." *TAPA* 126:77–99.

Burkert, W. 1960. "Das Lied von Ares und Aphrodite." *RhM* 103:130–44.

———. 1972. "Die Leistung eines Kreophylos." *MH* 29:74–85.

———. 1979. "Kynaithos, Polycrates, and the *Homeric Hymn to Apollo.*" In *Arktouros,* ed. G. Bowersock, W. Burkert, and M. C. Putnam, 53–72. Leiden.

———. 1987. "The Making of Homer in the Sixth Century B.C.: Rhapsodes vs. Stesichoros." In *Papers on the Amasis Painter and His World,* ed. D. von Bothmer, 43–62. Malibu.

———. 1992. *The Orientalizing Revolution.* Trans. M. Pinder and W. Burkert. Cambridge, Mass.

Calame, C. 1995. *The Craft of Poetic Speech in Ancient Greece.* Ithaca.

Carey, C. 1992. Review of *Pindar's Homer: The Lyric Possession of an Epic Past,* by G. Nagy. *AJP* 113:283–86.

Carlier, P. 1984. *La Royauté en Grèce avant l'Alexandre.* Strasbourg.

Chadwick, N., and V. Zhirmunsky. 1969. *Oral Epics of Central Asia*. Cambridge.

Clarke, M. E. 1986. "Neoanalysis: A Bibliographic Review." *CW* 79:379–94.

Clay, J. S. 1983. *The Wrath of Athena: Gods and Men in the* Odyssey. Princeton.

Combellack, F. M. 1950. "Contemporary Unitarians and Homer's Originality." *AJP* 71:337–64.

Connelly, B. 1986. *Arab Folk Epic and Identity*. Berkeley and Los Angeles.

Cook, E. 1995. *The* Odyssey *in Athens*. Ithaca.

Crane, G. 1988. *Calypso: Backgrounds and Conventions of the* Odyssey. Frankfurt.

Danek, G. 1998. *Epos und Zitat: Studien zu den Quellen der Odyssee*. Wiener Studien 22. Vienna.

Davies, M. 1981. "The Judgement of Paris and *Iliad* XXIV." *JHS* 101:56–62.

———. 1988. *Epicorum Graecorum Fragmenta*. Göttingen.

———. 1989. *The Epic Cycle*. Bristol.

de Jong, I. F. 1985. "*Iliad* 1.366–392: A Mirror Story." *Arethusa* 18:1–22.

———. 1987a. *Narrators and Focalizers*. Amsterdam.

———. 1987b. "The Voice of Anonymity: *Tis*-speeches in the *Iliad*." *Eranos* 85:69–84.

———. 1992. "The Subjective Style in Odysseus' Wanderings." *CQ* 86:1–11.

de Vet, T. 1996. "The Joint Role of Orality and Literacy in the Composition, Transmission, and Performance of the Homeric Texts: A Comparative View." *TAPA* 126:43–76.

Dihle, A. 1970. *Homer-Probleme*. Opladen.

Doherty, L. 1995. *Siren Songs: Gender, Audiences, and Narrators in the* Odyssey. Ann Arbor.

Donlan, W. 1973. "The Tradition of Anti-aristocratic Thought in Early Greek Poetry." *Historia* 22:145–54.

———. 1979. "The Structure of Authority in the *Iliad*." *Arethusa* 12:51–70.

———. 1981–82. "Reciprocities in Homer." *CW* 75:137–75.

Dowden, K. 1996. "Homer's Sense of Text." *JHS* 116:47–61.

Edmunds, L. 1997. "Myth in Homer." In *A New Companion to Homer*, ed. I. Morris and B. Powell, 415–41. Leiden.

Edwards, A. 1985. *Achilles in the* Odyssey. Beiträge zur klassichen Philologie 171. Königstein.

Edwards, M. 1980. "Convention and Individuality in *Iliad* 1." *HSCP* 84:1–28.

———. 1986. "Homer and Oral Tradition: The Formula." Part 1. *Oral Tradition* 1:171–230.

———. 1988. "Homer and Oral Tradition: The Formula." Part 2. *Oral Tradition* 3:11–60.

Erbse, H. 1972. *Beiträge zum Verständnis der Odyssee*. Berlin.

Fehling, D. 1979. "Zwei Lehrstücke über Pseudo-Nachrichten (Homeriden, Lelantischer Krieg)." *RhM* 122:193–210.

Fenik, B. 1968. *Typical Battle Scenes in the* Iliad. Hermes Einzelschriften 21. Wiesbaden.

———. 1974. *Studies in the* Odyssey. Hermes Einzelschriften 30. Wiesbaden.

Fentress, J., and C. Wickham. 1992. *Social Memory*. Oxford.

Finkelberg, M. 1990. "A Creative Oral Poet and the Muse." *AJP* 111:293–303.

————. 1998. *The Birth of Literary Fiction in Ancient Greece*. Oxford.

Finnegan, R. 1977. *Oral Poetry: Its Nature, Significance, and Social Context*. Cambridge.

Fittschen, K. 1969. *Untersuchungen zum Beginn der Sagendarstellungen bei den Griechen*. Berlin.

Flueckiger, J. 1988. "He Should Have Worn a Sari." *Drama Review* 32:159–69.

Flueckiger, J., and L. Sears. 1991. *Boundaries of the Text: Epic Performances in South and Southeast Asia*. Ann Arbor.

Foley, J. M. 1985. *Oral-Formulaic Theory and Research: An Introduction and Annotated Bibliography*. New York.

————. 1990. *Traditional Oral Epic: The* Odyssey, Beowulf, *and the Serbo-Croatian Return Song*. Bloomington, Ind.

————. 1991. *Immanent Art: From Structure to Meaning in Traditional Oral Epic*. Bloomington, Ind.

————. 1995. *The Singer of Tales in Performance*. Bloomington, Ind.

————. 1999. *Homer's Traditional Art*. University Park, Pa.

Ford, A. 1992. *Homer: The Poetry of the Past*. Ithaca.

————. 1997. "The Inland Ship." In *Written Voices, Spoken Signs: Tradition, Performance, and the Epic Text*, ed. E. Bakker and A. Kahane, 83–109. Cambridge, Mass.

Fowler, R. L. 1987. *The Nature of Early Greek Lyric: Three Preliminary Studies*. Toronto.

Friedrich, R. 1975. *Stilwandel im homerischen Epos*. Heidelberg.

Friis Johansen, K. 1967. *The* Iliad *in Early Greek Art*. Copenhagen.

Garvie, A. F. 1994. *Homer: Odyssey Books VI–VIII*. Cambridge.

Genette, G. 1980. *Narrative Discourse: An Essay in Method*. Trans. J. Lewis. Ithaca.

Gerrig, R. J. 1989. "Suspense in the Absence of Uncertainty." *Journal of Memory and Language* 28:633–48.

Giacomelli, A. 1980. "Aphrodite and After." *Phoenix* 24:1–19.

Gordesiani, R. 1980. "Zur Interpretation der Duale im 9. Buch der Ilias." *Philologus* 124:163–74.

Griffin, J. 1977. "The Epic Cycle and the Uniqueness of Homer." *JHS* 97:39–53.

————. 1980. *Homer on Life and Death*. Oxford.

————. 1995. *Homer: Iliad IX*. Oxford.

Griffith. M. 1983. "Personality in Hesiod." *ClAnt* 2:37–65.

————. 1990. "Contest and Contradiction in Early Greek Poetry." In *The Cabinet of the Muses*, ed. M. Griffith and D. Mastronarde, 185–207. Atlanta.

Gschnitzer, F. 1991. "Zur homerischen Staats- und Gesellschaftsordnung: Grundcharakter und geschichtliche Stellung." In *Zweihundert Jahre Homer-Forschung*, ed. J. Latacz. 182–204. Stuttgart.

Hansen, W. 1982. "The Applied Message in Story-Telling." In *Folklorica: Festschrift for Felix J. Oinas*, ed. E. Zygas and P. Voorheis, 99–109. Bloomington, Ind.

Haslam, M. 1997. "Homeric Papyri and Transmission of the Text." In *A New Companion to Homer*, ed. I. Morris and B. Powell, 55–100. Leiden.

Haubold, J. 2000. *Homer's People: Epic Poetry and Social Formation*. Cambridge.

Heubeck, A. 1954. *Der Odyssee-Dichter und der Ilias.* Erlangen.

———. 1974. *Die homerische Frage.* Darmstadt.

Higbie, C. 1995. *Heroes' Names, Homeric Identities.* New York.

Hobart, A. 1987. *Dancing Shadows of Bali: Theatre and Myth.* London and New York.

Hobsbawn, E., and T. Ranger, eds. 1983. *The Invention of Tradition.* Cambridge.

Holoka, J. P. 1983. "'Looking Darkly' (Ὑπόδρα Ἰδών): Reflections on Status and Decorum in Homer." *TAPA* 113:1–16.

———. 1991. "Homer, Oral Poetry Theory, and Comparative Literature: Major Trends and Controversies in Twentieth-Century Criticism." In *Zweihundert Jahre Homer-Forschung,* ed. J. Latacz, 456–81. Stuttgart.

Hölscher, U. 1990. *Die Odyssee: Epos zwischen Märchen und Roman.* 3d ed. Munich.

Howald, E. 1924. "Meleager und Achill." *RhM* 73:402–25.

Janko, R. 1982. *Homer, Hesiod, and the Hymns.* Cambridge.

———. 1998. "The Homeric Poems as Oral Dictated Texts." *CQ* 48:1–13.

Jensen, M. S. 1980. *The Homeric Question and the Oral-Formulaic Theory.* Copenhagen.

Jones, P. V. 1992. "The Past in Homer's *Odyssey.*" *JHS* 112:74–90.

———. 1995. "Poetic Invention: The Fighting around Troy in the First Nine Years of the Trojan War." In *Homer's World: Fiction, Tradition, Reality,* ed. O. Andersen and M. Dickie, 101–12. Bergen.

Jörgensen, O. 1904. "Das Auftreten der Götter in den Büchern ι-μ der Odyssee." *Hermes* 39:357–82.

Kahane, A. 1994. *The Interpretation of Order: A Study in the Poetics of Homeric Repetition.* Oxford.

———. 1997. "Hexameter Progression and the Homeric Hero's Solitary State." In *Written Voices, Spoken Signs: Tradition, Performance, and the Epic Text,* ed. E. Bakker and A. Kahane, 110–37. Cambridge, Mass.

Kakridis, J. T. 1949. *Homeric Researches.* Lund.

Kannicht, R. 1982. "Poetry and Art: Homer and the Monuments Afresh." *ClAnt* 13:70–76.

Katz, M. A. 1991. *Penelope's Renown: Meaning and Indeterminacy in the* Odyssey. Princeton.

Keeler, W. 1987. *Javanese Shadow Plays, Javanese Selves.* Princeton.

Kelly, S. 1990. *Homeric Correption and the Metrical Distinctions between Speeches and Narrative.* New York.

Kiparsky, P. 1976. "Oral Poetry: Some Linguistic and Typological Considerations." In *Oral Literature and the Formula,* ed. B. Stoltz and R. Shannon, 73–106. Ann Arbor.

Kirk, G. S. 1962. *The Songs of Homer.* Cambridge.

Knox, B. M. W. 1985. "Books and Readers in the Greek World: From the Beginnings to Alexandria. In *The Cambridge History of Greek Literature,* ed. P. E. Easterling and B. M. W. Knox, 1–15. Cambridge.

Köhnken, A. 1975. "Die Rolle des Phoinix und die Duale im I der Ilias." *Glotta* 53:25–36.

Koljević, S. 1978. "Noch einmal Phoinix und die Duale." *Glotta* 56:5–14.
———. 1980. *The Epic in the Making*. Oxford.
Kraus, Walter. 1955. "Die Auffassung des Dichterberufs im frühen Griechentum." *WS* 68:65–87.
Krischer, T. 1971. *Formale Konventionen der homerischen Epik*. Zetemata 56. Munich.
Kullmann, W. 1955. "Die Probe des Achaierheeres in der Ilias." *MH* 12:253–73.
———. 1956. *Das Wirken der Götter in der Ilias*. Berlin.
———. 1960. *Die Quellen der Ilias*. Hermes Einzelschriften 14. Wiesbaden.
———. 1985. "Gods and Men in the *Iliad* and the *Odyssey*." *HSCP* 89:1–23.
Kurke, L. 1991. *The Traffic in Praise: Pindar and the Poetics of Social Economy*. Ithaca.
Lamberton, R. 1988. *Hesiod*. New Haven and London.
Lang, M. 1983. "Reverberation and Mythology in the *Iliad*." In *Approaches to Homer*, ed. C. Rubino and C. Shemerdine, 140–64. Austin.
———. 1989. "Unreal Conditions in Homeric Narrative." *GRBS* 30:5–26.
———. 1995. "War Story into Wrath Story." In *The Ages of Homer*, ed. J. Carter and S. Morris, 149–62. Austin.
Latacz, J. 1996. *Homer*. Trans. J. Holoka. Ann Arbor.
Leaf, W. 1900–1902. *The* Iliad. 2d ed. 2 vols. London. Reprint, Amsterdam, 1971.
Lenz, A. 1980. *Das Proöm des frühen griechischen Epos: Ein Beitrag zum poetischen Selbstverständnis*. Bonn.
Lohmann, D. 1970. *Die Komposition der Reden in der Ilias*. Berlin.
Lord, A. B. 1960. *The Singer of Tales*. Cambridge, Mass.
Louden, B. 1993. "Pivotal Counterfactuals in Homeric Epic." *ClAnt* 12:181–98.
———. 1999. *The* Odyssey: *Structure, Narration, and Meaning*. Baltimore and London.
Lowenstam, S. 1993. *The Scepter and the Spear: Studies on Forms of Repetition in the Homeric Poems*. Boston.
———. 1997. "Talking Vases: The Relationship between the Homeric Poems and Archaic Representations of Epic Myth." *TAPA* 127:21–76.
Lowry, E. 1991. *Thersites: A Study in Comic Shame*. New York.
Lutgendorf, P. 1991. *The Life of a Text: Performing the* Ramcaritmanas *of Tulsidas*. Berkeley, Los Angeles, and Oxford.
Lynn-George, M. 1988. *Epos: Word, Narrative, and the* Iliad. Basingstoke and London.
Mackie, H. 1996. *Talking Trojan: Speech and Community in the* Iliad. Lanham, Md.
———. 1997. "Song and Storytelling: An Odyssean Perspective." *TAPA* 127: 77–95.
MacLeod, C. 1982. *Homer:* Iliad *24*. Cambridge.
Malkin, I. 1998. *The Returns of Odysseus: Colonization and Ethnicity*. Berkeley.
March, J. 1987. *The Creative Poet: Studies of the Treatment of Myth in Greek Poetry*. *BICS* Supplement 49. London.
Marg, W. 1956. "Das erste Lied von Demodocus." In *Navicula Chilionensis: Festschrift Felix Jacoby*, 16–29. Leiden.
———. 1971. *Homer über die Dichtung*. Münster.
Martin, R. 1989. *The Language of Heroes: Speech and Performance in the* Iliad. Ithaca.

———. 1992. "Hesiod's Metanastic Poetics." *Ramus* 21:11–33.

———. 1993. "Telemachus and the Last Hero Song." *Colby Quarterly* 29:222–40.

Merkelbach, R. 1948. "Zum Y der *Ilias*." *Philologus* 97:303–11.

Meuli, K. 1921. *Odyssee und Argonautika*. Berlin.

Miller, A. 1983. "*Ingenium* and *Ars* in *Persae* 101–114." *ClAnt* 2:77–81.

Mills, M. 1989. *Rhetorics and Politics in Afghan Traditional Storytelling*. Philadelphia.

Minchin, E. 1992. "Homer Springs a Surprise: Eumaios' Tale at *Od*. o 403–484." *Hermes* 120:259–266.

Mondi, R. 1983. "The Homeric Cyclopes: Folktale, Tradition, and Theme." *TAPA* 113:17–38.

Morris, I. 1986. "The Use and Abuse of Homer." *ClAnt* 5:81–138.

———. 1988. "Tomb Cult and the 'Greek Renaissance': The Past in the Present in the Eighth Century B.C." *Antiquity* 62:750–61.

Morrison, J. 1992a. "Alternatives to the Epic Tradition: Homer's Challenges in the *Iliad*." *TAPA* 122:61–71.

———. 1992b. *Homeric Misdirection: False Predictions in the* Iliad. Ann Arbor.

———. 1997. "*Kerostasia*, the Dictates of Fate, and the Will of Zeus in the *Iliad*." *Arethusa* 30:273–96.

Most, Glenn. 1989. "The Structure and Function of Odysseus' *Apologoi*." *TAPA* 119:15–30.

Moyle, N. K. 1990. *The Turkish Minstrel Tale Tradition*. New York.

Muellner, L. 1996. *The Anger of Achilles:* Mênis *in Greek Epic*. Ithaca.

Mühlestein, H. 1987. *Homerische Namenstudien*. Beiträge zur klassischen Philologie 183. Frankfurt am Main.

Murnaghan, S. 1987. *Disguise and Recognition in the* Odyssey. Princeton.

Murray, O. 1980. *Early Greece*. Stanford.

Nagler, M. 1974. *Spontaneity and Tradition: A Study in the Oral Art of Homer*. Berkeley.

Nagy, G. 1974. *Comparative Studies in Greek and Indic Meter*. Cambridge, Mass.

———. 1979. *The Best of the Achaeans: Concepts of the Hero in Archaic Greek Poetry*. Baltimore.

———. 1990a. *Greek Mythology and Poetics*. Ithaca.

———. 1990b. *Pindar's Homer: The Lyric Possession of an Epic Past*. Baltimore.

———. 1992. "Mythological Exemplum in Homer." In *Innovations of Antiquity*, ed. R. Hexter and D. Selden, 311–31. New York.

———. 1996a. *Homeric Questions*. Austin.

———. 1996b. *Poetry in Performance*. Cambridge.

———. 1997. "Ellipsis in Homer." In *Written Voices, Spoken Signs: Tradition, Performance, and the Epic Text*, ed. E. Bakker and A. Kahane, 167–89. Cambridge, Mass.

———. 1998. "Performing Homer." *New York Review of Books* 45, no. 6:81.

Narayan, K. 1989. *Storytellers, Saints, and Scoundrels: Folk Narrative in Hindu Religious Teaching*. Philadelphia.

Nesselrath, H. G. 1992. *Ungeschenes Geschehen: "Beinahe-Episoden" im griechischen und römischen Epos von Homer bis zur Spätantike*. Stuttgart.

Newton, R. M. 1987. "Odysseus and Hephaestus in the *Odyssey*." *CJ* 83:12–20.

Nicolai, W. 1983. "Rezeptionssteuerung in der Ilias." *Philologus* 127:1–12.

Niditch, S. 1996. *Oral World and Written Word: Ancient Israelite Literature.* Louisville.

Nilsson, M. P. 1993. *Homer and Mycenae.* London.

Noé, M. 1940. *Phoinix, Ilias, und Homer.* Leipzig.

O'Keefe, K. O'Brien. 1990. *Visible Song: Transitional Literacy in Old English Verse.* Cambridge.

Olson, S. D. 1989. "*Odyssey* 8: Guile, Force, and the Subversive Poetics of Desire." *Arethusa* 22:135–45.

———. 1995. *Blood and Iron: Stories and Storytelling in Homer's* Odyssey. Mnemosyne Supplement 148. Leiden.

Ong, W. 1982. *Orality and Literacy.* London.

Page, D. L. 1955. *The Homeric Odyssey.* Oxford.

———. 1959. *History and the Homeric* Iliad. Berkeley.

———. 1972. "The Mystery of the Minstrel at the Court of Agamemnon." In *Studi classici in onore di Quintino Cataudella,* 1:127–32. Catania.

Parry, M. 1971. *The Making of Homeric Verse: The Collected Papers of Milman Parry.* Ed. A. Parry. Oxford.

Parry, M., and A. B. Lord. 1954. *Serbo-Croatian Heroic Songs.* Vol. 1, *Novi Pazar: English Translations.* Cambridge, Mass.

Parry, M., A. B. Lord, and D. Bynam. *Serbo-Croatian Heroic Songs.* Vol. 3, The Wedding of Smailagić Meho: Avdo Međedović. Cambridge, Mass.

Peradotto, J. 1997. "Homer, Parry, and the Meaning of Tradition. In *Hommage à Milman Parry,* ed. F. Létoublon. Amsterdam.

Pratt, L. 1993. *Lying and Poetry from Homer to Pindar.* Ann Arbor.

Pucci, P. 1987. *Odyseeus Polytropos: Intertextual Readings in the* Odyssey *and the* Iliad. Ithaca.

———. 1998. *The Song of the Sirens: Essays on Homer.* London.

Qviller, B. 1981. "Dynamics of the Homeric Society." *Symbolae Osloenses* 56: 109–55.

Raaflaub, K. 1991. "Homer und die Geschichte des 8. Jh.v.Chr." In *Zweihundert Jahre Homer-Forschung,* ed. J. Latacz, 205–56. Stuttgart.

———. 1997. "Homeric Society." In *A New Companion to Homer,* ed. I. Morris and B. Powell, 624–48. Leiden.

Rabel, R. 1991. "Agamemnon's *Iliad*." *GRBS* 32:103–17.

———. 1997. *Plot and Point of View in the* Iliad. Ann Arbor.

Rabinowitz, R. 1987. *Before Reading: Narrative Conventions and the Politics of Interpretation.* Ithaca.

Redfield, J. 1975. *Nature and Culture in the* Iliad: *The Tragedy of Hector.* Chicago.

Reinhardt, K. 1960. *Tradition und Geist.* Göttingen.

———. 1961. *Die Ilias und ihr Dichter.* Göttingen.

Reynolds, D. 1995. *Heroic Poets, Poetic Heroes.* Ithaca.

Richardson, S. 1990. *The Homeric Narrator.* Nashville.

Richman, P., ed. 1991. *Many Ramayanas: The Diversity of a Narrative Tradition in South Asia.* Berkeley and Los Angeles.

Rose, P. 1992. *Sons of the Gods, Children of Earth.* Ithaca.

———. 1997. "Ideology in the *Iliad: Polis, Basileus, Theoi.*" *Arethusa* 30:151–99.

Rosen, R. 1990. "Poetry and Sailing in Hesiod's *Works and Days.*" *ClAnt* 9:99–133.

Rösler, W. 1980. "Die Entdeckung der Fiktionalität in der Antike." *Poetica* 12:283–319.

Ross, J. A. 1980. "Old French." In *Traditions of Heroic and Epic Poetry*, ed. A. T. Hatto, 79–133. London.

Rubin, D. 1995. *Memory in Oral Traditions: The Cognitive Psychology of Epic, Ballads, and Counting-Out Rhymes.* New York and Oxford.

Russo, J. 1997. "The Formula." In *A New Companion to Homer*, ed. I. Morris and B. Powell, 238–60. Leiden.

Rüter, Karl. 1969. *Odysseeinterpretationen: Untersuchungen zum ersten Buch und zur Phaiakis.* Hypomnemata 19. Göttingen.

Saïd, S. 1979. "Les Crimes des Prétendants, la maison d'Ulysse, et les festins de l'Odyssée." In *Études de littérature ancienne*, ed. S. Saïd, F. Desbordes, J. Bouffartigue, and A. Moreau, 9–49. Paris.

Sale, W. M. 1987. "The Formularity of the Place Phrases in the *Iliad.*" *TAPA* 117:21–50.

———. 1989. "The Trojans, Statistics, and Milman Parry." *GRBS* 30:341–410.

———. 1993. "Homer and Roland: The Shared Formular Technique." *Oral Tradition* 8:87–142, 381–412.

———. 1994. "The Government of Troy: Politics in the *Iliad.*" *GRBS* 35:5–102.

Scaife, R. 1995. "The *Kypria* and its Early Reception." *ClAnt* 14:164–91.

Schadewaldt, W. 1966. *Iliasstudien.* 3d ed. Darmstadt. Reprint of 2d ed., Leipzig, 1943.

Scodel, R. 1982. "The Autobiography of Phoenix: *Iliad* 9.444–95." *AJP* 102:214–23.

———. 1992a. "Absence, Memory, and Inscription: Epic and the Early Greek Epitaph." *SIFC* 10:57–76.

———. 1992b. "The Wits of Glaucus." *TAPA* 122:73–84.

———. 1998. "The Removal of the Arms, the Recognition with Laertes, and Narrative Tension in the *Odyssey.*" *CP* 93:1–17.

———. 1999. *Credible Impossibilities: Conventions and Strategies of Verisimilitude in Homer and Greek Tragedy.* Stuttgart.

Scott, J. A. 1921. *The Unity of Homer.* Berkeley.

Scully, S. 1981. "The Bard as the Custodian of Homeric Society: *Odyssey* 3.263–72." *QUCC* 37:67–83.

———. 1990. *Homer and the Sacred City.* Ithaca.

Seaford, R. 1994. *Reciprocity and Ritual: Homer and Tragedy in the Developing City-State.* Oxford.

Sealey, R. 1957. "From Phemius to Ion." *REG* 70:312–55.

Sears, L. 1986. "Text and Performance in Javanese Shadow Theatre: Changing Authorities in an Oral Tradition." Ph.D. diss., University of Wisconsin.

Segal, C. 1968. "The Embassy and the Duals of *Iliad* 9.182–89." *GRBS* 9.101–14.

———. 1983. "*Kleos* and Its Ironies in the *Odyssey.*" *AC* LII:22–47.

———. 1992. "Bard and Audience in Homer." In *Homer's Ancient Readers*, ed. R. Lamberton and J. J. Keaney, 3–29. Princeton.

————. 1994. *Singers, Heroes, and Gods in the* Odyssey. Ithaca.

Shils, E. 1981. *Tradition.* Chicago.

Shive, D. 1987. *Naming Achilles.* New York and Oxford.

Slatkin, L. 1991. *The Power of Thetis: Allusion and Interpretation in the* Iliad. Berkeley and Los Angeles.

Slings, S. 1990. "The I in Personal Archaic Lyric." In *The Poet's I in Archaic Greek Lyric,* ed. S. Slings, 1–36. Amsterdam.

Slyomovics, S. 1987. *The Merchant of Art: An Egyptian Hilali Oral Epic Poet in Performance.* University of California Publications in Modern Philology 120. Berkeley and Los Angeles.

Smith, J. D. 1991. *The Epic of Pabuji.* Cambridge.

Smith, P. 1981. "Aineiadai as Patrons of *Iliad* XX and the *Homeric Hymn to Aphrodite.*" *HSCP* 85:17–58.

Snodgrass, A. M. 1974. "An Historical Homeric Society?" *JHS* 94:114–25.

Stanford, W. B. 1967. *The* Odyssey. 2d ed. London.

Stanley, K. 1993. *The Shield of Homer.* Princeton.

Starr, C. 1962. *The Origins of Greek Civilization.* London.

Sternberg, M. 1978. *Expositional Modes and Temporal Ordering in Fiction.* Baltimore.

Stinton, T. C. W. 1965. *Euripides and the Judgment of Paris.* Society for the Promotion of Hellenic Studies, Supplementary Paper 11. London.

Strasburger, G. 1954. "Die kleine Kämpfer der *Ilias.*" Ph.D. diss., Frankfurt am Main.

Strasburger, H. 1953. "Der soziologische Aspekt der homerischen Epen." *Gymnasium* 60:97–114.

Svenbro, J. 1976. *La parole et le marbre.* Lund.

Tandy, D. 1997. *Warriors into Traders: The Power of the Market in Early Greece.* Berkeley, Los Angeles, and London.

Taplin, O. 1990. "The Earliest Quotation of the *Iliad?*" In *Owls to Athens: Essays on Classical Subjects Presented to Sir Kenneth Dover,* ed. E. M. Craik, 109–12. Oxford.

————. 1992. *Homeric Soundings.* Oxford.

Thalmann, W. G. 1988. "Thersites: Comedy, Scapegoats, and Homeric Ideology in the *Iliad.*" *TAPA* 118:1–28.

————. 1998. *The Swineherd and the Bow: Representations of Class in the* Odyssey. Ithaca.

Thomas, R. 1989. *Oral Tradition and Written Record in Classical Athens.* Cambridge.

————. 1992. *Literacy and Orality in Ancient Greece.* Cambridge.

Thornton, A. 1978. "Once Again the Duals in Book 9 of the *Iliad.*" *Glotta* 56: 1–4.

————. 1984. *Homer's* Iliad: *Its Composition and the Motif of Supplication.* Göttingen.

Touchefeu-Meynier, O. 1968. *Thèmes Odysséens dans l'art antique.* Paris.

Traill, D. 1990. "Unfair to Hector?" *CP* 85:299–303.

Trevor-Roper, H. 1983. "The Invention of Tradition: The Highland Tradition of

Scotland." In *The Invention of Tradition,* ed. E. Hobsbawn and T. Ranger, 15–42. Cambridge.

Tsagarakis, O. 1979. "Phoenix's Social Status and the Achaean Embassy." *Mnemosyne* 32:221–42.

Ulf, C. 1990. *Die homerische Gesellschaft: Materialien zur analytischen Beschreibung und historischen Lokalisierung.* Munich.

van der Valk, M. 1953. "Homer's Nationalistic Attitude." *AC* 22:5–26.

Vansina, J. 1973. *Oral Tradition: A Study in Historical Methodology.* Trans H. W. Wright. London.

———. 1985. *Oral Tradition as History.* Madison, Wis.

van Wees, H. 1992. *Status Warriors: War, Violence, and Society in Homer and History.* Amsterdam.

Visser, E. 1987. *Homerische Versifikationstechnik: Versuch einer Rekonstruktion.* Frankfurt am Main.

von Scheliha, R. 1943. *Patroklos: Gedanken über Homers Dichtung und Gestalten.* Basel.

Wackernagel, J. 1953. *Kleine Schriften.* Göttingen.

Wade-Gery, H. T. 1952. *The Poet of the* Iliad. Cambridge.

Walsh, G. 1984. *The Varieties of Enchantment.* Chapel Hill.

Woodhouse, W. 1930. *The Composition of Homer's* Odyssey. Oxford.

West, M. L. 1966. *Hesiod:* Theogony. Oxford.

———. 1988. "The Rise of the Greek Epic." *JHS* 108:151–72.

———. 1997. *The East Face of Helicon.* Oxford.

Whitley, J. 1988. "Early States and Hero-Cults: A Re-appraisal." *JHS* 108:173–82.

Whitman, C. H. 1958. *Homer and the Heroic Tradition.* Cambridge, Mass.

Wilamowitz-Moellendorff, U. von. 1884. *Homerische Untersuchungen.* Philologische Untersuchungen 7. Berlin.

———. 1916. *Die Ilias und Homer.* Berlin.

———. 1930. "Lesefrüchte." *Hermes* 45:141–53.

Willcock, M. M. 1964. "Mythological Paradeigmata in the *Iliad.*" *CQ* 14:141–51.

———. 1977. "Ad Hoc Invention in the *Iliad.*" *HSCP* 81:41–53.

Wyatt, W. F. 1985. "The Embassy and the Duals in *Iliad 9.*" *AJP* 106:399–408.

———. 1988. "Homer in Performance: *Iliad* I.348–427." *CJ* 83:289–97.

Zanker, G. 1994. *The Heart of Achilles.* Ann Arbor.

Zumthor, P. 1990. *Oral Poetry: An Introduction.* Minneapolis.

General Index

Aeschylus, 10, 189
Aethiopis, 109
Ainos, 125
Alcaeus, 45
Alhā, 16
Analysis, 49, 162
Anonymous speech, 194–98
Archilochus, 181
Argo, 37, 51, 91
Aristophanes, 176
Authorial audience, 62, 64, 68, 126,
    141, 155, 173

Bakhtin, M., 15–16
Bakker, E., 66
Balinese puppet-theater, 11
Bani Hilali (Egyptian epic), 9, 10, 16,
    20, 32, 48, 56, 57, 91, 177
Bataille Loquifer, 59–60
Bible, 50
Biebuyck, D., 48
Borges, J. L., 41

Callimachus, 58
Candaini, 7–8, 10, 42
Canons, 3–4, 16–17, 18, 69, 88
Chanson de Roland, 17–18
Character-narrators, 91, 124–25, 126,
    137
Cleisthenes of Sicyon, 88
Composition-in-performance, 1–2,
    88
Contest of Homer and Hesiod, 111
Contextually bound, 18, 29–30, 48–49,
    96, 98, 126, 132, 139, 140, 145,
    149, 165
Cypria, 14, 55, 58, 141, 151–52, 189

Destruction de Romme, 60
Dhalang, 34–36, 39, 42
Dhola, 11
Disinterestedness, 65, 70, 74, 88–89
Doublets, 27

Egyptian epic. *See* Bani Hilali
Epic Cycle, 22, 37, 53, 129
    See also titles of individual epics
Epic distance, 32
Epigoni, 37, 111, 122, 139
Epithet, 12–15, 20–21, 30, 52, 66, 94,
    108, 114, 115, 156–59
    See also Formula

Fate, 68–69
Festival (site of performance), 43–44,
    55–56
Finkelberg, M., 65–66
Flueckiger, J., 7–8
Flyting, 76
Focalization, 94, 98, 112, 143–44, 145,
    163, 211
Foley, J. M., 11–12
Ford, A., 73
Formula, 1–2, 3, 12–13, 19, 21, 28, 66,
    69, 70, 71, 78–79, 108, 126, 133,
    139, 157–58, 167, 194, 199
Functions, 139

Garvie, A. F., 152–53
Genealogical poetry, 37, 47, 179
Genealogy
    African, 3
    in Homer, 67, 72, 75–77, 80, 93, 98,
        115, 120–22, 130–32, 133, 150–51
Great Foray, 150

Traditional referentiality, 11–12, 15,
    88, 138, 142
Transparency, assumption of, 23,
    62–63, 126, 132, 138–39, 155
Type scene, 26

Vansina, J., 6

Wayang, 33–36, 39, 40–41, 42
Webster, John, 10
West, M. L., 27, 46, 178–79
Willcock, M. M., 24–25, 28, 139–40
Wyatt, W., 8

Zenodotus, 162

Index of Passages Cited